韩国考古学重大发现

2002~2007

MOMENTOUS DISCOVERIES IN KOREAN ARCHAEOLOGY

韩国国立文化财研究所 编著

科学出版社

北京

图书在版编目(CIP)数据

韩国考古学重大发现. 2002~2007 / 韩国国立文化财研究所编著. —北京：科学出版社，2011
ISBN 978-7-03-031828-2

Ⅰ. ①韩… Ⅱ. ①韩… Ⅲ. ①考古发现—韩国—2002~2007 Ⅳ. ①K883.126

中国版本图书馆CIP数据核字(2011)第135055号

责任编辑：孙 莉 刘 能 / 责任校对：刘亚琦
责任印制：赵德静 / 封面设计：谭 硕

科学出版社 出版
北京东黄城根北街16号
邮政编码：100717
http://www.sciencep.com

北京雅昌彩色印刷有限公司 印刷
科学出版社发行 各地新华书店经销
*
2011年6月第 一 版　开本：889×1194 1/12
2011年6月第一次印刷　印张：24 1/2
印数：1—1600　　　字数：522 000

定价：298.00元
(如有印装质量问题，我社负责调换)

编 委 会

总 策 划	金英嫒
策划编辑	尹光镇　林承庆
正　　文	韩国国立文化财研究所
记　　事	池炳穆
翻　　译	方京一
审　　稿	朴淳发　郑大宁　韦　正
校　　对	郑大宁　金洪洙　崔镐玹
	全孝彬　孙　璐　王飞峰
摄　　影	吴世允

Director	Kim Young-Won
Chief Editor	Yun Gwang-Jin　Lim Seng-Kyeong
Author(Main Text)	NRICH of ROK
Author(Discussion Paper)	Ji Byong-Mok
Translateor	Fang Jing-Yi
Supervisor	Park Soon-Bal　Jeong Dae-Young　Wei Zheng
Assistant Editor	Jeong Dae-Young　Kim Hong-Soo　Choi Ho-Hyun
	Chun Hyo-Bin　Sun Lu　Wang Fei-Feng
Photographer	Oh Sae-Yoon

凡　例

1. 本书为介绍 2002～2007 年韩国国立文化财研究所进行的考古发掘调查成果的图录。
2. 本书按照百济—新罗—伽倻—高丽—朝鲜的顺序，分别对各王朝及其相应文物进行介绍。
3. 图片标记的顺序为编号、名称、出土地点、大小。文物同遗迹的时代不一致时另加时代名。
   文物以厘米为单位，并选择"H(高)、W(宽)、L(长)、D(直径)"中的一项来标明文物的大小。
4. 遗址的发掘调查机构见图片目录。
5. 本书使用学术界通用术语，韩语的固有名词以脚注形式加以说明。
6. 本书所载的文物曾在 2007 年韩国国立中央博物馆进行过展出。

序 Preface

　　自 1969 年韩国国立文化财研究所成立以后，其始终以发掘和管理物质文化遗产和非物质文化遗产为己任，是韩国唯一的国家级综合学术调查研究机构。作为国立研究机构，我所每年都要承担 20 余项田野考古发掘。

　　《韩国考古学重大发现（2002～2007）》一书的面世，是以向韩国普通读者和学术界介绍国立文化财研究所的重要成果为目的，而汇集成册的。本书囊括了百济王宫、伽倻古墓、新罗王京、高丽王陵和朝鲜景福宫等，曾经矗立在韩国历史中心、广受注目的遗址。积累如斯，本书汇集了近 40 年的考古学成果，堪称韩国此类书籍之翘楚。同时，我所为了向难以接触到韩国最新考古学成果的中国普通读者和对此关心的学者介绍最新成果，计划隆重推出中文版《韩国考古学重大发现（2002～2007）》。以此为契机，我们计划出版系列性的中文版韩国考古学学术资料。这样的出版业务，必将提高人们对两国历史和文化的考古学认识；同时，我们期待着，它能为双方更活跃、更积极、更广泛的学术交流，架构一座更坚固的桥梁。

韩国国立文化财研究所所长　金英媛

　　The National Research Institute of Cultural Heritage (NRICH) is the sole research institute in Korea that has been responsible for the excavation, investigation, restoration and preservation of the country's important tangible and intangible cultural properties since its foundation in 1969. As a national research institute, it conducts 20 archaeological investigations every year.

　　Momentous Discoveries in Korean Archaeology (2002~2007) was originally published in 2007 to introduce important research results of the NRICH to the public and academic circles. The publication includes the results of investigations of historic sites such as the royal palace of Baekje (百济), Gaya tombs, Wanggyeong, the ancient capital (王京) of Silla (新罗), royal tombs of the Goryeo (高丽) Dynasty, and Gyeongbokgung, (景福宫) a royal palace of the Joseon (朝鲜) Dynasty. It is the only book that covers the accomplishments of Korean archaeology over the past 40 years.

　　The NRICH has published this Chinese edition of *Momentous Discoveries in Korean Archaeology (2002~2007)* to introduce the latest achievements in archaeological investigations to the public and scholars in China. We plan to continue publication of Chinese editions of academic materials on Korean archaeology in the future. It is hoped that this publication will promote archaeological awareness in regard to the two countries' history and culture and signal the start of more active academic exchange.

Director-General of the National Research Institute of Cultural Heritage　Kim Young-Won

推荐意见 A Letter of Recommendation

中文出版的韩国考古学论著不多，特别是最新考古学发现与研究介绍的更少。在世界日益全球化的今天，学术的全球化不仅必须而且必然。在人类历史上，各种古代文化都不是封闭的，而是通过不断地接触，在交流互动中发展。东亚是一个文化圈，各地发现的遗迹遗物，显示出了共性与个性，各个文化之间的联系值得探索。

21世纪韩国考古学的发现和研究都有突破性进展，《韩国考古学重大发现（2002～2007）》一书，将大量的遗迹、遗物展示在人们面前，并做出研究解读，令人耳目一新。它不仅为研究韩国古代社会的生产、生活、信仰、艺术，提供了前所未有的资料，也揭示了古代东亚世界的文化交融发展。

古人在进行物质文化创造的同时也把精神文化移植到物品上来。韩国考古新发现是研究历史的生动鲜活的事物标本，但由于语言文字的阻隔，这些珍贵的、需要共享的资料，并不被中国学界更多的人了解，因此翻译出版这本书具有意义。

北京大学教授　齐东方

In Korea, there are not very many archaeological books published in Chinese; especially, there have very few books that introduce recent archaeological results. With rapid globalization, it is inevitable and necessary to globalize scientific works. Historically, all the ancient civilizations were not closed and became prosperous with continuous cultural exchange and interaction. East Asian countries have formed a cultural area, and actually have relics in common with each other, but at the same time, they have differences. Thus, it is worthwhile to study intercultural differences.

The Korean archaeology of the 21st century has accomplished remarkable feats not only in excavation but in studies. The book *Momentous Discoveries in Korean Archaeology (2002 ~ 2007)* introduces many relics and explains them with research findings in order that readers may take the new fun out of reading. This book deals with productive activities, daily lives, religions and arts of ancient Korean society by using groundbreaking data, and moreover, explains cultural exchange and cross-fertilization in ancient East Asian countries.

Ancestors reflected moral culture in material civilization. The new findings in Korean archaeology are expected to be the living examples of histological studies. Nevertheless, valuable and useful materials have not been introduced to Chinese due to the barrier of language. This book is significant in the sense that it has been translated into Chinese.

Professor of Peking University　Qi Dong-Fang

韩国国立文化财研究所最新发掘成果和韩中交流

韩国国立文化财研究所所长 金英媛

一、国立文化财研究所和考古学发掘

考古学是一门通过遗址和遗物，研究人类活动和文化的学问，它既可以探悉由于文献的缺失而无法了解到的历史，也可以成为证明文献记载的重要基础。为此，考古学者毕其一生心血，发掘了曾经生活在这一片热土的人类遗址和遗物，为寻找我们祖先的灿烂文化，进行了不懈的努力。

但是，考古学学者的个人努力，在时间、金钱和规模等方面，受到诸多限制。因此，为了有计划、大规模地进行发掘和研究，韩国在政府主导下，于1969年设置了文化财研究室。这一机构在1975年，正式更名为国立文化财研究所，并沿用至今。

国立文化财研究所从成立开始，到2007年为止，直接参与发掘调查的遗址有：朝鲜半岛古代国家新罗、伽倻、百济和统一新罗遗址；高丽和朝鲜王朝遗址；新罗的王京、月城护城河、皇南洞遗址、皇龙寺址、芬皇寺、四天王寺址、传·仁容寺址、天官寺址以及荪谷洞、勿川里遗址等代表性的遗址；伽倻的松岘洞古墓群、内山里古墓群、城山山城等遗址；百济的风纳土城、扶苏山城、官北里遗址、宫南池、王宫里遗址、王兴寺址、北岩里古墓群等遗址；高丽的江华岛高丽王陵和实相寺等遗址；朝鲜的景福宫和洛山寺等，堪称具有韩国历史象征意义的代表性遗址。

但是，从现实的理由而言，国立文化财研究所无法直接涉足朝鲜半岛北部的古代国家遗址。由此，本书中自然无法记录与之相关的一鳞半爪之内容。但是，因为拥有相当数量的可以判断为从中国传来的遗物，通过本书的介绍，我们试图与朝鲜半岛南部出土的遗物进行比较。

二、韩国古代王国到朝鲜（王朝）的代表遗址

新罗是由位于朝鲜半岛东南一隅的辰韩十二国中，庆州地区的斯卢国成长发展而来的国家，他们较早地接受了律令制度和佛教文化，并以此作为政治和思想基础，形成了古代国家的雏形。同时，在统一三国之后，新罗不仅兼容了高句丽、百济的文化，而且并蓄了唐朝和西域的文物制度，形成了民族文化发展的坚实基础。同时，为统一大业提供了精神支柱的佛教，变得更为盛行，并深深地植根于社会和文化中。

以庆州为中心，与新罗至统一新罗相关的遗址，被大规模发掘调查。其对象，不仅有新罗王京和月城护城河，而且包罗了皇龙寺址、四天王寺址、芬皇寺、传·仁容寺址、天官寺址等寺院遗址；皇南洞建筑遗址和三国时代生产陶器和木炭的荪谷洞、勿川里生产遗址等多种性质的遗址。这样的发掘调查，为复原新罗王京的构造、规模、当时生产体系和生活面貌，提供了重要的资料。

位于弁韩旧土洛东江中下游的伽倻，以丰富的铁资源为后盾，成长为古代国际贸易中心。伽倻初期以庆尚南道金海的金官伽倻为中心，后期以庆尚北道高灵的大伽倻为中心发展迅猛。伽倻虽然具有联盟体的性质，但是又分别创造了独具特色的文化，它们自始至终维持着紧密的相互交流关系。

通过发掘调查，我们探明伽倻地区的遗址有着多种古墓和山城形态。它们不仅蕴藏着伽倻

的地区性文化特征，而且出土了大量被推断为与新罗和百济具有密切关系的遗物。尤其值得一提的是，作为铁的王国，马具、武器、农具等铁制品纷纷出土，可谓实至名归。同时，这里出土了大量木简，为考察韩国古代文书行政的一个侧面，提供了重要的文字资料，并由此引起了关注。

在汉江流域发展的百济，在三国鼎立的历史长河中，因为两次迁都，形成了汉城、熊津、泗沘三个时期，并以每座都城为中心，形成了独具特色的文化。百济人在汉城期的风纳土城、泗沘期的官北里一带，筑造了规模庞大的城池和大型砖瓦建筑，并设计了道路和上下水设施；同时，他们经营了各种工场和窑炉，并拥有了耕地、贮藏设施和厕所等多种多样的基础设施。他们以佛教、文字和度量衡为基础发展国力，并且通过和周边国家的积极交流，创造了洗练的百济文化。荣山江流域的伏岩里古墓，以独特的文化面貌，在古代韩日关系的研究中，被评价为不可或缺的重要遗址。

定都"开京"的高丽王朝，为了抵抗蒙古帝国的战争，迁都江华岛，驻跸长达39年。其结果为大量和王室相关的宫城、王陵和寺院等江华时代的遗址得以保存至今。江华岛上的王陵级古墓有：硕、坤、嘉三陵和陵内里石室墓，通过对它们的发掘调查，我们可以观察到古墓构造特征和这一时期高丽王陵的典型特征。另外，据传创建于统一新罗时期的实相寺，作为禅宗九山禅门中最早的伽蓝道场，在高丽时代香火鼎盛，信徒如云。在发掘调查中，我们探悉了实相寺既保持了香火的长盛不衰，又有随时代变迁变化伽蓝布局的情形。从包括高丽木塔址在内的众多建筑遗址中，我们至今仍能管中窥豹，了解到实相寺鼎盛时期的面貌。

景福宫，在朝鲜王朝的五大宫殿中，以正宫地位居首，它从太祖三年（1394年）开始修建，又被人们称为"北阙"。在壬辰倭乱的战火中被夷为一片废墟的景福宫，在高宗时代被重建，但是在日帝强占期，大量亭台楼阁被拆除，代之以朝鲜总督府办公楼等与殖民统治密切相关的建筑。最近为了复原和修缮被破坏的景福宫，国立文化财研究所在1990~2010年期间，大力推进了对景福宫的发掘调查工作。

另一方面，对于在2005年因发生山火，而给圆通宝殿和铜钟带来极大破坏的洛山寺，随着其复原和修缮计划的确定，发掘和调查工作正式启动。其成果是，从相传为洛山寺创建期的统一新罗时期到朝鲜时代的大量遗物被确认，这成为了人们重新审视洛山寺悠久历史和原貌的契机。

三、韩中两国考古学界交流现状回顾与展望

韩中两国，一衣带水，自古以来，在政治、经济、军事、文化等各个领域相互影响、相互促进。因为这样的原因，众多韩国历史学者在学习中国历史之余，孜孜不倦地深入研究了韩中两国的交流关系。与此同时，中国的历史学者对韩国历史也给予了持续的关注，并参与到我们的研究之中。

但是，在考古学领域，韩中两国的研究人员的交叉研究并不多，这也是无可争议的现实。我们认为，这是因为与以文献资料为中心的历史学不同，以现场发掘调查和遗址及出土品的分析和解释为基础的考古学学术特征，带来了这样不同的结果。

实际上，在20世纪中期以后，两国由于现实的政治问题，在相当长的时间内，不可能进行直接的交流。自然而然，由于双方没有机会直接参与到对方的发掘调查现场，因此导致了几十年来都缺乏积极的研究人员的遗憾局面。

因为这样的理由，即便是1992年韩中建交之后，我们也很难期待短时间内会出现研究人员大幅增加的情况。建交之后，部分韩国研究人员到中国留学，开始研究中国考古学；同时，中国的研究人员也开始访问韩国，或开始参与到实际的发掘调查，或开始学习韩国考古学。但是，到目前为止，它还处于蹒跚起步的阶段。

综上所述，韩中两国往来交流的历史绵延数千年，直到今天，才有机会重新相互审视。目前，韩国很多大学都开设了"中国考古学概论"这一课程，成为了大学生们了解中国考古学的一条途径。但是，目前为止，在韩国还没有出现宏观地介绍中国考古学的概论性书籍。这是因为，在韩国研究中国考古学的人员仍然在学术界人微言轻的缘故吧。

这样的问题，对中国的韩国考古学研究人员也不会是例外。事实上，在中国，介绍韩国考古学的概论性书籍和讲座，都是凤毛麟角。

与此相关，韩中两国之间的考古学交流还处于零星状态，作为韩国文化财研究的代表机构——国立文化财研究所，将责无旁贷地制订计划，先行出版我所的考古发掘调查成果。如果说这本书最大的遗憾的话，莫过于前面所提到的，由于本研究所无法涉足而遗漏的朝鲜半岛北部的古代国家遗址。

虽然仍然会有这样那样的不足之处，但是，第一本系统地介绍韩国考古学成果的中文版图书即将付梓。以这本书的出版为契机，我们期待着，在中国掀起对韩国考古学关注的热潮，并且也希望这本书能够成为广大中国读者初步了解韩国考古学的捷径。

国立文化财研究所将在这本书之外，准备将更多的研究成果翻译成中文出版。我们深深地期待着，处于起步阶段的考古学领域内的韩中交流，能够通过这本凝结了无数心血的画册，变得更加活跃。

Archaeological Achievements of NRICH, Its Excavations of Major Korean Sites and Korea-China Exchange

Kim Young-Won (Director-General of NRICH)

1. NRICH and Archaeological Excavations

As the study of human activities and culture through remains and relics, archaeology not only provides verification of history that could not be confirmed due to the lack of documentary evidence but also corroborates historical facts handed down in written records. Many archaeologists have, therefore, worked hard to discover the culture of the ancestors through excavation of their remains and relics.

Archaeologists' individual efforts, however, often came up against problems in terms of time and finances or even scale. Hence the Research Office of Cultural Heritage was established by the Korean government in order to conduct large-scale and well-organized excavations. It was reorganized into the National Research Institute of Cultural Heritage (NRICH) in 1975.

From 1975 to 2007, the NRICH excavated and investigated the major ruins of ancient Korean states such as Silla, Gaya (伽倻), Baekje, and Unified Silla, as well as the Goryeo and Joseon dynasties: (1) Silla: Wanggyeong (王京), the ancient capital of Silla (present day Gyeongju); Weolseong Moat (月城护城河); the remains of Hwangnamdong (皇南洞); Hwangnyongsa Temple site (皇龙寺址); Bunhwangsa Temple, Sacheonwangsa Temple site (四天王寺址); the presumed site of Innyongsa Temple site (传·仁容寺址); Cheongwansa Temple site (天官寺址); and the remains of Songokdong (苏谷洞) and Mulcheollri (勿川里); (2) Gaya: tombs of Songhyeondong (松岘洞); tombs of Naesalli (内山里); Tombs, and Seongsan-sanseong (城山) mountain fortress; (3) Baekje: Pungnap-toseong (风纳) earthen wall fortress; Busosanseong (扶苏) mountain fortress; the remains of Gwanbungni (官北里), Gungnamji Pond (宫南池), the remains of Wanggungni (王宫里), Wangheungsa Temple site (王兴寺址), and the tombs of Bogamni (伏岩里); (4) Goryeo: royal tombs of Goryeo in Ganghwado (江华) and Silsangsa (实相) Temple; and (5) Joseon: Gyeongbokgung Palace and Naksansa (洛山) Temple. All the above are archaeological sites symbolic of the history of Korea.

For practical reasons, the NRICH was not able to directly excavate the remains of ancient kingdoms located in the northern part of the Korean Peninsula and accordingly they are not included in this book. However, as many relics presumed to be of Chinese origin have been handed down in Korea, an attempt has been made in this book to compare them with relics excavated on the Korean Peninsula.

2. Excavation of Major Sites from Korea's Ancient Kingdoms to the Joseon Dynasty

Silla is an ancient kingdom that developed out of Saroguk (斯卢国), situated in Gyeongju (庆州), one of the 12 states of the Jinhan (辰韩) confederacy in the southeast part of the Korean Peninsula. With its early introduction of laws and Buddhism, it laid the groundwork for politics and thought and thereby established the basic systems of an ancient state. After unifying the Three Kingdoms, Silla assimilated the cultures of Tang (唐) China and the Western regions (西域) (countries bordering Western China) as well as the cultures of the Goguryeo (高句丽) and

Baekje kingdoms to lay the foundations for its own culture. Buddhism, the spiritual base for the unification of the Three Kingdoms, further flourished and became deeply rooted in Silla society and culture.

Large-scale excavations were carried out on various types of sites from Silla and Unified Silla located in and around Gyeongju. They include Silla's capital Wanggyeong (王京) and Weolseong Moat (月城护城河), the site of buildings in Hwangnamdong (皇南洞), temple remains such as Hwangnyongsa Temple site (皇龙寺址), Bunhwangsa Temple (芬皇寺), the presumed site of Innyongsa Temple (传·仁容寺址), and Cheongwansa Temple site (天官寺址), etc., and sites revealing` earthenware and charcoal remains from the Three Kingdoms period including Songok-dong (苏谷洞) and Mulcheolli (勿川里). The excavations yielded important materials for study of the organization and size of the Silla capital and the production system and life in those times.

Gaya, situated in the middle and lower reaches of the Nakdonggang River (洛东江) [former territory of the Byeonhan (弁韩) confederacy], developed into a center for international trade thanks to the rich iron deposits in the region. In the early period it was centered around the state of Geumgwan Gaya (金官伽倻) in Gimhae (金海), Gyeongsangnam-do Province (庆尚南道), and in the latter period around Daegaya (大伽倻) in Goryeong (高灵), Gyeongsangbuk-do Province (庆尚北道). In nature Gaya was an alliance of city-states, which maintained mutual exchange each other while developing their own individual cultures.

The excavated Gaya sites comprise various types of tombs and mountain fortresses, which have revealed differing cultural characteristics according to region. Relics assumed to be related to Silla and Baekje have often been excavated at these sites. In particular, many iron relics such as horse trappings, weapons, and agricultural tools have been discovered, as expected of a state known as the "kingdom of iron." Another notable discovery is a large number of wooden tablets that served as documents, important relics facilitating study of ancient documentation and administration.

In the midst of continued conflict between the Three Kingdoms, Baekje, which first flourished in Han River basin, moved its capital twice, dividing Baekje history into three periods—Hanseong (汉城), Ungjin (熊津) and Sabi (泗沘). During each period, a unique culture developed in each of the capitals. In the Hanseong period, the Baekje people constructed Pungnap-toseong (风纳), an earthen wall fortress assumed to have formed a major walled capital, and in the Sabi period large fortresses and tiled-roof buildings all over Gwanbungni (官北里). They built roads and water supply facilities, operated craft workshops and kilns, and created diverse infrastructure including arable lands, storage facilities, and toilets. With state administration underpinned by Buddhism, literacy in Chinese characters, a system of weights and measures, and active exchange with neighboring countries, Baekje succeeded in creating an original and highly sophisticated culture. The Bogamni (伏岩里) tombs in the Yeongsangang River (荣山江) basin in particular are regarded as remains essential to uncovering the unique culture of Baekje and its relationship with Japan.

In the Goryeo Dynasty, in the face of Mongol invasion the court transferred the capital from Gaegyeong (开京) to Ganghwado Island (江华岛) and remained there for 39 years. Remains from the Ganghwado period include a royal palace, a Buddhist temple connected with the royal family, and royal tombs including Seongneung (硕陵), Golleung (坤陵), Gareung (嘉陵) and a stone-chamber tomb in Neungnaeri (陵内里). Excavation of these sites has enabled researchers to examine the structural features of the tombs and the archetype of Goryeo royal tombs of this period. Silsangsa (实相) Temple, the first Buddhist temple of the Nine Mountain Zen School

(九山禅门), known to date to the Unified Silla period, flourished during the Goryeo Dynasty. Excavations of the temple shed light on the way the layout changed while the influence of the temple was maintained over a long period of time. Numerous building sites including that of a wooden pagoda give an idea of how Silsangsa looked in its heyday.

Gyeongbokgung (景福宫), one of the five main palaces of the Joseon Dynasty, was first constructed in 1394, the third year of King Taejo's (太祖) reign. Originally called Bukgweol (北阙), meaning "northern palace", it was destroyed by fire in the Imjin Woeran (壬辰倭乱), or the Japanese Invasion of Korea in 1592, and rebuilt in the Gojong (高宗) era. It was put through many trials during the Japanese colonial period (1910~1945), when many of the palace buildings were demolished and replaced by buildings serving Japan's colonial rule. One example of such was the former Japanese Government-General Building. The NRICH conducted excavations of Gyeongbokgung in its damaged state from 1990 and to 2010 in preparation for its repair and restoration.

Another important excavation was that carried out on Naksansa (洛山) Temple when plans were made for its repair and restoration following a big fire in 2005 that destroyed the temple's main hall, Wontongbojeon (圆通宝殿), and the bronze temple bell. The investigations unearthed a large number of relics ranging in time from the Unified Silla to Joseon periods, enabling confirmation of the long history and real appearance of the temple.

3. Present State and Prospects of Korea-China Archaeological Exchange

Korea and China have influenced each other in all aspects such as politics, economics, society, culture, and military matters due to their geographical contiguity since ancient times. Many Korean historians have studied Chinese history and researched exchange between the two countries. Chinese historians have displayed continued interest in Korean history and are taking part in such studies also.

However, few Korean or Chinese scholars have conducted research on each other's archaeology. This can be attributed to the nature of archaeology, for contrary to study of documented history it is based on site excavation as well as analysis and interpretation of the site and the relics discovered there.

For political reasons, it has been impossible for the two countries to carry out direct exchange since the mid-20th century. Hence there have been few opportunities over the past several decades for researchers of the two countries to participate in each other's excavation projects.

This being the case, it was difficult to expect a noticeable increase in the number of such researchers even after the establishment of diplomatic ties between Korea and China in 1992. Since normalization of ties, however, Korean researchers have been going to China to study Chinese archaeology, and at the same time, Chinese researchers are coming to Korea to participate in excavations or study Korean archeology. Yet it is true that such exchange is still very much in its infancy.

As indicated by the above, new opportunities are emerging to build mutual understanding between Korea China, which have a long history of exchange over thousands of years. Presently, many universities in Korea have established Introduction to Chinese Archaeology courses, through which students can gain a basic understanding in this field. But as the number of Chinese archaeology scholars in Korea is still small, currently there is no Korean textbook that gives a macroscopic view of the subject.

The situation is little different when it comes to the study of Korean archaeology in China, where textbooks or courses giving an introduction to Korean archaeology are still rare.

It was this tenuous archaeological exchange between Korea and China that motivated the NRICH, the representative research institute of Korean cultural heritage, to publish a book on the results of past excavation projects. It is highly regretted that the remains of Korea's ancient kingdoms located in the northern part of the Korean Peninsula could not be directly excavated and were therefore not included in this book, as mentioned above.

Publication of the Chinese edition of this book introducing the achievements of Korean archaeology is just the beginning. It is our hope that this book will provide a good a basic introduction to Korean archaeology for Chinese readers and stimulate greater interest among Chinese scholars.

In addition, the NRICH is preparing further publication of archaeological research results in the Chinese language. While Korea-China archaeological exchange is still in its early stages, it is anticipated that publication of this book in Chinese will promote greater interaction between the two countries in this field.

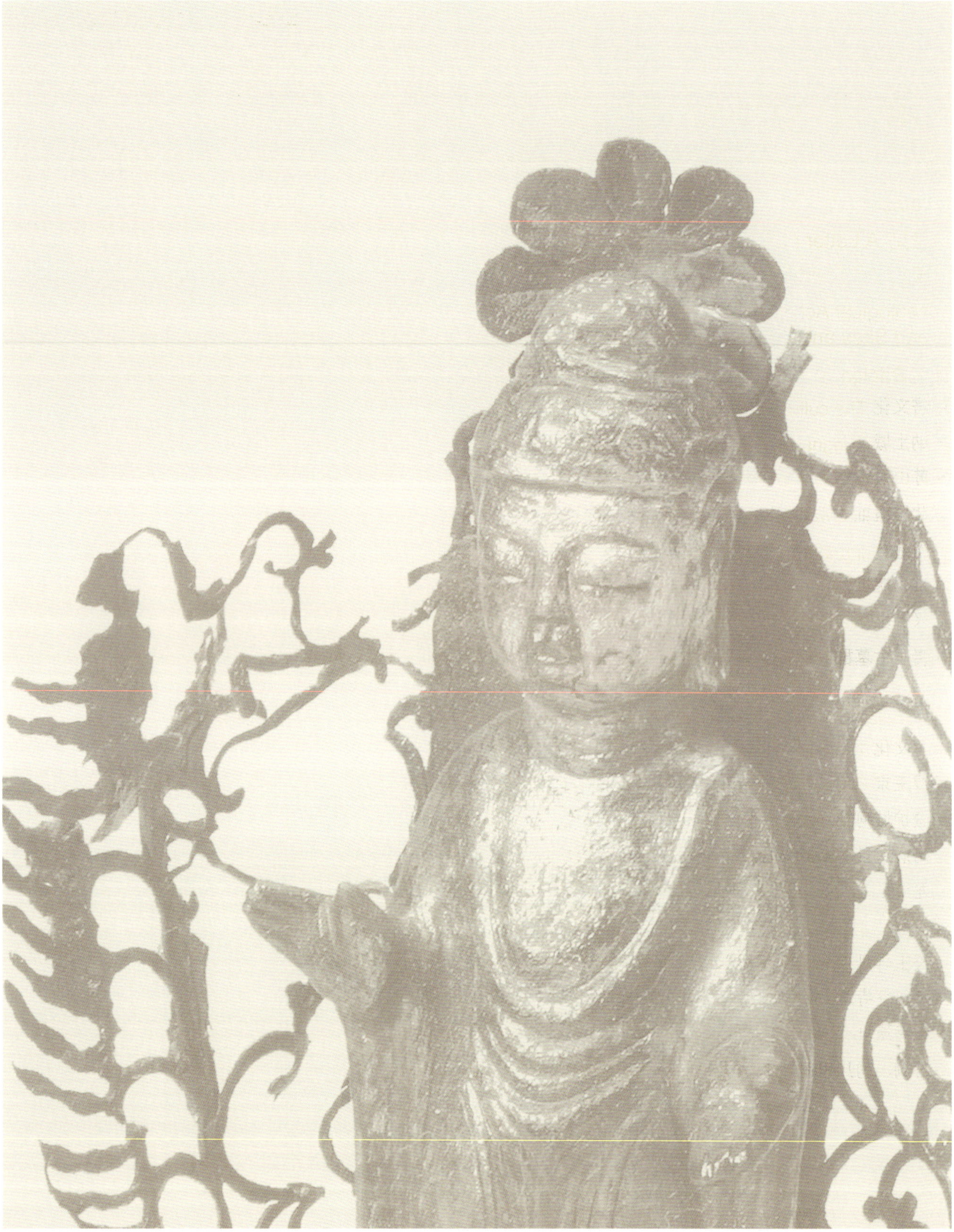

目录 | Contents

序 Preface	1
推荐意见 A Letter of Recommendation	2
韩国国立文化财研究所最新发掘成果和韩中交流	3
Archaeological Achievements of NRICH, Its Excavations of Major Korean Sites and Korea-China Exchange	6
百济 | Baekje	13
百济文化 The culture of Baekje	15
风纳土城 Pungnap Mud Fortress Wall	16
扶苏山城 Busosanseong Fortress	28
官北里遗址 Gwanbungni Baekje Archaeological Site	32
宫南池 Gungnamji Archaeological Site	46
王宫里遗址 Wanggungni Archaeological Site	50
王兴寺址 Wangheungsa Temple Site	62
伏岩里古墓群 Bogamni Tomb Complex	66
新罗 | Silla	73
新罗文化 The culture of Silla	75
新罗王京 Royal Capital of Silla	76
月城护城河 Wolseong Moat	86
皇南洞遗址 Hwangnamdong Archaeological Site	92
皇龙寺址 Hwangnyongsa Temple Site	96
芬皇寺 Bunhwangsa Temple	106
四天王寺址 Sacheonwangsa Temple Site	124
传·仁容寺址 Inyongsa Temple Site (Alleged)	136
天官寺遗址 Cheongwansa Temple Site	144
荪谷洞、勿川里遗址 Songokdong·Mulcheolli Archaeological Site	148

伽倻 ｜ Gaya	157
伽倻文化 The culture of Gaya	159
松岘洞古墓群 Songhyeondong Tomb Complex	160
内山里古墓群 Naesalli Tomb Complex	174
城山山城 Seongsansanseong Fortress	186
高丽 ｜ Goryeo	193
高丽文化 The Culture of Goryeo	195
江华高丽王陵 Goryeo Royal Tombs in Ganghwa	196
实相寺 Silsangsa Temple	206
朝鲜 ｜ Joseon	217
朝鲜文化 The Culture of Joseon	219
景福宫 Gyeongbokgung Palace	220
洛山寺 Naksansa Temple	236
附录 ｜ Appendix	245
国立文化财研究所在韩国田野考古学史上的成长足迹	246
The NRICH from the Perspective of Korea's Excavation History	256
韩国国立文化财研究所发掘年表 Chronicle of the Field Work of the NRICH	268
图片目录索引 Plates Index	278

Baekje 百济

韩国 考古学重大发现（2002~2007）

根据《三国史记》的记载，百济是公元前18年建国，公元660年被新罗和唐朝联军灭亡。根据其都城的迁移及文化特征的变化，百济可分为汉城时期、熊津时期和泗沘时期。百济文化通过与唐文化、高句丽文化、新罗文化等不断地文化交流而发展，并在其发展过程中体现出独特的文化特征。后来百济文化还传播到日本，并对日本古代飞鸟文化的形成起到了重要的作用。

汉城时期（前18～475年），温祚王先在汉江以北建立国家，此后，又在汉江以南修建风纳土城作为都城，并以此为基础逐步发展起来。后来又在风纳土城附近修筑梦村土城，形成了"两城制"的都城制度。风纳土城是以版筑技术修建的六角形土城，其内部以道路为界分布有官署、公共建筑、礼制建筑等遗址，出土了百济初期的瓦类等大量精美的文物。

熊津时期（475～538年），百济迁都公州的公山城。这一时期由于和新罗结盟，百济还企图收复汉江流域。

泗沘时期（538～660年），是百济文化最繁荣的时期，佛教于本阶段传入（384年）。此阶段百济经济持续稳定发展，和佛教文化一起进入一个繁荣的时期。百济圣王自公州迁都扶余，修建了环绕都城外的罗城和扶苏山城以及官厅所在的官北里遗址和王宫南侧的宫南池。都城建设是有计划地划分为5部5巷进行的，与此相关的铭文瓦也已经发现。武王时期因为有再次迁都的计划，在益山地区还修筑了宫城。但是关于当时真迁都与否的意见并不一致。在王宫里遗址发现宫城遗址外，还发现了制作金、银、铜和玻璃等的作坊遗址，这是研究这一时期生产和消费关系的重要遗址。

另外，伏岩里古墓群的发掘，为确认6世纪中期以后百济加强对湖南地区[①]荣山江流域的统治提供了证据。

According to Korea's history book "The Chronicles of the Three Kingdoms (三国史记)", Baekje is an ancient country which was founded in 18 B.C. and brought to the ground by the allied forces of Silla and Tang in 660 A.D. The history of Baekje is divided into three periods according to transfer of the capital and the change of cultural aspects: Hanseong (汉城), Ungjin (熊津) and Sabi (泗沘). Baekje developed its cultures gradually through constant cultural exchanges with China and its neighboring countries Goguryeo and Silla to create its original culture. After that time, Baekje's culture exerted considerable influences on the formation of Japan's ancient Asuka (飞鸟) culture.

In the period of Hanseong (18 B.C.~475 A.D.), King Onjo (温祚王), first built up a country in the north of the Han River. Then, he went to south of the Han River and set up the capital in Pungnap (风纳) Mud Castle, located at Seoul. Baekje grew with it as the new capital starting point. It constructed Mongchon (梦村) Mud Castle near the capital to establish a system of dual castles. Pungnap Mud Castle is an earth wall built by ramming earth well down and has a shape of planar hexagon. Excavated were many of splendid relics such as roof tiles of the early years of the Baekje era together with public building and systematic construction sites, by starting from the roads in the castle.

The period of Ungjin (475~538 A.D.) was a time when Baekje attempted to rise again transferring of the capital to Gongsan (公山)Castle in Gongju (公州). In this period, Baekje formed an alliance with Silla and tried to recover the Han River basin.

---

① 湖南地区为韩国西南部的全罗南道和全罗北道的合称。

The period of Sabi (538~660 A.D.) was a time when Baekje's culture was most brilliant; it attained economic stability and created Buddhist culture after the introduction of Buddhism into it (384 A.D.). King Seong (圣) constructed Buso (扶苏) Mountain Castle, the internal castle of naseong (罗城) which surrounds the outskirts of the capital city, remains of Gwanbungni (官北里), where the government office site was identified, and Gungnamji (宫南池), known as a pond site in the south of the palace transferring the capital Gongju (公州) to Buyeo (扶余). He built up the capital as a planned city dividing it into 5 parts (部) and 5 towns (巷). This was confirmed by roof tiles into which words were carved. King Munmu (文武) planned to transfer the capital and constructed a royal palace in Iksan (益山). But, there are divergent opinions about whether the capital was transferred. The remains of Wanggungni (王宫里) are important ruins showing the relationship between production and consumption of those days in that facilities which produced gold, silver, bronze and glass were identified in the remains, together with a royal palace.

The remains of Bogamni's (伏岩里) were excavated which give proofs for the fact that Baekje strengthened its control over the Yeongsan River (荣山江) basin in the Honam (湖南) district after the mid-6th century.

百济文化 | The culture of Baekje

在汉江流域成长的百济王国，在三国鼎立的历史环境中，历经两次迁都，分为汉城、熊津、泗沘三个时期，以各个时期的都城为中心，形成了独具特色的文化。百济人在汉城期的风纳土城和泗沘期的官北里一带，建造了规模巨大的城郭和大型砖瓦建筑，铺设了道路和供水设施，修建了作坊和陶窑。除此之外，还筹建了耕地、贮藏设施和卫生设施等大量的基础设施。他们以佛教、文字和度量衡为基础发展国力，并且通过和周边国家的积极交流，创造了灿烂的百济文化。另一方面，位于荣山江流域的伏岩里古墓，以其独特的文化面貌，在古代对日关系的研究中，被评价为不可或缺的重要遗址。

The three Baekje capitals, Hanseong, Ungjin and Sabi, left distinctive remains, showing that each city made characteristic cultural achievements. The latest discovery to excite historians came from the site of the Pungnap Mud Fortress Wall, which many believe was the kingdom's first capital city, and that of a huge fortified city built in today's Gwannbuk-ri area during the Sabi period. The latter site contains the trace and remains of large tile-roofed buildings, roads, a water supply system, workshops, kilns, farming fields, storage facilities and event toilets.

The findings from the sites offer further evidence that Baekje developed a unique and refined culture through a process of exchange with neighboring kingdoms, and ran the state on the basis of Buddhism, characters, and standard weight and measures. The great variety of Baekje relics excavated recently contains an ample source of information concerning the techniques, systems and ideas developed by the Baekje people. Currently, archaeologists are paying increasing attention to the Bogamni Tombs, as they offer important clues that are essential to understanding the relationship between the kingdom's central power and the native local society at Yeongsangang River which succeeded in maintaining its own distinctive culture and tradition for a considerable period.

风纳土城 | Pungnap Mud Fortress Wall
（首尔市松坡区风纳洞 | 史迹第11号 | 三国时代）

位于汉江江畔的风纳土城，是百济汉城时期的大型平地城，南北向，呈长椭圆形或船形。土城城墙周长3.5公里（现存2.1公里），除因临近汉江而损坏严重的西墙之外，其余部分保存完好。1925年汉江大洪水时城内暴露出百济文化层，其中发现了中国制造的青铜鐎斗和铐带装饰片等重要遗物，在1964年的调查中，发现了两层百济时代的居住面以及"风纳里式无纹陶器"等公元前后至公元5世纪的遗物。

此后，从20世纪90年代后期开始，通过对风纳土城的正式发掘工作，发现了宽（墙基部）43米、高11米的巨大城墙和用版筑技法筑城的事实，同时确认了包括"吕"字形特殊建筑地基

Baekje 百济

和与祭祀有关的灰坑遗址在内的各种遗迹。此外，还出土了包括"大夫"铭陶器在内的大批百济初期的遗物，这大大提高了风纳土城是百济初期首都——河南慰礼城的可能性。

承担风纳土城的长期年度调查的国立文化财研究所在最近的调查区域中，发现了韩国最古老的道路遗迹，推测为内城墙、居住址、生产设施等大量的遗址，出土了数以万计的反映当时人们生活的百济陶器、瓦、金属遗物等。风纳土城，无论是城内的重要遗址和遗物，还是临近大江的选址条件以及周边的王陵级石村洞古墓群和山城等，可以说并不逊于高句丽的国内城、新罗的月城。

Located by the side of the Hangang in Seoul, the Pungnap Mud Fortress Wall is major fortress of the early Baekje period, built in an oval shape on level ground. The circumference of the fortress wall was originally 3.5 kilometers long, and most of the remaining wall (2.1 kilometers) is in relatively good condition, although much of the western part of the wall has been washed away by the river.

Full-scale excavation of the site started in the late 1990s and revealed that the wall, originally as wide as 43 meters and as high as 11 meters, was built using the traditional "hardening and heaping" technique. The excavation also revealed the remains of large buildings in unique forms and facilities related with religious events.

It is also at this site that archaeologists found the earliest road discovered so far in the south of the Korean peninsula, along with a large amount of relics from the early Baekje period including dwelling and production facilities. Located near a large river, with grand tomb comparable to the tombs of great rulers and mountain fortifications built in the vicinity, it is highly possible that the Pungnap Mud Fortress Wall once formed the center of the capital of early Baekje.

1. 风纳土城全景 View of Pungnap Fortress

2. 南北道路 North and South Road

3. 遗物出土状况 Remains

4. 居住遗址 Housing Site

5. 木筑井全景 Wooden Well

6. 取水用陶器出土状况 Pottery for Well-bucket

7. 井内部遗物出土状况 Remains in the Well

8、9. 取水用陶器 Pottery for Well-bucket
风纳土城 H16厘米

水 井

在风纳土城，人们为了获得必要的饮水而利用地下水，开凿了水井。在三国时代，人们已经开始使用石材或木料砌水井。在百济初期的都城——风纳土城外围，我们发现了用方木榫卯形式构筑的水井，其"井"字形态，和安岳三号墓中壁画上的水井极其相似。水井木方现存14层，高为2.5米左右，但是实际上此井可能更深。在水井内，发现了大批百济陶器和木制吊桶、顶圈和各类种子。部分陶器中发现了在颈部用绳子系过的痕迹，据此，判断这些陶器是人们使用过的吊桶。另外，在水井中还同时发现了为打捞掉入井中的吊桶而使用过的箭头形的木制品。也有学者认为，人们曾经在水井周围举行过某种盛大的祭祀活动。

10. 井内出土木制品 Wooden Ware
风纳土城 W27厘米

城墙的筑造技法

建于汉江沿岸的风纳土城，先堆起梯形土垒，以它为中心倾斜着堆出内外墙壁，这时使用一种叫做版筑法的建筑技法。使用版筑法首先平整土地以一定的区间为单位，立起木板为柱并进行固定，固定后按照一定的厚度将砂土和黏土交替堆积成层，最后用原木棍进行夯打。墙的内壁和外壁上部堆砌石块以保护土垒，土垒的最下层用河泥或黏土混合果皮或稻草之类的植物废弃物层层抹砌，这种方式是中国和日本也都有发现的重要的古代筑城法之一。

由此我们对当时的筑城规划可窥一斑，亦可以了解到以这样的规划为基础的精巧的测量技术在当时已经存在了。现在发现的城墙大概宽43米、高11米以上，如果对尚未调查的下部进行发掘的话，想来规模恐怕还要更大。

11. 城墙剖面状态 Section of Fortress Wall

12. 城墙出土陶器 Potteries
风纳土城 大型 H40.5厘米

13. 城壕出土陶器 Potteries
风纳土城 大型 H35厘米

百济陶器

百济陶器作为与百济国家同步发展的陶器群,是指具有百济固有的典型样式的陶器,它们大概从百济发展到古代国家时期就开始出现。从特征上看,百济陶器不尚纹饰而更加注重实用功能,戳压纹作为其特征持续了很长时间。

在汉城期,除出现了百济传统的陶器——黑陶和三足陶器之外,直口短颈壶、卵形陶器、豆形器等也相继出现。黑陶为了表现漆器的质感,使用了磨光陶器表面的技艺,一般认为它们主要是统治阶层使用的器物。

14. 黑陶 Black-polished Jar
 风纳土城 W16厘米

15. 百济陶器 Baekje Potteries
 风纳土城 缸 H29.5厘米

16. 风纳土城出土陶器 Potteries
 风纳土城

17. 瓦 Roof Tiles
风纳土城 L35.5厘米

汉城期的瓦

百济汉城期开始制作瓦，其制作可能是在陶工的主持下或合作下完成的。这样的推测来自于汉城期瓦的几个制作技艺特点，比如在没有瓦筒（制瓦模具）的情况下，用泥条盘起成型，打捺格子纹、水磨整面，都是这类特征。

汉城期筒瓦瓦当，仅在风纳土城、梦村土城和石村4号墓等地少量出土。这一时期筒瓦瓦当边轮高高突起，早期的筒瓦较小，逐渐发展变大，其纹饰以植物纹、圆纹、菱形纹和莲花纹等多见。

18. 瓦当 Roof-end Tiles
风纳土城 W17.7厘米

19. 础石 Cornerstone
风纳土城 W34.3厘米

20. 陶管 Pipes
风纳土城 L40.5厘米

21. 陶管底面 Bottom of the Pipe

22. 中国瓷器 Chinese Ceramics
    风纳土城

23. 石臼、网坠 Stone Mortar, Fishing Net-sinkers
    风纳土城 臼 H11厘米

24. 网坠 Fishing Net-sinkers
    风纳土城 小型 L14厘米

风纳土城的国家祭祀

　　在古代社会，牛和马是祭祀天地的重要牺牲，民间不能滥杀。在风纳土城敬堂地区 9 号坑遗址中，发现了作为牺牲的 12 匹马的马头、马形陶俑、马镫、玻璃珠、鱼骨、梅子、云母和以三足器、豆形器等特殊器具为主的一组陶器。在这些陶器中，有直口短颈壶 2 件，其肩部有用尖锐工具刻下的"大夫"、"井"等文字。这些文字意味着百济官员的等级或担任祭仪的官职，水井则有可能和避邪有关。而且，此次出土的云母在中国、韩国、日本等古墓中都曾发现过，由于云母在道教中象征着长生不老的灵丹妙药，所以被认为反映了百济与中国南朝各国的交流过程中引进的宗教观念。在风纳土城有可能共存由国家和王室主管的大规模祭祀和民间祭祀，可以推测以马为牺牲品的祭祀目的很可能就在于祈雨。

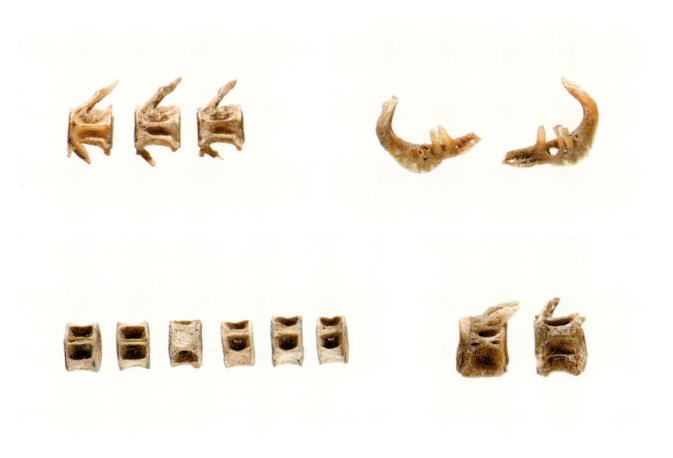

25. 鱼骨　Fish Bones
风纳土城

26. 马骨　Horse Bones
风纳土城 L11~27厘米

27. 牛骨　Cattle Bones
风纳土城 L4~21.5厘米

扶苏山城 | Busosanseong Fortress
（忠清南道扶余郡扶余邑双北里等 | 史迹第5号 | 三国时代）

为了百济的复兴，百济在圣王16年（538年）从熊津（今公州）迁都泗沘城（今扶余）。目前推测泗沘城的王宫位于官北里一带，扶苏山城为王宫的背后山城，和罗城以及周边的青山城、青马山城一起，起到了防御泗沘城的作用。在《三国史记·百济本纪》记载，泗沘城和所夫里城被认为大约是在迁都前后建造的。

扶苏山城位于以半月状环抱扶余邑西部地区的白马江相邻的扶苏山上，综合了泗沘期的包谷式山城和之后的沿山脊式山城的特点建造而成，其周长为2495米，面积达到74万平方米。

通过1980～2001年的长期发掘工作，不仅发现了东门、南门、北门遗址，还同时发现了竖穴居住遗址、建筑遗址和军库遗址等与山城有密切关系的各种设施。另外，在城墙的剖面调查中，发现了永定柱和横长木的使用痕迹，这些都证明了百济人拥有的杰出的筑城技术。

出土遗物有戳印瓦、莲花纹筒瓦瓦当、坛子、三足盘、鎏金背光等百济遗物，也出土了晚至朝鲜时代的各类遗物。尤其是在东门遗址中出土的"大通"铭的戳印瓦，其与公州大通寺址出土遗物具有同样的形态，这是证明熊津期的建材在新建王都中被重新使用的重要材料。

在城内，不仅有应付紧急情况的军事设施，而且也有迎日楼、泗沘楼、半月楼、皋兰寺、宫女祠和落花岩等休闲设施。它们可能是平时用于观赏白马江和扶苏山美景的花园。

It was in 538 that Baekje, one of the three Korean kingdoms, moved its capital from Ungjin (today's Gongju) to Sabi (today's Buyeo) as part of an effort to rejuvenate the kingdom.

Busosanseong Fortress was built during this period as one of many fortifications designed to protect the kingdom's new royal capital.

Constructed during the period in which Baekje moved the capital, the fortifications had a 2,495-meter-long wall combined with various structures built for military purposes.

In the excavation conducted between 1980 and 2001, archaeologists discovered features of the fortress' east, south and north gates and other defense facilities including and arsenal. They also discovered that the Baekje people had advanced skills in fortress wall construction. The findings include roof tiles showing that many of the buildings in the new capital were built by re-using materials taken from the early capital.

28. 扶苏山城远景 View of Busosanseong Fortress

29. 城墙筑造状况 Fortress Wall

30. 扶苏山城城墙 Fortress Wall

31. 背光 Aureole
扶苏山城 D12.6厘米

这是1991年在扶苏山城东门址附近发现的佛像或菩萨像的背光,其中央有个可以在佛像头部背面安放插销的小孔。其正面是纯金装饰板,背面用金铜板来支撑。放在佛像头部后侧的背光,其中心部分用金片剪成莲花花瓣,表现得富有立体感;其外围部分则用镂刻技法施以唐草纹。莲花与唐草纹之间的联珠纹区分两个纹样带,纹样内部刻有精致的点线和阴刻线条,使其显得更加华丽端庄。

背面的鎏金板下端刻有"何多宜藏法师"铭文,这应该是与光背的制作有关的人名,尤其是"法师"标记,应该是一位僧侣。如果铭文揭示的真是背光的制作者,那么这将成为研究几乎不见物勒工名的韩国古代美术史和手工业史的重要材料。

32、33. 背光 Aureoles
扶苏山城 D14.4厘米

扶苏山城出土的黑釉瓷器

中国的黑釉瓷器出现于东汉时期，与青瓷一同发展。东晋至南朝初期黑釉瓷器产于南方（今浙江地区）的瓷窑，北朝东魏时期，北方地区也开始制造黑釉瓷器。北齐时期更为成熟，渐渐形成中国施釉瓷器的一个潮流。在韩国，相当于中国六朝到隋时期的黑釉瓷器主要出土于百济，扶苏山城出土的黑釉瓷器应该是隋朝和唐朝初期制作的。通过出土于风纳土城、梦村土城、扶苏山城、天安龙院里、公州武宁王陵、公州水村里古墓等遗址的黑釉瓷器，可以推断出这些瓷器与青瓷一起，以几乎同样的制作水平传入了韩国。

34. 扶苏山城出土黑釉瓷器 Black-glazed Wares

35. "大通"铭板瓦 Roof Tile
扶苏山城 L16.8厘米

在扶苏山城东门址发现的戳印瓦。"大通"是中国南朝梁武帝在527~529年使用过的年号。公州市班竹洞遗址也发现过类似的瓦，据《三国遗事》记载，"大通元年为梁武帝立大通寺于熊川州"，由此发现了班竹洞一带就是大通寺址。

通过此瓦可知，百济从公州迁至扶余之前，已经在扶苏山外围修筑山城等整顿了都城的防御设施。

36. "大通"铭板瓦细部 Detail of Roof Tile

官北里遗址 | Gwanbungni Baekje Archaeological Site
（忠清南道扶余郡扶余邑官北里 | 史迹第428号 | 三国时代）

　　官北里遗址，作为百济泗沘期（538～660年）的王宫或相关设施所在之处，位于扶苏山南麓。通过1982年开始的连续调查，清理出了百济时期井然有序的古代道路、莲池和各种建筑遗址等泗沘都城的主要设施。

　　最近在这里发现了被评价为王宫正殿级殿堂的大型建筑遗址，其大小为面阔7间（东西35米），进深4间（南北18米）。作为基础设施，使用了磉墩[1]，建筑的中心部是形成通间的两层瓦房。如果将这样的大型殿堂建筑和历史状况联系起来看的话，让人非常容易想起武王三十一年（630年）二月重修泗沘宫殿，或义慈王十五年（655年）二月修缮太子宫的文献记录。

　　现在在史迹遗址一带发现的大型殿堂或供水设施，大约是泗沘期末期修建的。迁都到泗沘城时，作坊和各种地下仓库等王宫附属生产和贮藏设施已经先期营造完毕，以后为了扩建王宫，堆土台基不断扩大，在此土台之上，有计划地修筑和安置了道路、排水设施、建筑和池塘等设施。

　　通过发掘调查可知，在官北里遗址，百济泗沘期王宫和相关的各种设施，在不同的时期，以不同形态，被不断建造。同时也出土了大量描绘当时人面的陶器、带"首府"铭文的瓦、木简、草鞋和果实的种子等遗物。可以预见的是，随着对遗址和周边一带发掘与调查的持续进行，这里可以为复原百济王宫和泗沘都城的生活史提供比想象更多的基础材料。

Located on the southern slopes of Busosan, the archaeological site in Gwanbungni of Buyeo is believed to have once been the site of the royal palace of late Baekje (538~660). A series of excavations conducted from 1982 revealed that the first buildings erected in the new capital were workshops and subterranean storage facilities associated with the new palaces. The following expansion of the capital involved the systematic construction of new roads, drainage ditches, lotus ponds, palace buildings and landscape facilities.

A recent excavation revealed that the site contains the vestiges of palace buildings, including one that can be regarded as a throne hall measuring 7 by 4 han (one kan being the distance between the two columns, that is, 35 by 18 meters), and water supply facilities. With the palace facilities built in regular sequence for various purposes, the Gwanbungni site provides valuable information about the changes that occurred in the development of loyal palaces during the late Baekje period.

---

[1] 韩国传统建筑的承重构件之一，在地上挖坑后，用小石头和土夯成基础，柱础安放其上，以此承柱。

37. 莲池遗址 Pond Site

38. 官北里遗址全景 View of Gwanbungni Site

39. 官北里遗址大型建筑物址 Large Building Site

40. 大型建筑物复原图 Presumed Elevation of Large Building

41. 木椁仓库 Wooden Warehouse

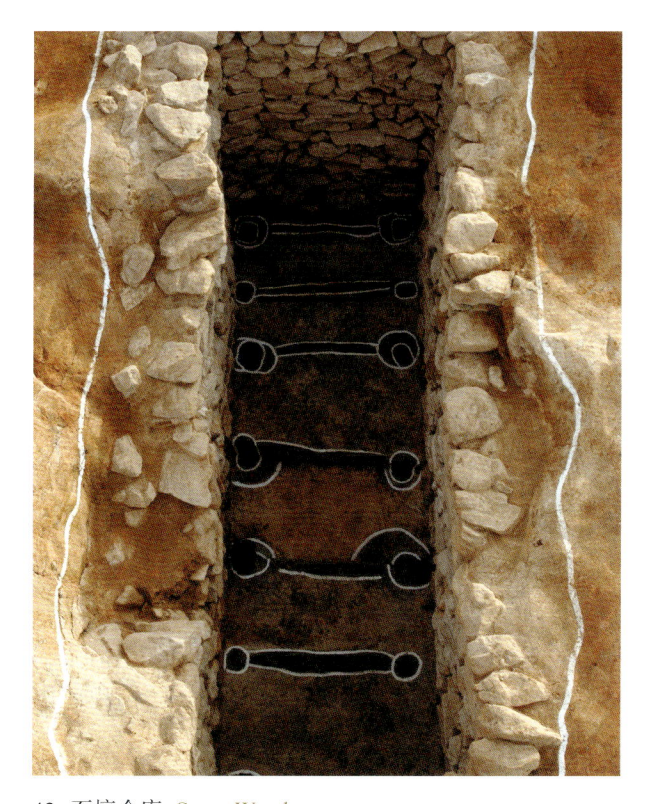

42. 石椁仓库 Stone Warehouse

43. 上水道设施 Water Supply Facilities

44. 人面纹陶器 Pottery with Human Face Design
官北里 D10.7厘米

戳印瓦

在一侧用圆圈或四边形围出边界，然后刻上1~4个字的瓦片，人们因其"在瓦上戳印"故名"戳印瓦"。在百济地区，出土过戳印瓦的遗址有扶余官北里、扶苏山城、定林寺址、益山王宫里、弥勒寺址等泗沘期都城相关遗址和寺院遗址。戳印瓦上戳印的文字，虽然大部分很难确认其准确内容，但是有些表现干支或泗沘期五部官署的名称，作为历史资料其使用价值很高。

45. "下部乙瓦"铭

46. "前部乙瓦"铭

47. "午-斯"铭

48. "首府"铭

49. 戳印瓦 Roof Tiles
官北里 W13~23厘米

50. 瓦当 Roof-end Tiles

51. 瓦当 Roof-end Tiles
官北里 D15～16厘米

泗沘期百济瓦

迁都泗沘(538年)后，百济不仅调整了国家体制，加强了地方统治，而且在都城内外不断地扩建各种衙署和寺院，因此就要生产大量的瓦。在泗沘期制造出来的具有各种形状和华丽花纹的筒瓦瓦当，让百济产生了独具特色的瓦当文化。

泗沘迁都后至6世纪后半期为止，百济仍然流行将花瓣末端表现为突起模样，然后轻轻反转的熊津后期的莲花纹筒瓦当，到7世纪左右花瓣末端变成了三角形或推出折角棱式样，有了比较明显的变化。风车纹瓦当、无纹筒瓦当、莲花花瓣中刻有花蕊形子叶的瓦当纷纷出现，作为新的流行时尚，筒瓦当逐渐出现了装饰华丽的倾向。

52. 唐瓦 Roof-end Tiles
官北里 大型 D12.2厘米

百济虎子

　　这是模仿老虎等动物模样制造的容器。一般被认为是当便器使用,但是有的认为它们是具有酒器、茶具、明器等特殊用途的器皿。在开城地区出土的青瓷虎子被认为是从中国传入的。扶余郡军守里出土虎子看似男用尿壶,是改进南朝虎子而成的。从这里我们可以看出百济文化通过与南朝交流,吸收南朝文化,而呈现出独特的文化面貌。

53. 虎子 Chamber Pot
官北里 L17厘米

54. 虎子侧面 Side of Chamber Pot

55. 器座 Pottery Stand
官北里 H50厘米

56. "合"铭陶器 Pottery
官北里 D19.6厘米

57. "合"铭陶器内部 Inside of the Pottery

"官"铭坩埚

"官"铭坩埚,在推测为百济泗沘期王宫所在的扶余官北里作坊址出土。坩埚盖和坩埚体上刻有"官"字,说明这里是泗沘期官营作坊址。

59. "官"铭坩埚细部
Detail of the Melting Pot

58. 官北里出土坩埚 Melting Pot
官北里

开元通宝

三国时期的遗址中出土的唐朝货币不仅是与唐朝进行文物交流的证据,而且有利于通过货币制作年代的研究,以确定缺少文字记录的遗址年代。开元通宝是从唐高祖武德四年(621年)开始使用的货币。这一时期开始不再使用重量单位来命名货币,而是用"通宝"、"元宝"、"重宝"等名称,其形状与制作方法成为东亚各国货币的基础。扶余百济遗址中发现的"开元通宝"在一些阶层被作为特殊用品使用,从而仅在有限的范围内流通。

60. 开元通宝 Chinese Coin
官北里 D2.3厘米

61. 竹尺 Ruler
官北里 L10厘米

用于测量长度、体积及重量的度量衡的统一，不仅给人们的经济生活带来方便，而且还有利于治理国家。因此，秦始皇统一天下后首先实行的也正是度量衡的统一。度量衡的基础是测量长度的尺子，因为只有有了衡量标准的"尺"，才能制造升、斗等计量单位的标准容器。因此，把什么当作衡量的标准尺度显然最为重要。

汉城期百济使用过从乐浪引进的23厘米左右的东汉尺。之后熊津期和泗沘期前半期用过25厘米左右的中国南朝尺，泗沘期后半期用过29.5厘米左右的唐尺。在官北里出土的尺子一个格是2.5厘米左右，因此是南朝尺的可能性比较大；而在扶余双北里出土的另外一把尺子则更趋于唐尺的标准。

62. 竹尺细部 Detail of the Ruler

63. 木简 Wooden Strips
官北里

43

64. 背光 Aureole
官北里 H16厘米

　　这是在官北里遗址出土的舟形鎏金背光。在中央下端有两个用来固定本尊像的小孔，二孔上下排列，从比例来推测，应是附着在单独立像上的背光。在衬托着佛像身体的头光与佛身部分外围，用二条刻线围绕，以区分外部的火焰纹。

　　在金边轮廓外，有六处可以附着天人像的方形孔突出于轮廓之外，是这个背光的特征。至今为止，在6世纪的三国时代佛像的背光中，还没有发现在轮廓上装饰方孔的先例。这样形态的鎏金背光是在6世纪前期的北魏盛行一时的作品，作为类似作品，可以举出日本根津美术馆保存的北魏普泰二年（532年）的铭文鎏金背光一例。但是，普泰二年铭文背光是左右雕有胁侍像的三尊像，从头光中有六朵莲花纹和火焰纹中有三个化佛的形式上看，它们之间也有相当的差异。同时，火焰纹的种类和雕刻手法也各有千秋，官北里出土的背光中，表现得更为柔和与平坦的莲花花瓣头光，让人不禁想到了百济的瓦当。目前，虽然无法判明这个鎏金背光的产地，但它为研究百济文化和佛教美术与中国关系，提供了更多可能的途径。从这一点上看，这件背光具有不可忽视的价值。

65. 鎏金佛立像 Gilt-glazed Standing Buddha
官北里 H8厘米

66. 鎏金佛立像 Gilt-glazed Standing Buddha
官北里 H7厘米

  从整体上看腐蚀严重，以致不能真切地看到更为细微的特征，但是从表现肉髻和"U"字形的衣服皱褶中，我们可以知道这是一尊披着袈裟的立式佛像。佛像与台座铸为一体，衣服皱褶是铸造之后刻上去的。背部没有任何雕琢痕迹，与板状佛像相似，在头和腰部有突起的痕迹，推测为可能是用来固定背光。

  两座佛像两臂均以上下倾斜的姿态抬起，保持了施无畏印和与愿印的姿势，但是我们无法得知佛像尊号。台座是中间较细的长鼓型，左侧佛像下端宽而平，右侧佛像下端为透雕，它们之间保持了相当的差异。

  这样简略的铸造法和单纯化的立像表现手法，在统一新罗时代后期的鎏金佛像中经常可以看到，至于佛像的制作年代则可以推迟到新罗末高丽初。

宫南池 | Gungnamji Archaeological Site
(忠清南道扶余郡扶余邑东南里、军守里等 | 史迹第135号 | 三国时代)

　　宫南池，作为人工水池遗址，被推测是百济泗沘时期的都城园林池苑，它和扶苏山南麓的王宫遗址和定林寺遗址一起，形成同一条南北中轴线，坐落于泗沘都城南端。据《三国史记·百济本纪》武王三十五年（634年）条记载："穿池于宫南，引水二十里，四岸植以杨柳，水中筑岛屿，拟方丈仙山。"又武王三十九年（638年）条有"春三月，王与嫔御泛舟大池"的记载，展现了宫南池的原貌。

　　宫南池因为和当时周边存在的花枝山别宫遗址、军守里寺址有密切联系，所以受到学术界特别重视。从1990年的外围调查为开始，1995年启动了对池塘内部和周边整体遗址的发掘工作。

　　在宫南池一带，与池塘的护岸设施一起，我们还发现了三国时代的道路、建筑遗址、水田耕地、排水设施、水井、蓄水槽等遗址，同时也出土了草鞋、漆器、木耜在内的木制品和百济陶器、砖瓦。它们为我们研究百济人的生活面貌提供了重要的资料。其中，最值得一提的是，有名为"西部后巷……"铭文的木简出土，为了解百济行政区域名称提供了重要的资料。

The Gungnamji Archaeological Site is believed to have been a garden pond forming part of the royal palace in Sabi, the capital of late Baekje. The site is located at the southern part on the south-north axis formed by the royal palace site to the north of the capital and the Jeongnimsa Temple Site in the central area.

According to historic record, "they made a pond by digging the ground at the south of the royal palace and drawing water from a source some 20-li (i.e. approx. 8 kilometers) away, planted willows around it, and made an islet at the center of the pond." Another record states that "in springtime, the king had a boat set on the water and got onto it with his queen."

Archaeologists have also discovered that the site contains traces of the revetment of the pond, road originating from the Three Kingdoms period, buildings, rice paddies, irrigation channels, a well and a reservoir. Other findings include wooden strips featuring inscriptions of the names of Baekje's administrative districts, straw-woven shoes, lacquer ware, wooden vessels and roof tiles.

67. 宫南池全景 View of Gungnamji Site

68. 蓄水槽遗迹 Water Tank

百济的草鞋

　　中国古代史书《晋书》中就有马韩人"穿草蹻"的记载。草蹻是草鞋的汉字名称，当时草鞋并不只是用草制作的，它泛指草本类的所有鞋子。百济的草鞋多次出土在扶余官北里、宫南池等遗址，可以认定为是百济泗沘期的产物。这类草鞋使用了生长在喜湿环境的蒲黄草，其经线、纬线和鞋系带线细密而精巧，类似于今天的麻鞋。通过其高超的工艺手法，可以认定它不是属于平民百姓的用品，而是属于特殊阶层的。

69. 草鞋 Straw Shoes
　　 宫南池 L26厘米

70. 宫南池出土陶器 Potteries
宫南池

锯痕与锯柄

锯子是锯或切开木头的工具。在韩国从新石器时代开始，人们就已经使用石锯。随着锯子的功能越来越多，其中的拉锯模仿弓的形态，从两边将锯条拉近以求其更强有力，由此制成了绞锯。在百济遗址发现了留有锯痕的木料和看上去很像锯柄的木把儿，这说明当时已经使用过锯子。在这个锯柄上，为防止拉锯线打滑还在手把末端特意削出刻痕。

71. 锯痕 Traces of Sawing
宫南池 L26厘米

72. 锯柄 Saw Grip
宫南池 L24.5厘米

韩国 考古学重大发现（2002～2007）

王宫里遗址 | Wanggungni Archaeological Site
（全罗北道益山市王宫面王宫里 | 史迹第408号 | 三国时代）

　　王宫里遗址，被认为百济武王（600～641年）时代建造的宫城遗址，它位于从弥勒山东侧向南端延伸的低矮的山脊线末端。益山王宫里五层石塔（国宝第289号）位于遗址内部，邻近帝释寺遗址和弥勒寺遗址。

　　通过1989年开始的长期发掘，测定了南北长490余米、东西宽240余米的石筑城墙，它围绕百济后期建设的大规模宫城和其后建造的寺院设施，相互之间有叠压打破关系。在宫城内部发现了仅在扶余地区才有的瓦积基坛建筑和面阔7间、进深4间规模的大型殿堂式建筑，另外还发现了可以显示百济杰出园林技术的庭院和围墙、排水沟、大型厕所、作坊及各种附属设施。除此之外，又发现了王宫里五层石塔及其相关的金堂、讲堂遗址，它们成排分布，是典型的统一新罗时期的寺院布局。

　　在王宫里遗址先后出土了近3000件遗物，其中既有刻着"王宫寺"、"大官官寺"铭文的瓦片和刻着"首府"字样的戳印纹瓦在内的瓦类，也有大量的陶器、金制璎珞、玻璃珠和中国青瓷片。

　　其中在作坊遗址中大量出土的坩埚，为宫城内可以大规模生产金属和玻璃制品提供了有力的证据。另外，通过对厕所遗址中出土的土壤样品和厕筹[①]的分析，我们可以复原古代人的饮食生活。

The Wangungni Archaeological Site contains relics of a Baekje palace built in the first half of the 7th century. The main discovery at the site consists of a large palace enclosed by fortified walls that run approximately 490 meters from north to south and 240 meters from east to west, containing many palace buildings, temples and other related facilities.

Well-preserved relics found at the site include a foundation made by pilling up roof tiles, an architectural element only found in the capital of late Baekje, the remains of a large 7 by 4-han building, a garden exhibiting the distinctive landscaping style of Baekje, walls, ditches, a large toilet, and workshops.

A total of over 3,000 items were discovered at the site including a large amount of crucibles that were discarded by the workshops. The vessels show that various glass and metal objects were mass produced by court artisans within the palace. Another important discovery - the remains of a large toilet containing woden tools used as toilet paper, provides valuable knowledge about the foodstuffs that nourished our ancient Korean forebears.

73. 王宫里遗址全景　View of Wanggungni Site

[①] 大便后用以拭秽的木竹小片。

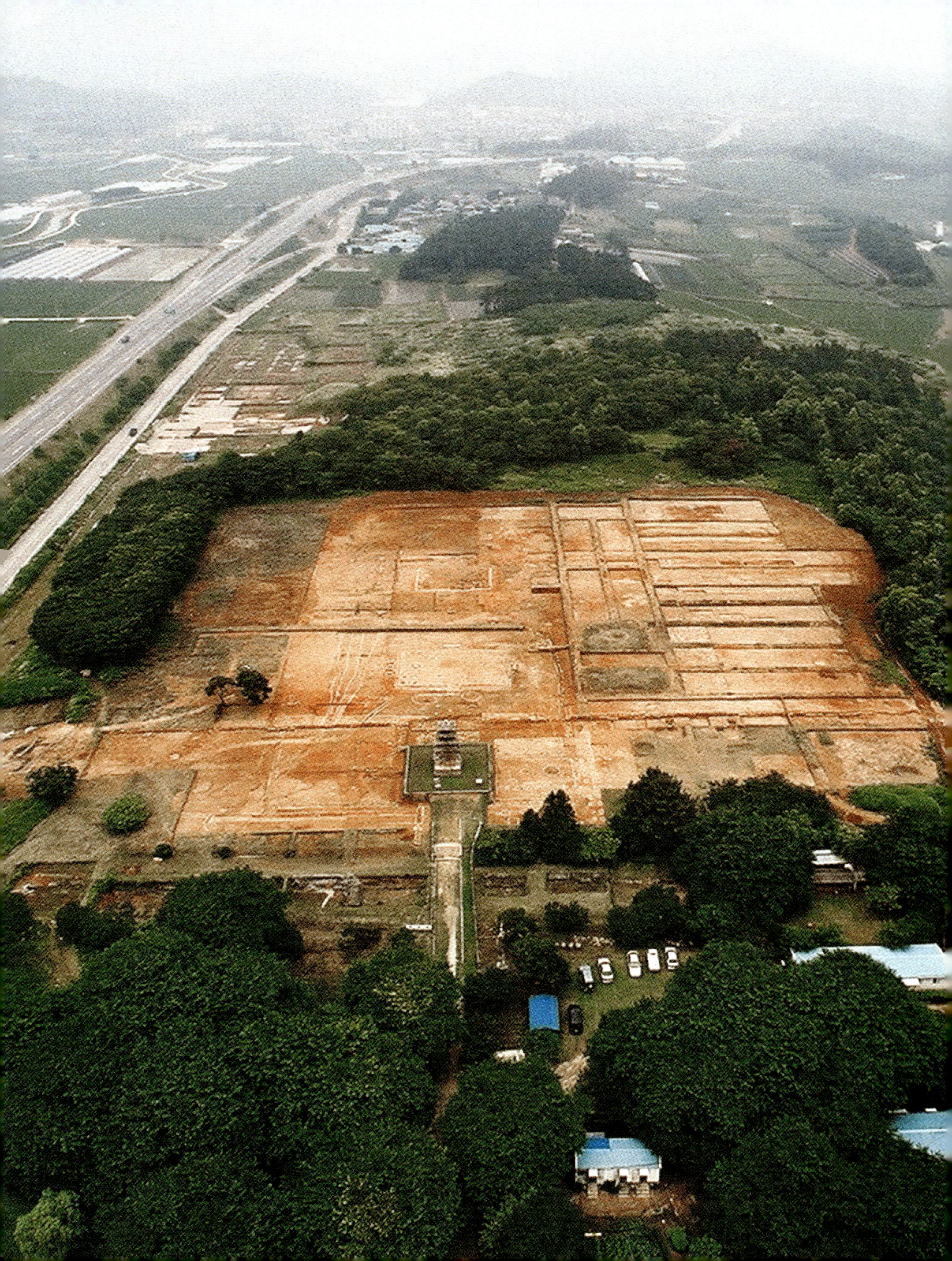

74. 东墙残存状态 Eastern Wall

75. 大型建筑遗址 Large Building Site

76. 排水沟 Drainage

77. 车轮痕迹 Traces of Wagon Wheel

78. 厕所遗址 Toilet Room

79. 厕所示意图 Presumed Elevation of Toilet Room

80. 施釉陶器 Glazed Ware
王宫里 H23厘米

王宫里的中国青瓷

中国商朝中期，被称为"原始青瓷"的早期粗糙瓷器出现之后，中国青瓷水平不断发展。汉朝时期，长江以南的浙江省地区正式生产了青瓷，经过东晋的飞速发展，不仅是南方，北方地区的瓷器制造也日渐发达。王宫里出土的中国青瓷使用贴花工艺，表明了这是南北朝至隋朝的瓷器，由此我们可以看到这一时期中国青瓷的发展水平。

81. 中国瓷片 Chinese Celadons
王宫里

82. 烟囱帽（烟囱装饰陶器） Chimney Head Cover
   王宫里 H28厘米

　　烟囱装饰陶器——烟囱帽，是安装在带有灶孔和烟道的建筑的烟囱上的部分，它一般是指安在圆筒形烟囱柱体之上，顶端饰有莲花花苞形状的球体。在球体中间有外沿，全身镂孔装饰，这些显然都是为了便于烟气均匀地从烟囱中排出而设置的。这样的烟囱装饰陶器是仅在扶余、益山有所发现的地区性器物，它们大量采用了泗沘期盛行的具有佛教含义的莲花花苞形态，是主要在都城地区制作的高级陶器之一。在扶余陵山里寺院遗址、官北里、花枝山、王宫里等地也有所出土，和中国集安的禹山下墓区M2325号出土品相比，可以看出它们受到了高句丽烟囱帽的影响。

灶形陶器

这是将炉灶形态缩小后当作便携式火炉使用的灶形陶器。炉灶一般用土或石质材料制成，将炊具置于其上用以加热，是跟火炉一起使用的炊事工具。从三国时代开始被人们广泛使用，甚至为了使用这种炉灶，还制作了专门的炊具。

在群山市余方里82号古墓中，出土了带有烟囱和灶孔的火盆形态陶器，其特征是灶与炊具结合在一起。它虽然与在王宫里遗址出土的炉灶形陶器以及灶，在灶孔部分、支脚部分、烟囱的组合构成上具有统一的形态，但在圆筒形炉体、短而粗的烟囱、支脚的大小等细微的形态上有一些差异。在日本，虽然也有些外形相似的实物被发现，但在是否带有小型烟囱和灶孔的形态上，可以看出差异。

83. 灶形陶器 Cooking Stove-shaped Pottery
    王宫里 H24厘米

84. 虎子 Chamber Pot
    王宫里 L31.5厘米

85. 便器 Toilet
    王宫里 L31.5厘米

86. 陶器 Potteries
王宫里 大型 H25.9厘米

87. 有萼陶器 Pottery with Extended Rim
王宫里 H7.7厘米

88. 瓶、盘 Bottle and Dish
王宫里 瓶 H11.8厘米

89. 带流陶器 Bottle with Spout
王宫里 H28厘米

90. "弥力寺"铭盖杯 Dish with Cover

91. "弥力寺"铭盖杯细部
Detail of the Cover

57

古代玻璃

　　在古代遗址中发现的玻璃，其产地与起源、色泽与形状、结构等种类繁多。据《三国志》记载，与黄金、丝绸相比三韩（马韩、辰韩、弁韩）之人更喜欢玻璃珠。韩国古代玻璃根据其构成成分可以分为四种类型，其中碱性玻璃至今仍被普遍使用。在古代遗址中发现最多的深蓝色圆珠大部分是碱性玻璃，迄今为止最古老的碱性玻璃是出土于海南君谷里贝丘的公元前1世纪左右的草绿色管玉。与此相反，钠玻璃在古代中国自汉代以后就几乎很少使用了，到隋唐时期又重新登场亮相。韩国目前已经在相当于4～5世纪的庆州和晋州地区遗址中有所发现，百济地区则出土于益山王宫里遗址与弥勒寺遗址等地。统一新罗时期，随着石塔里安置舍利子的舍利信仰的普及，玻璃舍利瓶深受人们欢迎，用钠玻璃制成的草绿色玻璃瓶大幅增加。钠玻璃被制成玻璃珠和玻璃容器，其用途非常广泛，只可惜发现较少，尚未弄清确切的使用方式。另外，通过检测制造钠玻璃所使用的原料方铅石的同位素来推定其产地，这个意义非常重大。

92、93. 玻璃、玻璃坩埚　Glass and Melting Pot for Glass
　　　王宫里　H17.4厘米

94. 金坩埚、金箔 Melting Pot for Gold and Gold Foil
　　王宫里 H2.5厘米

95. 金属坩埚 Melting Pot for Metal
　　王宫里 H8厘米

96. 砥石 Grindstones
　　王宫里 D5~10厘米

97. 牌形瓦制品 Tablet-shaped Earthenwares
    王宫里 L17.8厘米

98. 瓦当 Roof-end Tiles
    王宫里 D18.5厘米

99. 兽蹄形器足 Paw-shaped Pottery Leg
    王宫里 H18.1厘米

100. 造景石 Garden Stones
     王宫里 L26厘米

王兴寺址 | Wangheungsa Temple Site
（忠清南道扶余郡窥岩面新里｜史迹第427号｜三国时代）

据记载，王兴寺始建于百济法王二年（600年），竣工于武王三十五年（634年），是百济寺院中知其由来和名称的重要遗址。1934年，在寺址内发现了"王兴"铭瓦片，由此寺院位置得以确定。

王兴寺遗址位于德牧材山[①]东南麓，德牧材山隔环绕泗沘都城的白马江，与扶苏山城相对而视。在其山顶的蔚城山城，推测为记载于《三国史记·新罗本纪》的王兴寺岑城。

遗址的发掘工作始于2000年，带有瓦积基坛的回廊遗址、附属建筑遗址和疑似木塔遗址等百济时代寺院的相关设施，在寺内以南侧为中心的地带集中发现。同时，在寺内北侧发现有高丽时代建筑遗址和石础设施，并出土了镇坛具、铭文瓦片等大量遗物。

最近在寺内东侧外围，发现了从百济到高丽时代的十余座窑址，其中高丽窑址内出土了"王兴"铭瓦，确认了王兴寺一直维持到高丽时代。

王兴寺遗址的寺院布局，是典型的百济式一塔一金堂形式，与陵山里寺址非常相似，精确的规模和寺院布局，有赖于以后的发掘与调查加以探明。

Located at a site overlooking Busosanseong Fortress across the Baengmagang River which encircles Sabi, the last capital of Baekje, this archaeological site is the location of a Buddhist temple named Wangheungsa that was built on the early 7th century. A roof tile found at the site clearly shows exactly where the temple was located, and has the temple's name inscribed upon it.

Archaeologists discovered at the south of the temple precinct features of temple buildings exhibiting the characteristics of a Baekje temple, including those of galleries whose foundations were built by piling up roof tiles, a wooden pagoda, and other sites. At the northern end of the site they found inscribed roof tiles and prayer objects buried among the foundations, along with the remains of Goryeo buildings and a stone embankment.

At the eastern part of the site the vestiges of ten kilns built in the period between Baekje and Goryeo were also discovered. A roof tile inscribed with the temple's name excavated at a Goryeo kiln site showed that Wangheungsa continued to thrive until the Goryeo period.

---

① 音译。

101. 王兴寺址远景 View of Wangheungsa Temple Site

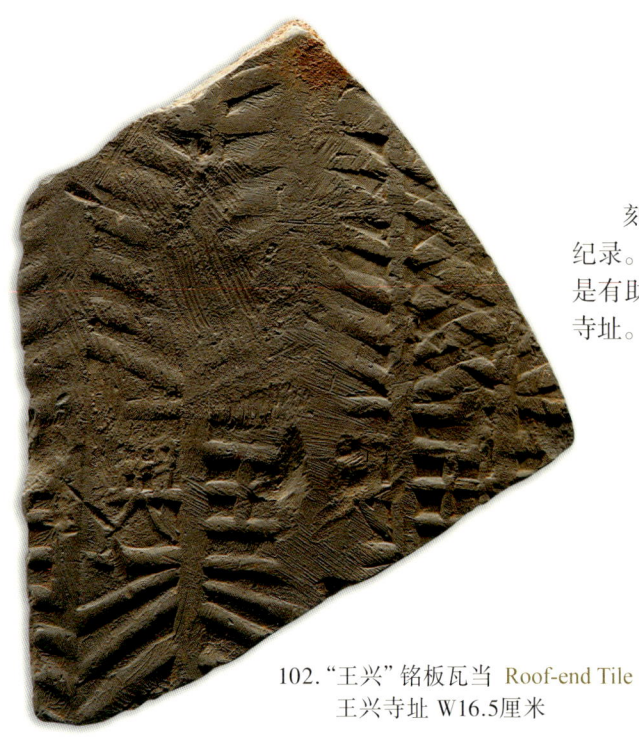

刻有寺院名称的瓦是提供寺院位置与存在的重要历史纪录。"王兴"铭板瓦瓦当虽然时间上晚于百济时期,但还是有助于推确定为百济武王时期竣工、传承到后世的王兴寺址。

103. "王兴"铭板瓦当细部 Detail of the Roof Tile

102. "王兴"铭板瓦当 Roof-end Tile
王兴寺址 W16.5厘米

104. 莲花纹筒瓦当 Roof-end Tiles
王兴寺址 W15~16厘米

瓦积基坛

百济建筑技术中，有一种叫做瓦积基坛，是将瓦片成层堆积垒砌成台基的技法，这种技法主要应用于百济泗沘期的王宫、寺院和一般建筑中。作为瓦片的堆积方式，有将瓦片放倒层层堆积的平积式，这是最普通的方式，外形简单但是使用瓦片最多，是最坚固的技法。将一块瓦片立在中央，在两侧立成"人"字形，许多组反复倾斜地堆积数层的合掌式技法，虽然有下端如果较大瓦片则容易被挤出的缺点，但是也有外形独特的优点。另外，在基坛外轮廓立瓦片，形成的垂直横列式技法，虽然使用的陶瓦较少，但是只能使用成品，有不能堆出较高基坛的局限性。在王兴寺址已经发现了平积式技法的基坛。这样的基坛筑造技术，在同一时期的高句丽和新罗遗址都没有发现，却在日本的京都和奈良等地得到了确认，可以认为这是百济建筑技法传到日本的最好实例。

105. 鸱尾 Ridge-end Tile
王兴寺址 L14.1厘米

106. 板瓦当 Roof Tiles
王兴寺址 L36厘米

107. 鸱尾 Ridge-end Tile
王兴寺址 H16厘米

伏岩里古墓群 | Bogamni Tomb Complex
（全罗南道罗州市多侍面伏岩里 | 史迹第404号 | 三国时代）

伏岩里古墓群是分布在荣山江支流——文平川一带的平地古墓群。多种形态的墓葬长时间内集中建造在同一坟丘之内，形成了具有共同墓葬性质的3号墓。通过对它的发掘，我们找到了研究荣山江流域独特古墓的特征以及当地土著势力与迁入的百济势力之间关系的切入点。

伏岩里3号古墓由1座木棺墓、22座瓮棺墓、3座竖穴式石椁墓、11座横穴式石室墓、1座石椁瓮棺墓、1座横口式石椁墓、2座横口式石室墓等，合计共41座墓葬组成。从修建方台形坟丘以前的大型瓮棺墓时期开始，经过将大型石室墓修建在坟丘中心，形成高冢化阶段，再进入先在方台形坟丘中挖出墓坑后再增加瓮棺或石室的扩大化阶段。

从3世纪专用瓮棺出现时期开始，到7世纪百济泗沘期石室墓为止，经过同一集团400年的经营，形成的伏岩里3号古墓，反映了荣山江流域的多人葬、复合葬墓葬的重要特点。

另外，在各种遗址中，出土了大量铜鎏金饰履、银鎏金冠饰等饰物以及三叶纹环首大刀等武器。此外，在这里也出土了大量各种陶器，这些发掘为研究百济中央政府如何扩大地方统治，以及如何频繁地与日本交流，提供了重要的资料。

A cemetery located mid-stream of the Yeongsangang River and used by the same tribal group for about 400 years, the Bogamni Tomb Complex consists of 21 tombs built in various styles, ranging from the jar-coffin tomb of the third century (Tomb #3) to the stone-chamber tomb of the 7th century. Archaeologists are particularly interested in the Bogamni Tomb #3 as it reflects the unique cultural heritage preserved in the area, which was characterized by multiple burials under the same mound. They also believe that the tomb provides an important clue as to the relationship between the native people of the region and those who arrived here at later period.

The artifacts found at the site, such as gilt-bronze shoes, gold and silver crown ornaments, and large swords with a ring pommel, also constitute and important source of knowledge concerning the expansion of Baekje in the area its effort to establish a centralized state and engage in active culture exchange with Japan.

108. 伏岩里3号墓 Tomb #3 of Bogamni Tomb Complex

109. 鎏金饰履 Gilt-bronze Shoe
伏岩里 L27厘米

鎏金饰履的前端基本上是圆形，其后跟已经破损得无法确认。两张侧板固定在脚背上，侧板下面叠成"L"形，用铜丝与底部缝在一起。鎏金饰履通体饰以龟甲纹，而且还嵌有圆珠璎珞，其底部更是添加了穗状纹和鱼纹璎珞。

这个鎏金饰履从制作工艺和形态上看，与益山笠店里、罗州新村里9号墓出土品形制相同，但是从龟甲纹来看，却与武宁王陵出土的鎏金饰履一脉相承。

110. 鎏金饰履底面 Bottom of the Shoe

111. 鎏金饰履侧面 Side of the Shoe

112. 冠饰 Crown Ornament
　　 伏岩里 L14.7厘米

113. 金制装饰 Gold Ornaments
　　 伏岩里 D2.5厘米

114. 石头枕 Stone Headrests
　　 伏岩里 大型 W36.7厘米

69

圭头大刀是装饰大刀的一种，手柄尾端类似于玉圭而得名。手柄末端的金铜板两侧刻有龙纹、云纹和忍冬纹，手柄部分缠上金线与银线。

在日本6世纪末～7世纪前期的遗址中大量出土此类大刀，它被认为是与畿内政权的统治有密切关联的遗物。

在韩国罗州伏岩里3号墓、5号石室和7号石室中，这类圭头大刀都有出土，它被认为是与日本交流的产物。

115. 圭头大刀 Sword
伏岩里 L87厘米

116. 三叶纹环头大刀 Sword with Pommel
伏岩里 L38厘米

117. 三叶纹环头大刀、圭头大刀 Swords

118. 马具 Horse Harness
 伏岩里

这是木芯铁板壶镫的一只，其大部分已经缺失，只剩镫柄和镫板。在铁板的边缘，有用于固定木芯的钉子，按 2～3 厘米的间距钉在上面。壶镫将轮部做成袋状，它是一种包裹骑手双脚的马镫。在陕川镫溪堤"TA-A"号墓和陕川玉田 75号墓中，均有出土。

119. 壶镫 Stirrup
 伏岩里 L25.5厘米

120. 广口带孔小壶 Jar with Hole
伏岩里 H15.7厘米

广口带孔小壶作为在朝鲜半岛南部地区经常发现的一种陶器，集中出土于荣山江流域。与生活遗址相比，它更多地以随葬品形式出土于墓葬，被认为是与礼仪有关的陶器。从初期形态来看，壶体比壶口直径大，脖颈短而粗，但是随着时间的流逝，逐渐出现了壶体变小、脖颈变长、壶口变宽的趋势。

相对于荣山江流域出土的其他物品，这件广口带孔小壶圈底、脖颈和壶体上的花纹等方面，更接近于日本的出土品，这一点备受学界关注。

121、122. 盛有朱漆的陶器 Pottery with Red-lacquer
伏岩里 H4.9厘米

Silla 新罗

新罗是由辰韩十二国之一的斯卢国发展而来的，主要由阏川杨山村（及梁）、突山高墟村（沙梁）、觜山珍支村（本彼）、茂山大树村（渐梁）、金山加利村（汉祇）和明活山高耶村6个村落和氏族构成。"新罗"一词有"德业日新，网罗四方"之意，是希望国家繁荣昌盛的意思。

公元前57年，据传新罗始祖朴赫居世受六部首领的推举建立国家，至敬顺王归顺高丽王朝，新罗历经56代国王，长达992年。建国初期不断吞并周围的小国并逐渐发展成为古代国家，根据《三国史记》的记载，新罗可以分为初期：朴赫居世至28代王真德女王（前57～654年），中期：25代王武烈王至36代王惠恭王（654～780年），晚期：37代王宣德王至56代王敬顺王（780～935年）三个时期。这样的时代区分是以古代国家的建国，三国统一和盛唐文化的吸收及发展，封建体制的崩溃及豪族势力出现和灭亡等事件为依据来判断的，目前韩国史学界依然沿袭这样的时代区分。

都城范围内有月城，雁鸭池和东西并列的建筑物独具特征。苑池遗址内分布有池塘、小岛及蜿蜒曲折的石筑湖岸。新罗王京遗址是受中国里坊制度影响而规划建设的都市，四边长约80米，坊内有20余座大小居住址。坊的四周没有发现坊墙，个别居住址的门和院墙连接道路，并有排水沟。作为宗教遗址的佛教寺院位于都城的各个地方。兴轮寺、灵妙寺、皇龙寺、芬皇寺、四天王寺、望德寺等大小寺院和石塔、木塔等"寺寺星星，塔塔雁行"，形象地表现了佛教国家的特征。作为生产遗址的陶窑遗址，主要位于都城外围，生产砖瓦、陶器和木炭等。王京内还发现了生产金属、漆器、玻璃等的作坊遗址，推测其中大部分为官营作坊。墓葬遗址主要包括木椁墓、瓮棺墓、积石木椁墓、横穴式石室墓、火葬墓等。4～6世纪墓葬位于都城内，7世纪以后逐渐转移至外围的丘陵地带。王陵采用积石木椁墓并陪葬金冠等，之后受唐文化影响，变为横穴式石室墓，周围也出现了人物像、狮子像和刻有十二生肖像的板石。

新罗文化在新罗统一三国的同时吸收了多种文化并通过与唐的交流发展成为具有东亚地区共性的文化。特别是在文学、宗教等方面与唐频繁交流，使得新罗文化成为韩国历史上文化的黄金时期。

Silla is a country into which Saro (斯卢), which as one of 12 countries of Jinhan (辰韩) developed. It consisted of 6 villages and clans: (1) Alcheon (阏川) Yangsan (杨山) Village [Geumnyang (及梁)]; (2) Dolsan (突山) Goheo (高墟) Village [Saryang (沙梁)]; (3) Jasan (觜山) Jinji (珍支) Village [Bonpi (本彼)]; (4) Musan (茂山) Daesu (大树) Village [Jeomnyang (渐梁)]; (5) Geumsan (金山) Gari (加利) Village [Hanji (汉祇)]; and (6) Myeonghwalsan (明活山) Goya (高耶) Village. "Silla (新罗)" stands for "deok eop il sin (德业日新) mang ra sa bang (网罗四方)" and means that a country flourishes.

Silla was founded by its progenitor Park Hyeokgeose (赫居世朴), selected as a king by 6 village heads, 57 B.C., and went out of existence by King Gyeongsoon's (敬顺) surrender to Goryeo. It was an ancient country governed by 56 kings for 992 years.

During the nation's founding, Silla developed gradually into a country annexing its neighboring small countries. According to "The Chronicles of the Three Kingdoms (三国史记)", the history of Silla is divided into three periods: (1) the early days (上代), Park Hyeokgeose (赫居世朴) to Queen Jindeok (真德), the 28th king of Silla (57 B.C.~654 A.D.); (2) the middle years (中代), King Muyeol (武烈), the 29th king of Silla, to King Hyegong (惠恭), the 36th king of Silla (654~780 A.D.); and (3) the late years (下代), King Seondeok (宣德), the 37th king of Silla, to King Gyeongsun (敬顺), the 56th king of Silla (780~935 A.D.). This periodization is based on the viewpoints of the foundation of ancient country, the unification of three kingdoms and the acceptance and development of High Tang's (盛唐) cultures, and the collapse of feudal system and the appearance and fall of powerful clans. Now the world of Korean history follows the periodization.

The remains of the capital city of Silla are the royal palace Weolsoeng (月城) and Anapji (雁鸭池). The buildings have a peculiar appearance; they are arranged in a row from east to west. The small squared pond (苑池) looks as if an island is in a pond. The curve of revetment and stone masonry expressed natural beauty. The ruins of Wanggyeong (王京) of Silla (i.e. the remains of dwelling site) constituted a planned city built under the influence of China's bangri (坊里) village system. There were approximately 20 large and small houses in bang (坊) measuring around eighty meters square. Bangjang (坊墙) surrounding bang (坊) is not identified. The doors and walls of individual houses adjoin the road. The drain was installed. The ruins of religion (i.e. Buddhist temples) are located around the capital city. Built were large and small Buddhist temples [e.g. Heungryun (兴轮) Temple, Yeongmyo (灵庙) Temple, Hwangnyong (皇龙) Temple, Bunhwang (芬皇) Temple, Sacheonwang (四天王) Temple, Mangdeok (望德) Temple, etc.] and stone and wooden pagodas. This confirms that Silla was a Buddhist country, as shown by the expression "sa sa seong seong (寺寺星星) tap tap an haeng (塔塔雁行)". The ruins of production, kiln sites (窑址), are situated in the outskirts of city. They produced roof tiles, earthenware and charcoal. There are workshops of metal, paint and glass. Most of them are presumed as governmental workshops. Ancient tombs, the ruins of graves, include wooden outer coffin tomb (木椁墓), jar coffin tomb (瓮棺墓), stone compiled wooden outer coffin tomb (积石木椁墓), stone chamber tomb with a tunnel entrance (横穴式石室墓), and crematory tomb (火葬墓). It is confirmed that these tombs were located in the city around the fourth to the sixth century and transferred gradually to the outskirts of the city after the seventh century. For a royal tomb, used was a stone compiled wooden outer coffin tomb (积石木椁墓) in which a golden crown and others were buried was used. Later, the burial system was changed to a stone chamber tomb with a tunnel entrance (横穴式石室墓) where a face stone (面石) on which figure (人物像), lion (狮子像) and 12 animals of the Chinese zodiac (十二生肖像) were carved, under the influence of China.

Silla accepted various cultures uniting the three kingdoms Silla, Goguryeo and Baekje. It developed in a common culture of East Asia, through exchanges with Tang (唐). In particular, active exchanges of literature and religion with Tang enabled those days to be the golden age of culture in Korean history.

新罗文化 | The culture of Silla

新罗是由朝鲜半岛东南部辰韩十二国之一的以庆州为中心的斯卢国发展起来的国家,从较早开始就接受了律令制度和佛教文化,并以此作为政治和思想基础形成了古代国家体系。在统一三国之后,新罗不仅兼容了高句丽、百济的文化,而且吸收了唐朝、西域文化,奠定了民族文化发展的坚实基础;作为统一三国的精神基础的佛教更加繁盛,深入到社会和文化各个角落。

以庆州为中心,我们对新罗到统一新罗的文化遗址,进行了大规模发掘和调查。在王京、月城护城河,乃至皇龙寺址、四天王寺址、芬皇寺、传·仁容寺址、天官寺址等寺院遗址,以及皇南洞建筑遗址、三国时代陶器和木炭的生产遗址——苏谷洞、勿川里遗址等不同类型的遗址内,出土了多种多样的遗物。这些调查与发掘为了解新罗王京的结构与规模,复原当时的生产和生活方式,提供了重要的资料。

Silla was an ancient Korean kingdom that developed from saroguk in today's Gyeongju area. The kingdom was instructed to buddhism and a legal system via china, and henceforth gradually accomplished the political and philosophical foundations on which to build a powerful kingdom with centralized government.

Currently, archaeologists are attracted to the features of the houses, temples and roads discovered in the Silla's royal capital and its vicinity. The discoveries made at these sites into indicated that the capital was built on the "district-block" system, by which it was divided into many square blocks composed of streets. The sites at which major archaeological investigations are taking place today include the site of Wolseong Moat, the temple sites of Hwangnyongsa, Sacheonwangsa, Bunhwangsa, Inyongsa and Cheongwansa, the building site in Hwangnam-dong, and pottery and charcoal production sites in Songokdong and Mulcheolli. The excavation and research activities conducted at all these sites have produced a wide range of materials that shed considerable light on the structure and size of Silla's royal capital, production systems, and various aspects of daily life.

新罗王京 | Royal Capital of Silla
（庆尚北道庆州市｜三国至统一新罗时代）

据《三国史记》记载，新罗是在公元前57年，由辰韩十二国中位于庆州地区的斯卢国成长发展而来。公元7世纪，新罗吞并了百济与高句丽之后，完成了统一大业。到公元935年，新罗作为历史悠久的古代国家，开创了灿烂的古代文化。

千年古都庆州由兄山江干流西川和支流北川、南川环绕，其外围由南山城、明活城、富山城、兄山城等山城代替罗城，守卫都城的四面八方。

公元5～6世纪，新罗开展了积极的对外交流和大规模的征服活动，在扩大版图的同时，对内强化了中央集权统治，以里坊制为基础，开始对王都进行了大规模的整顿。

新规划的王京以月城为中心，建立了棋盘式井然有序的道路网，在棋盘式道路网内，安排了包括民居在内的各种建筑设施。并按照居住者的身份和建筑用途，设定了不同的规模和位置。别宫、市场、皇龙寺、芬皇寺之类的大型寺院等横跨数个区域（坊）。这样的首都规划，显然不是一次完成的而是多次分阶段规划的，这一点在王京遗址持续的发掘与调查工作中得到了确认。

统一三国之后，扩建的新罗王京的规模和鼎盛期的面貌，我们可以通过《三国史记》、《三国遗事》等文献中记载的"王京内居178936户，1360坊，55里，35金入宅"等内容来了解。

A citadel consisting of mountain fortifications and enclosed by many rivers to make it a formidable stronghold, Gyeongju was the capital of Silla for one millennium. The kingdom greatly expanded its territory in the 5th and 6th centuries through aggressive diplomatic activities and military campaigns with and against neighboring kingdoms, and reorganized the capital under a newly introduced system of centralized power.

The newly developed capital featured a highly efficient, grid-like, road network consisting of houses, temples and markets arranged in a well-coordinated manner in areas that were divided in an orderly layout by interesting roads. The excavation in the following periods, until the last major development was completed just before the unification of the three Korean kingdom by Silla.

123. 皇龙寺东侧王京地区 East Side of Hwangnyongsa Temple

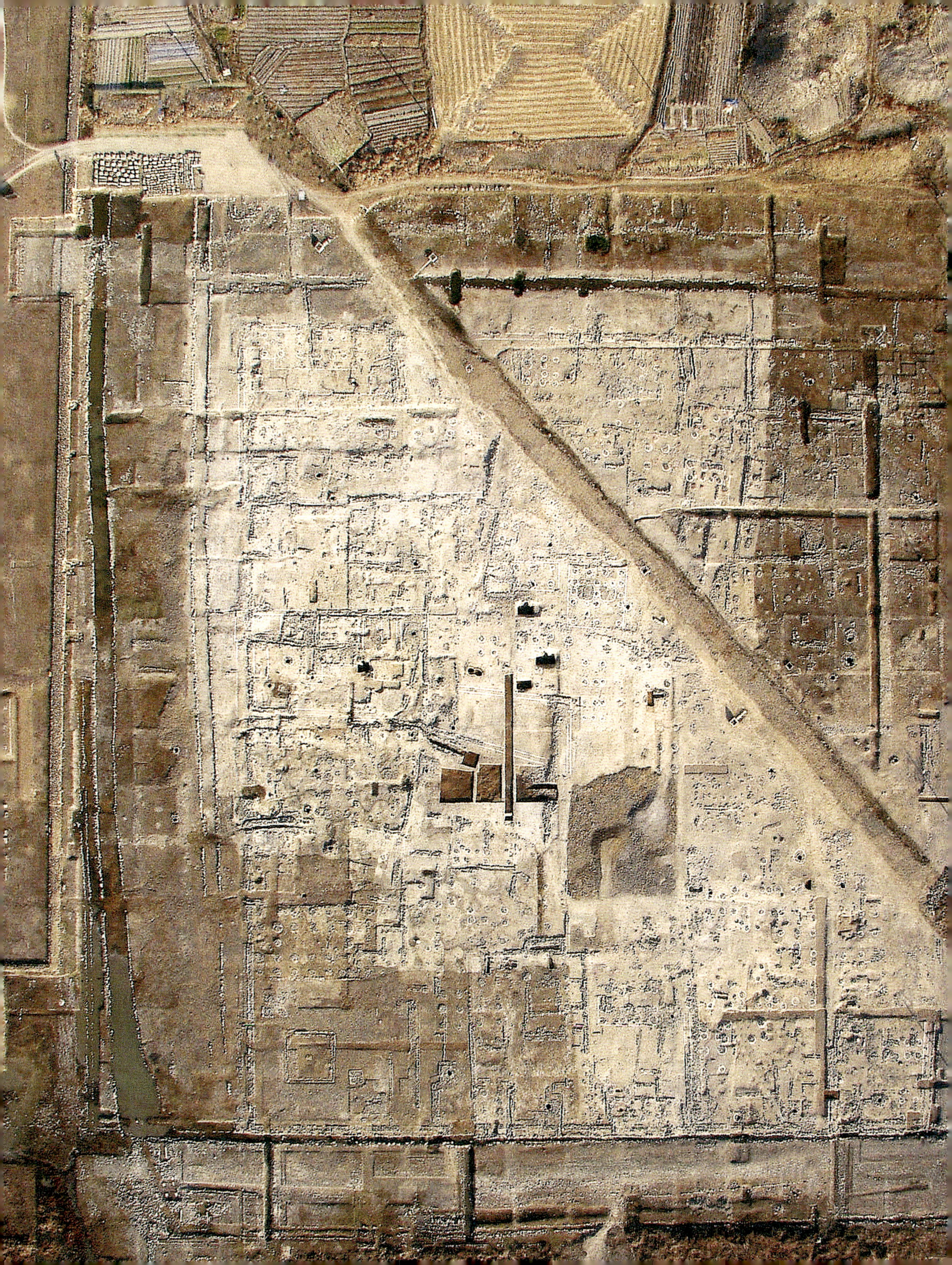

124. 东西大路 East and South Main Road

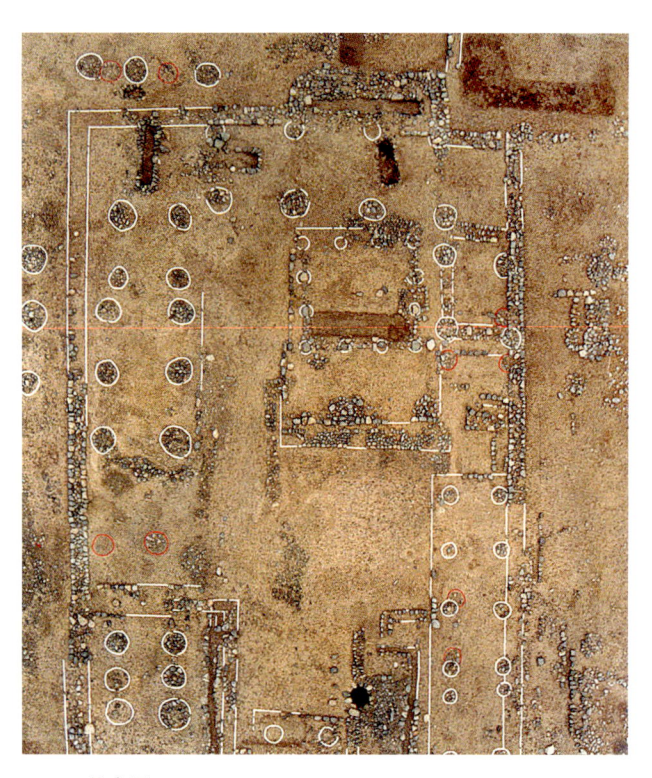

125. 2号房屋 House#2

126. 南北道路、大型排水道 North and South Road, Large Drainage

里坊制

　　新罗首都庆州在三国时代初期称为金城，5世纪末新罗国体确立之始又称为京都、王都、王京等。这一时期，伴随对中国文化的吸收，为了确立统治体制，引入了崭新的都城制度，建立了以王宫为中心的棋盘式道路网络，开始了系统的都城规划。

　　根据公元469年确定"坊里名"的文献记载来判断，可以认为新罗王京从5世纪中叶开始引入都城规划制度。但是从发掘调查的结果来看，最早的遗址出现在6世纪初到中期，其完成期则可以大概推测为8世纪上半叶。

　　按照里坊制规划的新罗王京规模，从《三国史记》和《三国遗事》的记录来看，南北长3075步，东西宽3018步，城内有1360或360个坊、35个或55个里；另外，王京的居住人口达到了178936户，大概有18万户。依照记录所载的新罗王京布局的复原正在持续进行，虽然对于"步"、"尺"、"里"的标准出现了争论，但是目前为止比较确切的"坊"的规模大约是160米×160米，其面积约为8000坪（1坪=3.3平方米）。就王京的具体位置和范围而言，文献记录的内容和实际发掘的内容有所差异，因而推算精确的数值比较困难，但是通过可以确认的道路遗迹发掘结果，王京南北纵深6公里，东西横跨5.5公里，以目前街区为中心的情况还是可以大概掌握的。城区向北可以延伸到隍城洞地区，向南到达西南山五陵的南部地区，向东可达狼山和普门洞一带，向西到达兄山江地区。

127. 新罗王京推定复原图 Presumed Reconstruction of Royal Capital of Silla

128. 兽面纹瓦 Roof-end Tiles
    新罗王京 W20厘米

129. 天马纹板瓦瓦当 Roof-end Tile
    新罗王京 W27.1厘米

130. 欂栱瓦 Roof-end Tile for Gable
    新罗王京 W26厘米

131. 戳印纹陶盒 Mounted Dish with Cover
　　新罗王京 H10.3厘米

　　在新罗王京出土的统一新罗时代陶器中，大部分都是戳印纹的圈足碗或盒。戳印纹陶器在统一新罗时期广泛使用，在6世纪后半期出现，9世纪初由盛行转向消失。

　　这个陶盒除了高圈足和盖把手以外，其他部分都印上了列点纹和菊花纹等戳印纹。尤其是列点纹，呈现出用多齿工具，以"之"字形连续戳印上的形态。

132. 多棱纹瓶 Bottle
　　新罗王京 H4.9厘米

133. 滑石印、陶印 Seals
　　新罗王京 W2.5~4.5厘米

81

134. 鎏金立佛 Gilt-bronze Standing Buddha
   新罗王京 H11.5厘米

　　这是佛身与莲花宝座连铸为一体的鎏金佛立像。表面呈现浅褐色，这一类型的镀金色，在统一新罗鎏金佛像中偶尔出现。宝座由三层八角形平台构成，其上由单层覆莲和仰莲形成了双层结构，但是并不给人繁琐的印象。法衣上的皱褶呈现"Y"字形，这是统一新罗佛立像服装皱折中一种重要的代表形态，被称为"甘山寺式"。

　　这个佛像身体比例和造型匀称端正，身体和服装有机地结合在一起，表现出一种造型上的匀称之美。这样的谐调与统一是统一新罗鼎盛时期佛教雕刻的典型形式。在佛像背面的腰间有一个铸造孔，左肩向后侧甩过去的袈裟末端形态生动，这些都是统一新罗时代鼎盛期鎏金佛像的明显特征。

135. 鎏金菩萨立像 Gilt-bronze Standing Bodhisattva
   新罗王京 H5.3厘米

136. 鎏金佛立像 Gilt-bronze Standing Buddha
新罗王京 H9厘米

这是左手持药碗的药师佛立像。右手末端虽然已经残缺,但是从举到胸口来看,可以视为施无畏印。袈裟以袒右肩式斜披在身上,一角从持药碗的左臂自然垂下,既有立体感又写实。背面头部和躯体上各有一个铸造孔,腰部内侧则横支着一个支架。

从面部表情和衣服皱褶上的独特形态,可以看出这是与统一新罗时代典型的鎏金立佛像不同的佛像类型。像这样左手持药碗,袒右肩的统一新罗时期鎏金药师佛像,还有几座现存于世,可供参考。

137. 鎏金药师佛立像 Gilt-bronze Standing Buddha
新罗王京 H9.4厘米

138. 鎏金异形装饰 Gilt-bronze Ornament
新罗王京 L17厘米

139~141. 鎏金异形装饰细部
Detail of Gilt-bronze Ornament

142. 羊形玉饰和滑石制玉饰 Ornaments
新罗王京 H4.2厘米

143. 祖形石 Stone Phallus
新罗王京 L8.1厘米

144. 石权 Weights
新罗王京 L5.6厘米

月城护城河 | Wolseong Moat

(庆尚北道庆州市仁旺洞 | 史迹第16号 | 三国至统一新罗时代)

月城自斯卢国初期婆娑尼师今二十二年（101年）建成以来，曾一度短期移居明活城。5世纪前后，月城成为名副其实的新罗王京的王城，一直持续到新罗灭亡。

月城的平面形态，像一轮初升的新月，因此被称为"月城"或"新月城"。然而，不仅在文献记录中，而且在铭文瓦中我们能确认的是"在城"这个称呼。直到今天，月城仍旧保存着宽50～70米，周长约1800米的城墙。

通过20世纪80年代开始的城墙的发掘工作，除了与蚊川（南川）接壤的南侧之外，我们在月城周围发现了石筑式或土圹式的城壕设施。城壕外侧警戒线上设置了护岸石的石筑城壕，应是在土圹式护城河废弃之后筑造的，其上发现了两次改建的痕迹。

三国统一之后，外敌入侵的威胁消失，城壕的防御功能可能被转换，成为像雁鸭池一类的观赏设施，在填平的城壕和周围，出现了宫殿和衙署等大型建筑物。

在城壕和周围遗迹中，不仅出土了古式莲花纹筒瓦瓦当之类的瓦器、陶器、金属遗物，而且在淤泥中收集到了漆器和木简等木质遗物和各种有机物。

最近，通过对月城内部进行的地下物理勘探，确认了文献中看到的宫殿和相关设施大规模地密集分布的情况，我们期待着对月城的研究能掀开新的篇章。

Located at the heart of the Gyeongju Basin, Wolseong (lit. "Moon Fortress"), Silla's royal castle, was fortified by earthen and stone walls whose layout consists of a crescent shape. The remaining fortress wall is 50 to 70 meters wide and 1800 meters long.

The latest excavations conducted outside the fortified wall have revealed that the fortress was protected by a moat made of earthen pits and a stone embankment. The ditch was designed to enclose the fortress, except for the southern part which faced a natural waterway. After the unification of the Three Kingdoms, which greatly reduced the threat of military conflicts with external forces, the defense facilities were turned into pleasure gardens such as Anapji ("Ducks and Geese Pond") or construction sites for large palace building and government offices.

145. 月城护城河 Wolseong Moat

146. 月城全景 View of Wolseong

147. 木简 Wooden Strips
月城护城河 L19~20厘米

和字老作之

问于板卅五

经中入用思买白不虽纸三斤

登流石奈生城上此本宜城今受不受郡云

芇八巷芇 卄三大舍麻断□□衣节草辛

149、150 鎏金装饰细部（正反面）
Detail of Gilt-bronze ornament

148. 鎏金装饰 Gilt-bronze Ornament
月城护城河 L7.1 厘米

  这是一件刀把形状的装饰品，上部缺失，柄端有直径 2.5 厘米的圆盘。圆盘两面使用浮雕技术雕刻了精巧的图案。这被认为是一种礼仪性佩刀。一面图案与扶余郡外里遗址出土的凤纹砖上的凤凰图案有相似之处。另一面雕有类似龙或兽面的图案。这两个图案和新罗与百济砖瓦中看到的图案均有类似之处。

151. 陶器 Potteries
月城护城河

152. 绿釉盖 Green-glazed Cover
月城护城河 H5.9厘米

绿釉盖是在表面施有低温铅釉系的绿釉的陶器。铅釉是在草灰水和沙子粉溶液（硅酸）中，掺入具有天然酸性质的碳酸铅，再掺入铜或铁粉，作为发色剂，抹在陶器上，可以烧制出青绿釉。如果氧气不足或铁粉过多，釉色会成为褐色。由于它的熔点在700～800℃，如果窑内温度超过这个限度，所有釉色将燃烧殆尽。月城护城河中出土的绿釉盖成色极佳，其顶上有宝珠形纽。

153. 鸭形陶器 Duck-shaped Pottery
月城护城河 L36.4厘米

154. 坩埚 Melting Pot
月城护城河 H15.8厘米

155. 陶球 Clay Balls
月城护城河 D2.5~3厘米

156. 渔网坠 Fishing Net-sinkers
月城护城河 D2~2.5厘米

皇南洞遗址 | Hwangnamdong Archaeological Site

（庆尚北道庆州市皇南洞 | 统一新罗时代）

新罗在文武王时代完成了统一大业之后，为了与焕发新春的国家地位相符，新罗开始大规模扩建都城，重修了月城宫殿作为王京正宫，并将已丧失防御功能的月城护城河埋入地下，以此为基础建造了大型宫殿和官署一条街等建筑，这些内容都在发掘调查中得到——确认。依《三国史记·地理条》中"新月城北有满月城"的记录进行推测的话，扩建后的月城就是满月城。

20世纪80年代末，在月城西北侧瞻星台和鸡林之间发现有大型积心型建筑群；2006年，对当时未能实施调查的部分（皇南洞123-2号一带）进行了补充调查后，其整体轮廓才为人所知。

在这个建筑群的北侧中央，有面阔3间，进深2间（两进三开）的中心建筑。南侧有南北向的长方形面阔10间、进深2间的建筑，东西向对立各有3间。同时，在这些回廊形态的建筑外侧，又有面阔13间、进深1间规模和面阔12间、进深1间规模的建筑各一座，也按对称结构排列。这些建筑因为与年代相近的日本藤原宫和平城宫内当作官僚政务场所的朝堂院几乎一致，所以更引起了人们的重视。

此外，在建筑群的南端，两座面阔2间、进深2间规模的方形建筑和北侧的中心建筑，以对称形式排列。在临近这些建筑的北侧，出现了有5个地镇具的围墙形态的石列地基遗址。在出土遗物中，收集了盛放可以散发金色的黄漆涂料的盒子，由此人们可以观察到古代装饰技术的一个重要侧面。

The unification of the three early Korean kingdoms by Silla in the 7th century led Silla to carry out an extensive renovation of its capital, as befitting a kingdom that had emerged as the major power of the region. It was during this period that Wolseong came to contain large, new palace buildings and government offices that were erected on the site prepared by filling in the moat encircling the fortress wall.

As for the large building complex located at the northwestern part of Wolseong, there was a main building at the northern center of the area, with other minor buildings arranged like galleries and standing face to face with each other from east to west. The latest discovery of two building sites has revealed an earthen, wall-like structure containing five religious objects that were used to sooth the earth's energy and a bowl containing "yellow lacquer" that was used for gold paint.

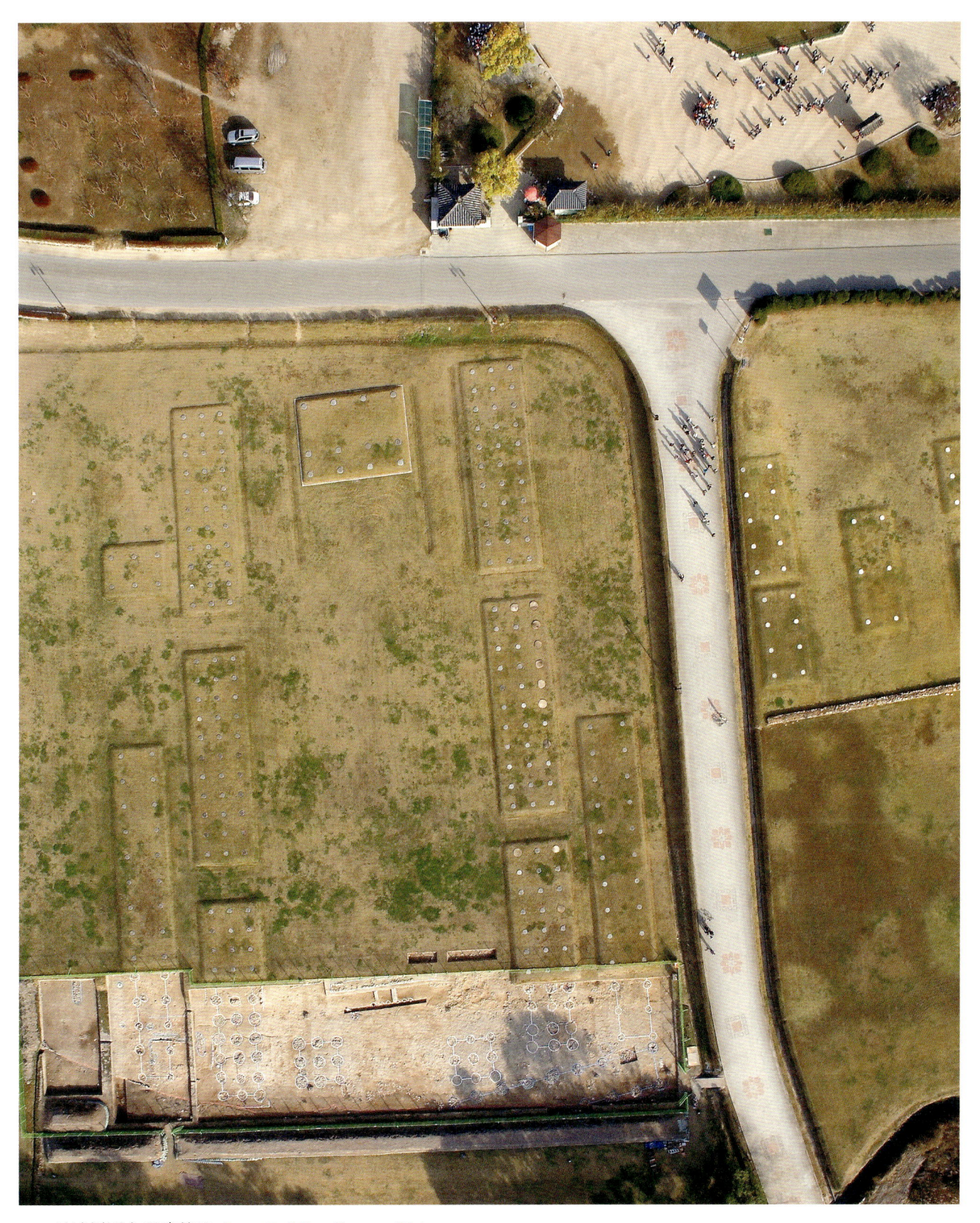

157. 月城周围大型建筑址　Large Building Site near Wolseong

地镇具

地镇具是指建造或维修建筑物时，出于防火防灾、避邪祈福的目的，埋入地下的用具。它主要有玉器、金属制品和各种容器等。公元7世纪后期开始以庆州为中心，在整个新罗文化圈内的皇龙寺址、九黄洞苑池和传·仁容寺址等主要寺院和建筑遗址中，经常可以见到这种用品。

158. 地镇具 Buried Ceremonial Protective Objects
    皇南洞 H33厘米

159. 皇南洞遗址地镇具出土状况 Buried Ceremonial Protective Objects

黄漆

黄漆树和漆树一样，是一种涂料用树，因其色黄，称金漆或黄漆。在黄漆树上割开小口后，为了愈合，黄漆树内会分泌树液，经过一段时间的阳光照晒，会变成金黄色。这一树种，仅生长在韩国南海和西海岸部分地区，是韩国特有的树种。意大利旅行家马可•波罗在他的游记《东方见闻录》中记载："铁木真的盔甲和大帐的金黄色，都使用的是这种树液，除了皇室之外，其他人等禁止使用。"又在中国的《通典》中记载："（百济）国西南海中有三岛，出黄漆树，似小檞树而大。六月取汁，漆器物若黄金，其光夺目。"据说统一新罗时代的海上王张保皋的贸易品中，黄漆也是最贵重的商品。为了满足中国紫禁城内龙床、御座等各种用品和天花板及墙壁的需要，从朝鲜征调了大量黄漆。丙子胡乱（丙子之役）（1636年）之后，清朝禁止朝鲜国王使用黄漆，作为世界唯一的黄漆生产地，全罗南道沿海地区被严格监视和限制。朝鲜著名学者丁若镛在他的著作《牧民心书》中记载："因为无法采集树液，百姓们只好在树干钻上小孔让它慢慢枯死，或者直接用斧头砍掉树木。"

在这次发掘中，第一次出现了仅见于记载的带有传说色彩的黄漆涂料，虽然它在戳印纹陶器中蒸发固化，但是黄漆这个传说中的珍宝终于得到了确认。陶器在有盖的状态下，被深深地埋藏在地下，好像有着特别的象征意义。

160. 黄漆盒
Detail of Covered Bowl with Yellow-lacquer

161. 盛有黄漆的戳印纹盒（黄漆盒） Covered Bowl with Yellow-lacquer
皇南洞

皇龙寺址 | Hwangnyongsa Temple Site
（庆尚北道庆州市九黄洞 | 史迹第6号 | 三国时代至高丽时代）

皇龙寺是新罗的护国寺院，在新罗真兴王十四年（553年）将原计划建造的宫殿改造为寺院。善德女王十四年（645年）建成九层木塔，才完成了寺院的整个布局。这次发掘调查中，确认了至高丽高宗二十五年（1238年）蒙古人烧毁为止，皇龙寺在700年间，经历了三次重建的情况。

寺院结构为南门、中门、九层木塔、中金堂和讲经堂处于南北中轴线上，在中金堂左右两边，设东西两间金堂，它们形成了一塔三金堂寺院的基本布局。根据里坊制的规定，边长为288米左右的方形寺院，占有新罗王京4坊之地，仅仅回廊内轮廓也是佛国寺的将近8倍之多的超大型佛寺，可见皇龙寺昔日的雄伟。

据说高达80米，面阔和进深均为7间的长方形九层木塔中央，支撑着中心柱的大型中心础石等各种基础设施依然保持着原样。另外，在面阔9间、进深4间的大型建筑遗址金堂址中，残存有包括超过5米的"丈六尊像"的超大型佛座在内的19具佛座。

我们在皇龙寺收集到了大量文物，其中包括大型鸱尾和瓦当在内的瓦器，以及作为生活用品如陶器、瓷器和各种金属、石制遗物等，其数量达到了40000余件。这些遗物让我们仔细观察到了韩国古代寺院的原貌。

Hwangnyongsa ("Temple of the Yellow Dragon") was designed to be a palace when its construction was first begun in 553, but it ultimately became a Buddhist temple and was revered as a state patron upon its completion, with a majestic nine-story wooden pagoda added to it in 645. The temple continued to thrive for about 700 years, during which time it underwent - as recent excavations have shown - three major expansion works up until 1238 when it was burnt down by Mongolian.

The layout of the temple after its completion featured the South Gate, Middle Gate, Pagoda, Central Golden Hall and Lecture Hall, all of which were constructed on the same straight line as the Eastern and Western Golden Halls that flank the Central Golden Hall, creating the layout of a single pagoda combined with triple prayer halls. The temple sanctuary formed a square measuring approximately 288 meters on each side covering an area of four smallest administrative units Silla had recently established. The massive size of Hwangnyongsa is well represented by that the area enclosed by the temple's inner galleries alone was times larger than the entire sanctuary of Bulguksa Temple.

162. 皇龙寺址全景 View of Hwangnyongsa Temple Site

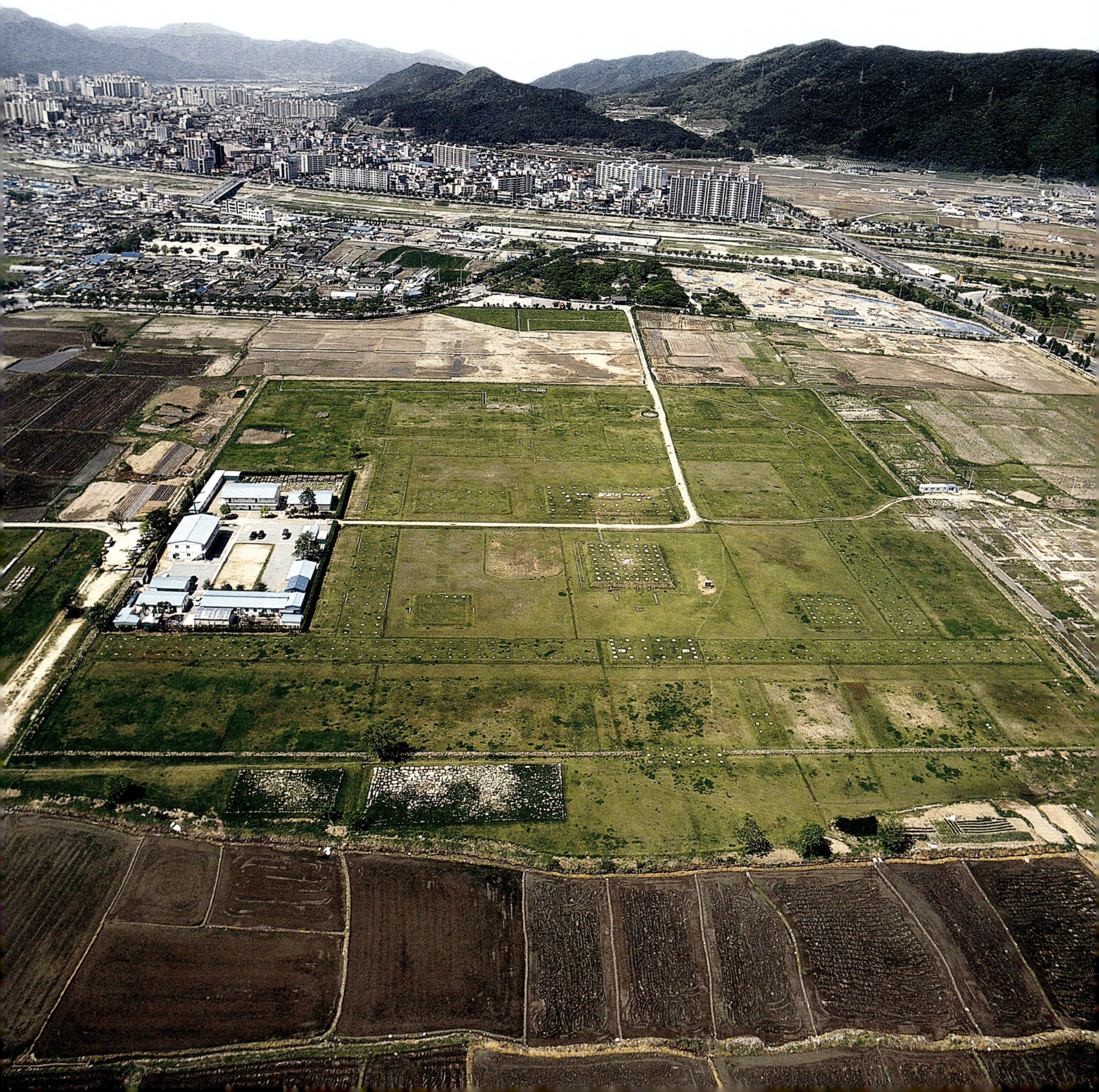

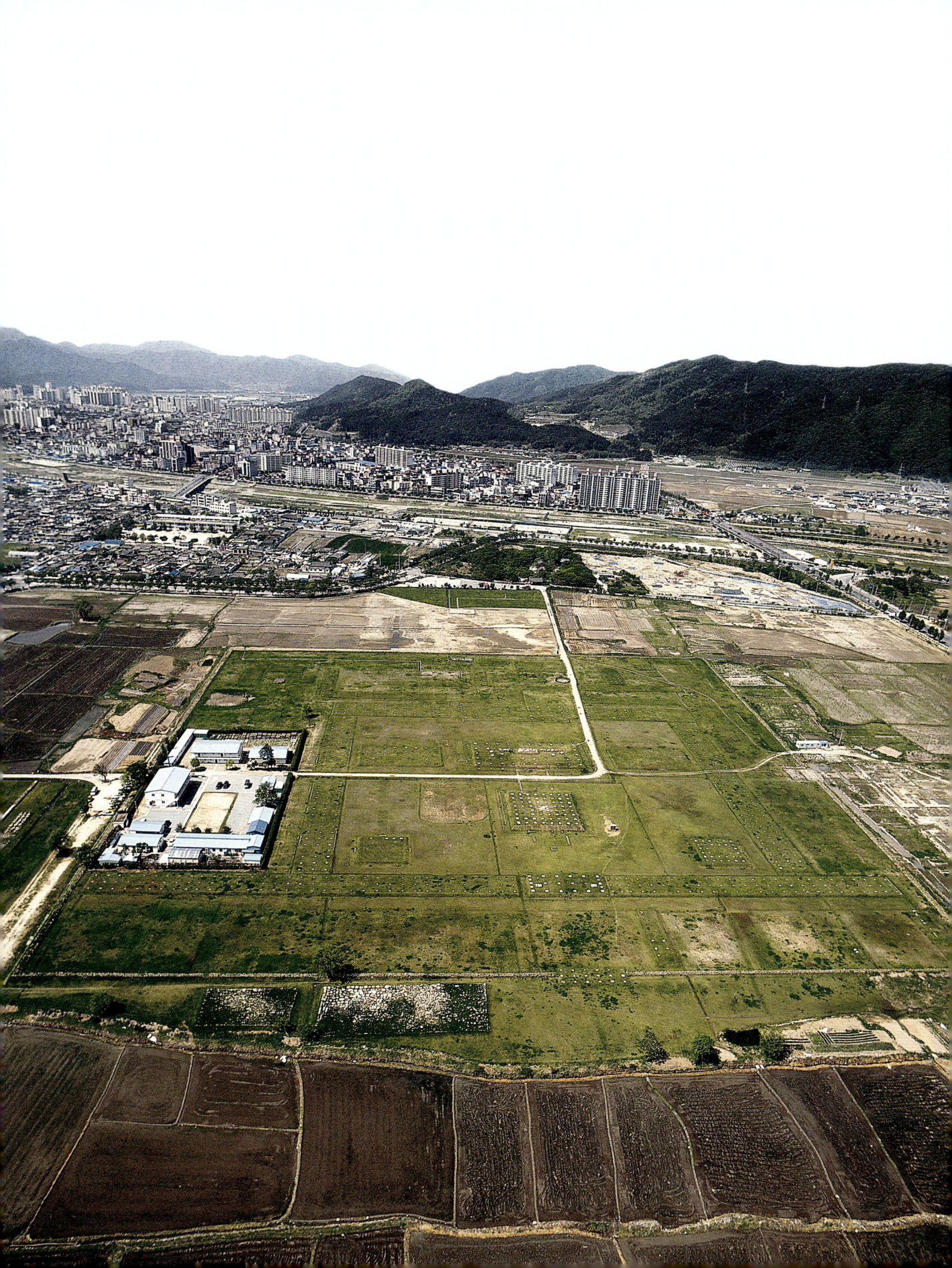

163. 木塔中心礎石
Foundation Stone of Wooden Pagoda

164. 中金堂佛座、木塔址 Central Golden Hall and Wooden Pagoda Site in Hwangnyongsa Temple Site

皇龙寺址出土的鎏金佛立像与雁鸭池出土的一批佛像一起，向我们展示了统一新罗时期庆州地区鎏金佛立像的时代变化。相对于身体而言过大的头部、土著化的面部、短短的胳膊等形体特征，可以看出它的制作年代可能比皇龙寺址出土的其他鎏金佛立像晚。

佛座和佛身铸为一体，仅留下一部分镂刻背光贴在佛像的背面。为了给人安全感和佛身粘贴在一起的背光部分采用了平板背光，头光部分用七叶莲花装饰，背光外侧用唐草纹装饰，边缘位置饰以火焰纹。这样形式的镂刻背光在雁鸭池遗址也有出土。但是从整体形态看，与目前保存在国立全州博物馆被推测为新罗末高丽初的全罗北道益山市王宫里五层石塔内出土的鎏金佛立像极为相似，可以看出它们是同一时期的雕刻样式。

165. 鎏金佛立像 Gilt-bronze Standing Buddha
皇龙寺址 H13厘米

166. 鎏金透雕装饰 Gilt-bronze Ornaments
皇龙寺址 小型 D4.1厘米

结跏趺坐的佛坐像，台座和一部分背光已经缺失。在头光和身光组成的背光内部，蕨菜纹之间饰有鱼子纹。在最外层的火焰纹之外，虽然还有其他花纹，但是想知道整体模样和结构并不容易。

虽然佛像看上去有保持阿弥陀手印的意思，但是左手置于腹部的处理手法，既不明确，也不和谐。袒胸，内着僧祇支，上刻菱形花纹。两个胳膊和躯体之间镂空，虽然让人联想到雁鸭池出土的板状佛像，但是在背面没有明显的铸造时的铁芯痕迹，显示出二者有所差异。和雁鸭池板状佛像比，该板佛形态较笨拙，其制作年代可能稍晚。

鎏金板状佛像本来是作为庄严具而贴在佛龛等物上的，从图像学上看，和统一新罗时期流行于唐朝与日本的砖佛与捶揲佛，有着比较密切的关系。在皇龙寺遗址，除了这个鎏金板佛坐像之外，还出土了在莲花座结跏趺坐的佛像下半身和身穿盔甲的神将坐像形态的鎏金板佛。作为韩国的鎏金板佛，还有更早的全罗北道金堤出土的佛像和统一新罗初期的庆州雁鸭池出土的佛像，这次皇龙寺遗址的出土品，再一次加深了人们对统一新罗佛教雕刻多样性的认识。尤其是最近九黄洞苑池发现的鎏金板菩萨坐像和雁鸭池板佛几乎一模一样，这说明因为当时流行着同一类的图像，所以出现了反复制作的情况。

167. 鎏金板佛　Gilt-bronze Plate of Seated Buddha
皇龙寺址 H9.7厘米

168. 青铜佛头　Bronze Buddha Head
皇龙寺址 H10厘米

169. 鎏金凤凰装饰 Gilt-bronze Phoenix-shaped Ornament
皇龙寺址 H23.3厘米

170. 鎏金凤凰装饰背部细部图
Detail of Gilt-bronze Phoenix-shaped Ornament

171. 人物土偶装饰灯盏 Lamplight Cup
皇龙寺址 H4厘米

172. 镕范、钗 Moulds and Hairpin
皇龙寺址 范 W14.5厘米

173. 兽面纹瓦 Roof-end Tile
　　皇龙寺址 W20.5厘米

174. 龙头 Dragon Head
　　皇龙寺址 H19.8厘米

175. 砚台 Inkstone
皇龙寺址 H10厘米

砚台基本以石制为主，但是瓦砚、陶砚、泥砚之类用土烧制的也不在少数。韩国从三国时代开始主要使用陶砚，主要有用多足支撑砚堂的百足砚和用圆筒形底座支撑砚堂的圆筒砚。石砚被认为在高丽时代以后才开始使用，据《高丽图经》记载："砚曰皮卢。"由此可知，高丽时代开始，砚就在韩国语中被称为"别卢"或"比卢"。通常把研墨的部分称为砚堂或墨道，研好的墨水或墨汁流向的凹陷部分称为砚池、砚泓或砚海。

在皇龙寺出土的被称为百足砚的砚台，用十条动物腿支起砚堂，在砚堂外壁绘三四道波纹。从砚堂部凹陷很深的痕迹来判断，这个砚台实际使用过的可能性很大。

105

芬皇寺 | Bunhwangsa Temple
（庆尚北道庆州市九黄洞 | 三国时代至今）

芬皇寺创建于新罗善德女王三年（634年），在公元七八世纪著名僧人慈藏和元晓大师等人曾经主持该寺并迎来了鼎盛期。至今为止，芬皇寺法灯延续近1370年之久。

通过20世纪90年代开始的发掘调查工作，我们确认了芬皇寺最初的寺院布局，在芬皇寺石塔（国宝第30号）北侧按"品"字形列有三座金堂，形成一塔三金堂的早期寺院的基本布局，同时也确认了至少经历了三次大的变化才缩小为一塔一金堂的变迁过程。

在寺院南北外侧，测得围墙之间的直线距离是195米，据此，可知芬皇寺在全盛时期的规模大小曾达到过皇龙寺的2/3。

尤其是在芬皇寺东侧外围（皇龙寺展示馆建立用地）发现了相当于雁鸭池1/15大小的统一新罗时代的苑池遗址。这个九黄洞苑池，以向芬皇寺北侧延伸的大型筑台为中心，在北部设有带着两个人工岛和护岸石的池塘以及排水沟、围墙等附属设施；南部有可以眺望池塘的楼亭等建筑遗迹及其相关设施等。

九黄洞苑池因地制宜地修筑护坡、开挖池塘以及利用怪石等造景，表现了富有自然美内涵的卓越的艺术性。同时，还在镇坛具和池塘内，出土了大量唐朝瓷器，有定窑、邢窑和越窑等多个窑口，被认为是展示8~10世纪新罗与唐朝交流关系的重要资料。

Bunhwangsa, a historic Silla temple establish in 634, enjoyed its heyday in the 7th and 8th centuries. The extensive series of excavations conducted so far have revealed that the temple's layout consider of a single pagoda combined with three main prayer halls arranged in a triangular layout situated to the north of the stone pagoda (designated as National Treasure #30). The original layout underwent three major changes at least after the 7th and 8th centuries, and the temple was transformed into a structure consisting of one pagoda and one main prayer hall.

Archaeologists discovered outside the eastern part of the Bunhwangsa sanctuary the features of a garden pond complete with two artificial islets and a stone revetment built during the United Silla period, as well as traces of buildings and their related facilities, including a garden pavilion. The Guhwangdong archaeological site is held in particularly high regard for the harmony between the pond and the stone revetment - which was designed to match the surrounding natural environment - as well as the stone landscaping used to enhance the natural beauty of the garden.

176. 芬皇寺全景 View of Bunhwangsa Temple

177. 芬皇寺仿砖石塔 Stone Pagoda in Bunhwangsa Temple

178. 九黃洞苑池 Garden Pond in Guhwangdong Site

179. 蜡石制菩萨像 Agalmatolite Bodhisattva
九黄洞苑池 H7.2厘米

180. 鎏金佛立像 Gilt-bronze Standing Buddha
芬皇寺 H3.6厘米

181. 鎏金板菩萨坐像 Gilt-bronze Plated of Seated Bodhisattva
    九黄洞苑池 H12.8厘米

182. 鎏金神将像 Gilt-bronze Buddhist Guardian
    九黄洞苑池 H19.2厘米

这是庆州九黄洞苑池出土的神将像。和苑池出土的其他板状佛像相比，其铸造和细部表现工艺相当粗糙。从其形态来看左手叉腰，右手握拳举于头上，右脚抬起，姿态生动。虽然穿着一身长甲，但是腰身纤细。在神将周围是火焰形背光，其轮廓中有许多凸起。左侧上下部，有将神像固定在某处用的触角向外伸展。

111

这是芬皇寺出土的青铜权。它可能是用来称量谷物、矿石和金属重量的。这个青铜权由狮子模样的权纽和权身组成。权身上部为球形，下部为上窄下宽的八角圆筒，每个侧面均为梯形。权纽的狮子像，保持昂首回望的坐姿，头部和向上翘起的尾部有非常浓密的鬃毛。而在狮子的嘴部，则有一个能通过绳子的较粗圆孔。这种造型与高丽时代印章纽的狮子像非常相似。

183. 狮子装饰青铜权 Bronze Weight
芬皇寺 H11.5厘米

184～186. 狮子装饰青铜权细部
Detail of Bronze Weight

187. 葡萄鸟纹铜镜 Bronze Mirror
    芬皇寺 D5.1厘米

　　这是用鸟纹和葡萄纹装饰的小型铜镜,可能是从唐朝进口的。很可能供奉在佛像或佛塔内。无论是日本殖民地时代的芬皇寺仿砖石塔修缮工程时出土的舍利具,还是1966年的佛国寺释迦塔的维修工程中出土的舍利盒均有铜镜,以此推测,当时的寺院可能在仪式中使用铜镜或供奉在佛塔中。

188. 勺范 Spoon Mould
    芬皇寺 W16厘米

189. 青铜容器 Gilt-bronze Bowls
    芬皇寺 大型器 H5.4厘米

芬皇寺中国陶瓷器

　　芬皇寺出土了大量不同时代的瓷器。其中，统一新罗时代瓷器中有越窑青瓷、长沙窑贴花壶和唐三彩等，与皇龙寺遗址、雁鸭池等附近出土的遗物一起，提供了观察中国瓷器输入过程的绝好机会。

　　越窑青瓷是在吴越之地的浙江省上虞、余姚和绍兴等地烧制而成的。它们延续了六朝以来的青瓷制作传统，到唐朝制作出了品质更好、更洗练的青瓷，被称为"秘色青瓷"而流传后世，并受到世人交口赞誉。

　　长沙窑位于湖南省长沙市北郊铜官镇瓦渣坪，又称为瓦渣窑或铜官窑。其技法特征是在涂有黄釉的器面贴上不同的花纹装饰，然后再涂以褐色或绿色颜料。它不仅满足了当时中国国内的需要，而且也大量生产外销瓷。

190. 唐朝瓷器（青瓷贴花壶残片）　Chinese Ceramics
　　　芬皇寺 H18.1厘米

191. 青瓷碗　Bowl, Celadon
　　　九黄洞苑池 H8.3厘米

192. 唐朝陶瓷　Chinese Ceramics
　　　芬皇寺

114

193、194. 镇坛具 Buried Ceremonial Protective Objects
九黄洞苑池 最外层碗 H13厘米

195. 鸭形杯 Duck-shaped Cup
九黄洞苑池 H7.5厘米

这只被认为是鸭子的鸟，脖颈向后扭，用喙叼着尾巴，鸭身为杯身。在其身体部分，用浮雕的手法，雕成红鹤或苍鹰之类的水鸟，在翅膀部分则以圆涡纹图案加以装饰。由于表面已经没有釉彩，我们无法确认其为白瓷还是唐三彩，但是和它类似的器形曾经出现在唐三彩中，由此可以推测为盛唐期7世纪后期的作品。同时，由于在其表面没有发现任何釉彩，也有可能原来就没有上釉。由于鸭状陶器和水的关系，我们推测是举行祈雨祭等活动时的重要器皿。

196. 虎子 Chamber Pot
芬皇寺 H20.5厘米

197. 动物形陶器 Animal-shaped Pottery
芬皇寺 H11.4厘米

198. 坩埚盖 Melting Pot Cover
九黄洞苑池 H5厘米

199. 装饰品 Architectural Ornament
芬皇寺 D32.5厘米

200. 棋盘砖 Brick of Baduk Board
芬皇寺 W42厘米

烧制之前，在砖面上横竖划上十五道线的围棋盘，其大小和线间距与当代棋盘非常相似。但是这件棋盘的特征是其上没有星位，而且与现代围棋的十九道线不同，仅有十五道线组成棋盘。中国春秋时代时，围棋盘为十三或十五道线，汉代出现十七道线的棋盘，推测后来才出现了与今天一样的十九道线棋盘。

201. 棋盘砖细部 Detail of Baduk Board

202. 鸱尾 Ridge-end Tile
芬皇寺 H36.3厘米

203. 莲花纹砖 Brick
九黄洞苑池 W33.5厘米

204. 瓦当 Roof-end Tiles
芬皇寺

芬皇寺瓦

在芬皇寺出土的瓦器中，板瓦当、筒瓦当占据了绝大部分，另外也有不少兽面纹瓦和铭文瓦。这里出土的囊括了从创建期开始的统一新罗、高丽王朝和朝鲜王朝所有时代的瓦当，也是其特征之一。

公元8世纪，芬皇寺在第一次重建中拆掉了创建时的三座金堂，代之以扩大创建期中金堂的方案。这一时期，出现了莲花纹、唐草纹、莲花宝相花纹、花草纹、龙纹和飞天纹等多种花纹。特别是创建期和第一次重建金堂时各自使用的筒瓦和板瓦成套出土引人注目。统一新罗时代的莲花宝相纹筒瓦和有宝相纹的双鸟纹板瓦成套地运用于创建期金堂，新罗末高丽初时代的花草纹筒瓦和双鸟纹板瓦则成套地运用在第一次重建的金堂之中。

第二次重建时使用的瓦器中，可以代表高丽时代样式的半球形兽目纹筒瓦瓦当成为主流，大部分在兽目纹周围用圆圈围绕，以珍珠纹或花纹装饰的瓦当也有发现。此外，用莲花纹和兽目纹装饰当心的和周围饰以草花纹的瓦当也有发现。第三次重建时的瓦器中，以朝鲜时代的莲花和花草纹筒瓦瓦当为主，其花瓣细长，末端尖锐，周边大部分没有花纹而凸出。其平面形态也是从圆形中将下颌部进行锐角化处理，给人以向下拉长的感觉，这种有所变形的作品，在朝鲜时代开始流行。

在朝鲜时代的板瓦中，很多有"万历十六年……化主法行"（1588年）和"万历四十五年丁巳"（1617年）等铭文，以此我们可以判断当时用瓦的寺庙年代。在出土的筒瓦、板瓦中，也有很多刻有铭文，例如带有"王"字的铭文筒瓦，我们知道它可能会和芬皇寺寺名有密切联系。

205. 创建期瓦当 Roof-end Tiles
芬皇寺 筒瓦瓦当 D14.9厘米

206. 第一次重建期瓦当 Roof-end Tiles
芬皇寺 筒瓦瓦当 D17.8厘米

207. 兽面纹瓦 Roof-end Tile
芬皇寺 W25.5厘米

208. 兽面纹筒瓦瓦当 Roof-end Tile
芬皇寺 D15.4厘米

209. 麒麟纹板瓦瓦当 Roof-end Tile
芬皇寺 W30厘米

210. 飞天纹板瓦瓦当 Roof-end Tile
芬皇寺 W22厘米

211. 龙纹板瓦瓦当 Roof-end Tile
芬皇寺 W34厘米

212. 莲花纹筒瓦瓦当 Roof-end Tile
芬皇寺 D15.8厘米

213. 莲花宝相花纹筒瓦瓦当 Roof-end Tile
芬皇寺 W14.3厘米

214. 莲花纹筒瓦瓦当 Roof-end Tile
芬皇寺 D13.9厘米

215. 莲花宝相花纹筒瓦瓦当 Roof-end Tile
芬皇寺 D13.6厘米

216. 莲花纹筒瓦瓦当 Roof-end Tile
芬皇寺 D12.7厘米 高丽以后

217. 双鸟纹筒瓦瓦当 Roof-end Tile
芬皇寺 D14.1厘米

218. 狮子纹筒瓦瓦当 Roof-end Tile
芬皇寺 D14.4厘米

219. 花草纹筒瓦瓦当 Roof-end Tile
芬皇寺 D14.4厘米 高丽以后

四天王寺址 | Sacheonwangsa Temple Site

（庆尚北道庆州市排盘洞 | 史迹第8号 | 统一新罗时代）

四天王寺是文武王十九年（679年）创建的双塔式寺院，通过《三国遗事》等与创建相关的记录，可以观察到当时新罗人的宇宙观和作为护国寺院而著称的四天王寺的全貌。四天王寺作为新罗"七处伽蓝之墟"之一，位于被认为神圣的神游林的狼山丘陵南侧。它采用了以金堂为中心，在东西两侧分别立塔的典型的统一新罗时代双塔式寺院布局。

最近以西塔与西回廊为中心，展开了发掘与调查工作，并确认了在金堂和西回廊之间曾有面阔9间、进深1间的廊庑；随着在西回廊的北侧发现了被推定为北回廊的遗址，我们能够了解寺院的整体布局。

在西塔址调查中，我们确认了特殊形态的框架式台基，其台基上粘贴了四天王像绿釉砖的壁砖。在台基的长条石之上，留有可以插入角柱或承重柱的基槽，承重柱两边向上叠起着用唐草纹装饰的砖石，其间粘贴着绿釉砖。

本来被认为围绕在宝塔四周的台阶，现在仅发现了北侧和西侧的部分。在石筑台基之上，用三角形的象眼树起之后，以垂带完成的台阶，以榫槽结合在一起的技法，向世人展示了精巧的石工技术。

在四天王寺址中，采集到了大量可以确认寺院名称和重修过程的铭文瓦，在塔址中出土的绿釉壁砖中，还发现了与以前采集的样品相似，在图像上可以视为同一人物上半身的残片，这些发现使得我们能够复原其完整的面貌。

Established in 679 as one of Silla's major "stage guardian temples", Sacheonwangsa ("Temple of the Four Heavenly Kings") consisted of the distinctive "twin-pagoda layout" established during the Unified Silla period, and offers previous insight into the concept of the universe developed by Silla people.

The latest excavation has revealed the features of a hallway built to link the Golden Hall with the Western Gallery, as well as traces of the Northern Gallery, offering an important clue to the size of the entire temple. Archaeologists were particularly delighted to discover at the excavation of the Western Pagoda site the use of green-glazed tiles in the foundation structure of the pagoda. The remaining parts of the foundations show that the stone stairs built in all four directions of the compass were fixed into each other using rabbets, indicating the advanced skills of Silla's masons. Other discoveries from the Sacheonwangsa Temple site include roof tiles inscribed with the name of the temple and a record of ancient renovation work.

220. 四天王寺远景 View of Sacheonwangsa Temple Site

221. 四天王寺全景 View of Sacheonwangsa Temple Site

222. 西塔址 Western Pagoda Site

223. 西塔址全景 View of Western Pagoda Site

224. 西塔台基细部 Stereobate of Western Pagoda

四天王寺址传说

善德女王元年（632年），新罗僧人明朗为了求得佛法真理，前往大唐学习密法。四年后，他在归国途中，受到龙王之邀，进入龙宫向龙王传授了密宗秘法后，从龙王那里得到了千两黄金的施舍，施展地遁法从自家水井现身回家。然后，他化家为寺，用龙王施舍的黄金为佛像和法堂镀色，寺院因之定名为金光寺，本人也投身于弘扬密教的事业中。

唐朝与高句丽战争之后，并没有将军队撤回本国，而是驻屯在百济旧地，准备与新罗战争。为此，文武王请来明朗大师请教退敌之策，明朗奏请在庆州狼山南侧的神游林中建立四天王寺，创设弘扬文豆娄秘法[1]的寺院。但是，薛邦率领众多唐军集结于国境线的急报传来，明朗急忙在狼山南侧神游林中，用彩帛建起了临时寺院，祭起密教魔法中的文豆娄秘法，唐军大败。文武王十九年（679年），明朗在以密教秘法击退唐军的庆州神游林创建了新寺，命名为四天王寺。新罗朝廷为此特设了叫作"四天王寺成典"的官署，并派重臣管理四天王寺[2]。

四天王像绿釉壁砖

四天王本来是印度传统的方位之神，佛教中升为天神，成为守卫佛法、安抚众生的守护神。其在印度被绘制为贵族或菩萨的模样，但是传经中亚之后，变成了手持武器，身着铠甲的威武彪悍形象。这样的四天王像，经中国传入韩国，以三国统一为契机，成为流行一时的护法神和护国神。

四天王寺以这样的四天王信仰为背景，于新罗统一三国之后文武王十九年（679年）创建，成为护国寺院。当时的四天王像为浮雕式壁砖，在最近发掘调查的四天王寺西侧木塔址台基之上发现了这种壁砖，使我们知道了其位置。通过日本强占期采集到的数十块残片，四天王像砖下半部已被世人所熟知。通过四天王匀称的身材与适当的身体比例、细致入微的盔甲、强有力的大腿肌肉以及被压坐的恶鬼表现出的痛苦表情，我们可以充分领略到统一新罗初期现实主义风格的雕塑精髓。同时，随着最近的发掘调查，四天王像砖的上半部残片也大量出土，可以更好地领略四天王像砖风姿。在以前公开的两座天王像之外，戴着头盔的另一个天王像的原貌被公开，引起了人们的关注。

225. 四天王像绿釉壁砖
Green-glazed Brick of Buddhist Guardian

---

[1] 文豆娄秘法为梵语的音译，指神印秘法。
[2] （高丽）一然著，李丙焘译著：《三国遗事·文虎王法敏条》，明文堂，1992年。

226. 四天王像绿釉壁砖 Green-glazed Brick of Buddhist Guardian
　　 四天王寺址 H86.2厘米

227. 四天王像绿釉壁砖示意图　Presumed Restoration of Buddhist Guardian
　　（姜友邦复原案）

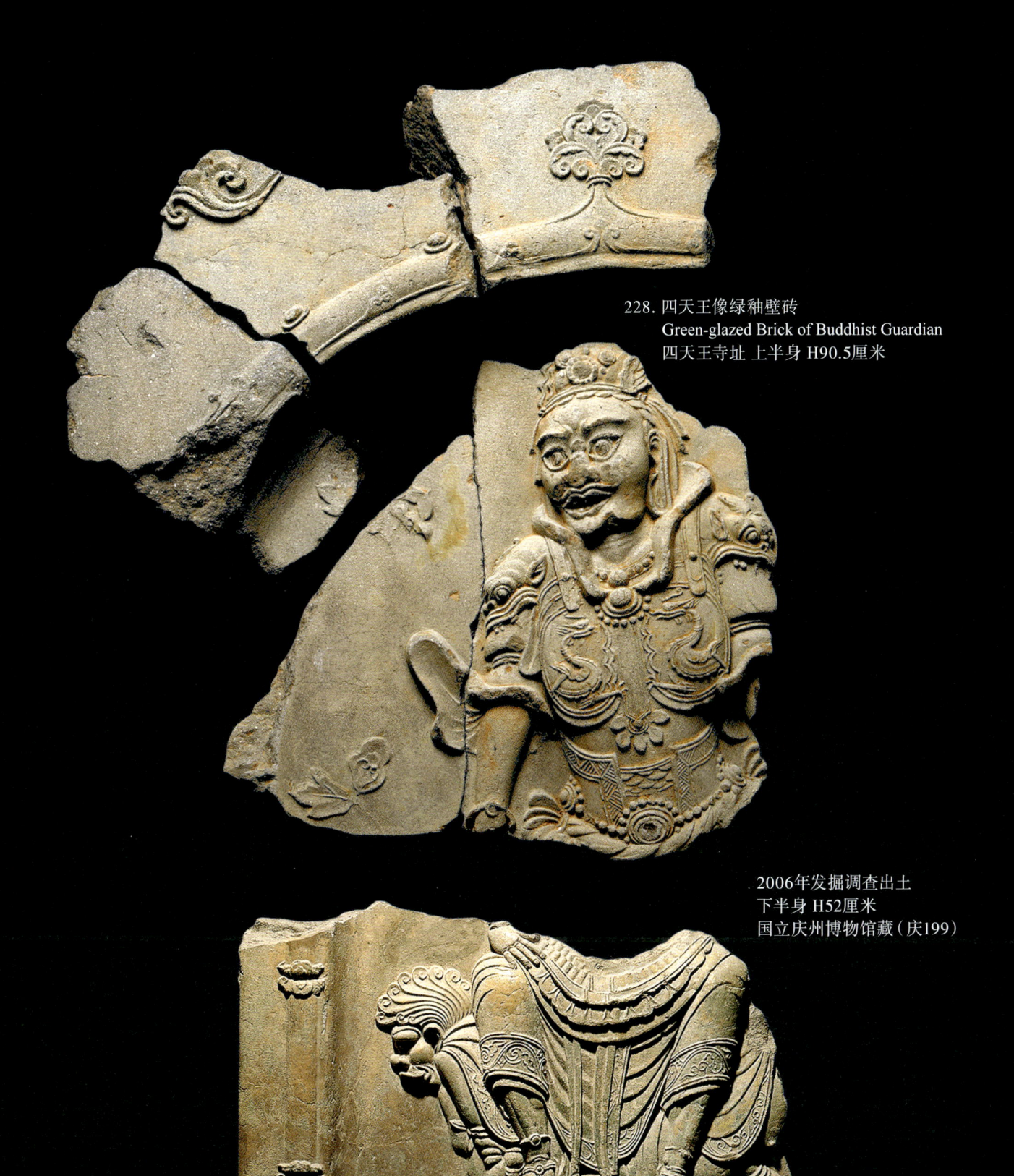

228. 四天王像绿釉壁砖
Green-glazed Brick of Buddhist Guardian
四天王寺址 上半身 H90.5厘米

2006年发掘调查出土
下半身 H52厘米
国立庆州博物馆藏（庆199）

229. 四天王像绿釉壁砖 Green-glazed Brick of Buddhist Guardian
    四天王寺址 H14.5厘米

230. 四天王像绿釉壁砖 Green-glazed Brick of Buddhist Guardian
    四天王寺址 H31厘米

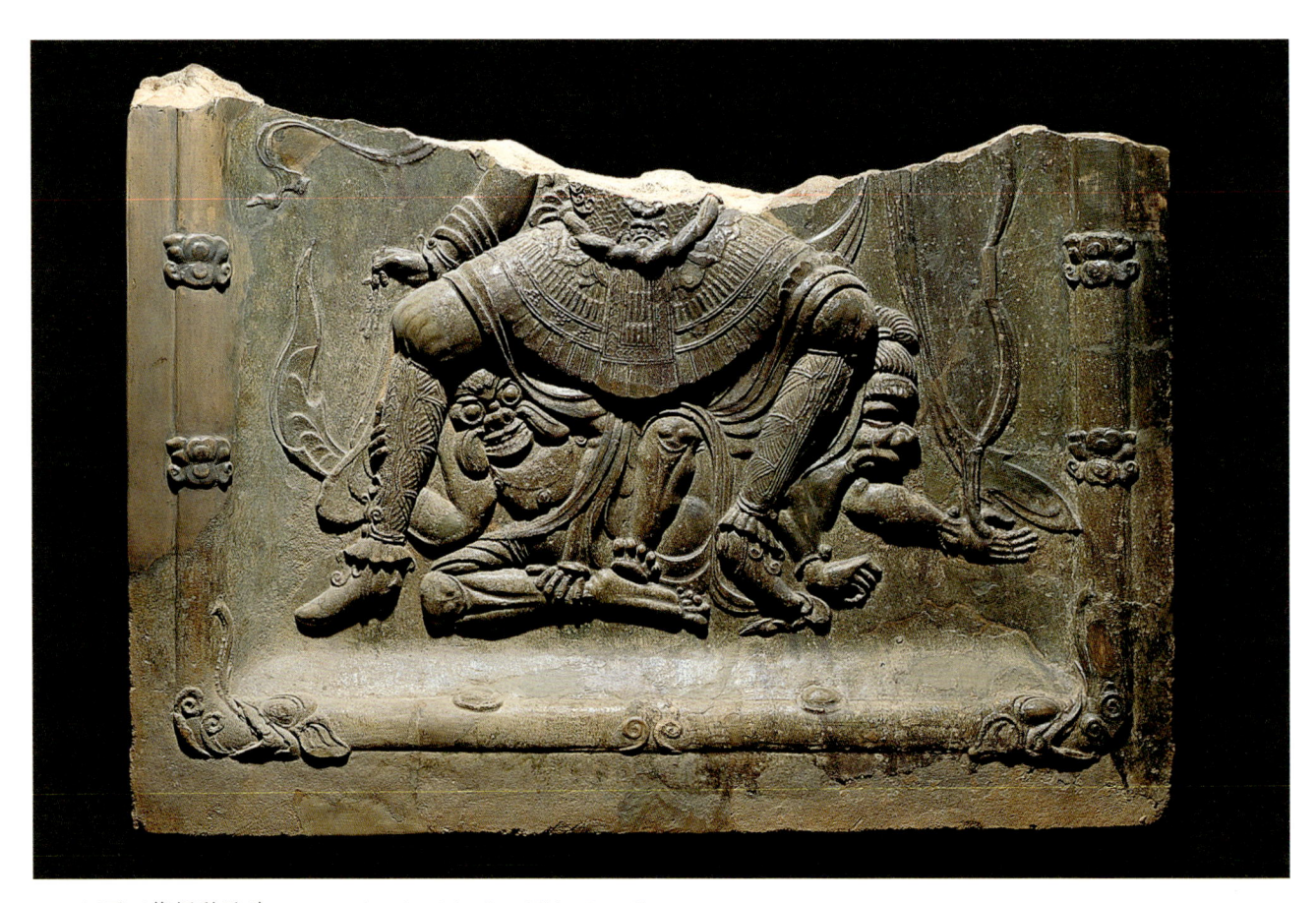

231. 四天王像绿釉壁砖 Green-glazed Brick of Buddhist Guardian
    四天王寺址 H69.5厘米 国立中央博物馆藏（本馆12495）

232. 四天王像绿釉壁砖示意图 Presumed Restoration of Buddhist Guardian
（姜友邦复原案）

233. 四天王像绿釉壁砖 Green-glazed Brick of Buddhist Guardian
    四天王寺址 W55厘米

234. 四天王像绿釉壁砖示意图　Presumed Restoration of Buddhist Guardian
（国立中央博物馆简图）

135

传·仁容寺址 | Inyongsa Temple Site (Alleged)

（庆尚北道庆州市仁旺洞 | 文化财资料第240号 | 统一新罗时代）

仁容寺，是新罗文武王时为派到唐朝担任宿卫的王子金仁问创建的，由于《三国遗事》保留的相关记载很少，其位置和详细的内容并没有流传下来。仅据推测，在环绕月城南端的蚊川南麓可能有仁容寺旧址，目前以东西塔址和留下的一部分基石的位置为中心，正在进行年度发掘。

以统一新罗时代典型的三层石塔的双塔址为中心，在其北端，有被推测定为金堂址的面阔5间、进深5间大小的大型建筑址；在塔址南端，有"十"字形的台基被推测为中门遗址，在其南侧还确认有南北向的方形池塘。同时，在这建筑中，还发现了环绕东西外围的回廊遗址。结合出土遗物和石塔的建筑风格，寺院的营造年代可以初步判定为8世纪中后期。

目前为止出土的800余件遗物中，大部分是砖瓦类遗物，其中包括有"右官"、"汉"、"皇"、"卍"、"寺"、"朱"、"四天王寺"等文瓦。同时还出土了精心雕刻着八部众像的石塔上层台基贴石、滑石制小塔和被推测为舍利庄严具的陶制小塔，还有小型鎏金佛像和鎏金菩萨立像等与佛教有密切关系的遗物。

Archaeologists believe that this site, located to the south of Wolseong, is where a temple named Inyongsa once stood during the United Silla period. Excavations at the site have revealed foundation stones and a stone slab inscribed with a chronology of events concerning a pagoda erected in the temple precinct.

Excavations have also revealed what the temple once had twin three-stone pagoda featuring the characteristic layout of Unified Silla temple. To the north of the pagodas there is a site containing a large building which experts believe was originally the temple's main prayer hall, while to the south there is a site containing a middle gate and the remaining features of a pond. Archaeologists also discovered vestiges of the temple's east and west galleries. Both the excavated relics - approximately 800 items including talc or earthen miniature pagodas and gilt-bronze Buddha images - and the style of the stone pagoda show that the temple was built during the mid to late 8th century.

235. 传·仁容寺址全景 View of Alleged Inyongsa Temple Site

236. 金堂遗址 Main Building of the Temple

237. 天龙八部像 Image of Eight Buddhist Guardians
传·仁容寺址 W158厘米

天龙八部是指聚集在释迦牟尼说法场所，接受感化的部众，他们分别被称为"天"、"龙"、"夜叉"、"乾达婆"、"阿修罗"、"迦楼罗"、"紧那罗"、"摩睺罗伽"。他们本来是佛教创立之前，印度神话中出现的神仙并且拥有强大的法力，随着佛教出现，逐渐发展成为守护佛法的神将。

传·仁容寺址的石塔由样式相同的东西双塔构成。石塔大部分构件都已流失，仅在东塔发现了刻有

天龙八部像的基坛石一枚。在出土的两个天龙八部像中，左侧像身穿盔甲，左手捧珠，右手持刀，两脚相向，坐于祥云之上。从嘴型为鸟喙的特征，可以推断其为迦楼罗像。右侧像身穿盔甲，左手持珠，右手不明，左脚放于右脚之上，以结跏趺坐姿势端坐于祥云之上。右侧像从坐于迦楼罗同一侧面来判断可能是"天"像，从手的位置和手持物等判断，也可以认定为"龙"像，目前尚无法确认。

传·仁容寺址佛像

从日本强占期开始,仁容寺址出土了小型菩萨立像和佛立像。左侧菩萨立像站在较高的莲台宝座之上,头戴装饰复杂的三叶状宝冠,右手举于胸前,左手低垂于腹部,如果仔细观察,还可以发现左手有持物的痕迹。从图像看,虽然是菩萨像,却如佛像一样身披袈裟,十分特别。这样身着袈裟的菩萨像,虽然在统一新罗佛教雕刻中非常少见,但是也确实发现了几尊,对此需要进一步考察和研究。不过也有可能是因为佛像太小,而引起了表现技术上的问题,也不能排除匠人在制作过程中错觉图像的可能。

右侧佛立像将佛身和背光铸为一体,背光一部已经缺失。从大小推测,这样的小型鎏金佛立像,也有可能是护身佛,庆州罗原里五层石塔中出土的鎏金佛像与之类似。尤其值得一提的是,其与小型蜡石制石塔一起被发现于传出土双石塔的仁容寺遗址中,这更增加了这些佛像就是与《无垢净光经》所宣扬的造塔信仰相关的塔内供奉物的可能性。

238. 鎏金菩萨立像、鎏金佛立像 Gilt-bronze Standing Bodhisattva and Buddha
　　 传·仁容寺址 菩萨 H6厘米 如来 H4.2厘米

239. 龙头 Dragon Head
传·仁容寺址 H5.5厘米

240. 小塔 Small Pagoda
传·仁容寺址 H6.5厘米

241. 传·仁容寺址出土中国瓷器 Chinese Ceramics

邢窑白瓷残片

传·仁容寺址中出土的中国白瓷是唐朝或五代十国时期邢州窑生产的白瓷碗残片，玉璧形的圈足高而宽，折沿向外翻卷。通过对窑址的发掘，我们得知邢窑的烧造历史始于北朝终于五代十国，它位于河北省临城县和内丘县，可以生产水平极高的白瓷。邢窑与浙江的越窑在唐代有"南青北白"之誉。

141

242. 瓦 Roof-end Tiles
传·仁容寺址

243. 鸱尾 Ridge-end Tile
传·仁容寺址 H62厘米

244. 兽面纹瓦 Roof-end Tile
传·仁容寺址 W27厘米

245. 施釉瓦片 Glazed Roof-end Tile
传·仁容寺址 L16厘米

天官寺遗址 | Cheongwansa Temple Site

（庆尚北道庆州市校洞 | 史迹第340号 | 统一新罗时代）

　　天官寺位于从月城过月精桥接近南山的入口处，和庆州南山最北端的南山土城及都堂山土城相邻。据说，天官寺因统一三国而名震天下的名将金庾信和天官之间的哀切爱情故事而闻名；同时，也有新罗第38代国王元圣王金敬信因梦到跳入天官寺水井而登基为王的记录。

　　通过天官寺址发掘工作，确定了石塔址、石灯址等多个建筑物和台基、围墙、门址、水井等寺院相关设施的位置。石塔是在两层方形石坛之上起建的塔身八角形的异形塔，推断其大致建于8世纪中叶。

　　虽然无法精确地了解寺院的布局，但是在多座建筑基址之间，有3座大型的建筑，间距14米左右，南北排列，其中有一座正方形建筑基址为类似于瓦积台基的抬梁式台基。

　　天官寺遗址出土小型金铜如来立像、滑石质权等520多件遗物。其中，有半切偏口瓶，这是将瓶身垂直切开，然后再将切面重新贴上的陶器。当然，最引人注目的是骑马人物陶器，它能让人联想到马将熟睡的金庾信将军驮到天官家门口的传说。

　　Cheongwansa is a Buddhist temple related with the tragic love story involving General Kim Yu-Sin, Silla's great military leader who played a decisive role in the unification of the three Korean kingdoms, and a young woman named Cheongwan, hence the name. Excavations of the temple site have revealed remains of various Buddhist buildings and structures including a stone pagoda and a lantern. The stone pagoda, which is believed to have been built after the mid 8th century, featured a singular style in which the octagonal body was erected on the double-tiered square foundation.

　　Archaeologists recovered from the site a great variety of relics totaling some 520 items, including a miniature gilt-bronze standing Buddha. Historians are particularly interested in an earthenware vessel with the shape of a mounted warrior as it appears to be associated with the famous story in which the general's clever horse carried its master, who happened to have fallen asleep on its back, to his lover's house only to face a tragic end.

246. 天官寺址全景 View of Cheongwansa Temple Site

247. 骑马人物形陶器出土状态 Disclosure of Remains

天官寺址传说

　　这是关于为统一三国做出贡献的金庾信和天官女的民间传说，但是在《三国史记》或《三国遗事》中并没有出现过天官女。《破闲集》和《新增东国舆地胜览》中记载了由天官女创作的《天官怨词》或《怨歌》的由来。据说，金庾信在花郎时节听从母亲的劝告，下定决心和相爱的名妓天官女断绝往来。但是，有一天金庾信大醉之后，骑马回家时，所乘之马习惯性地将他拉到了天官女家门前，庾信酒醒之后，用刀斩落马首，返回家中。天官女目睹此情景，创作了埋怨金庾信无情的怨歌。此后，天官女伤心而亡，金庾信为了安慰死去的天官女的灵魂，在天官女家建立了寺院，称为天官寺，这个寺院据说就在五陵之东。

248. 骑马人物形陶器　Horse Rider-shaped Pottery
天官寺址　H12.5厘米

249. 权 Weights
天官寺址 H5.8厘米

权是测量重量的基本工具，在交纳租税和贡赋时或在日常生活的物物交换时，在市场交易时，都是必不可少的。使用一定重量单位的权，可以在交纳租税或进行物物交换时减少不必要的纠纷，提高准确度和效率。这样的权在三国时代已经被人们广泛地使用，王京遗址或天官寺址等建筑遗址中大量出现。

目前在遗址中调查和发掘出土的权由石、陶、青铜和铁等多种材料制成，其形态共同点是在顶端有一个可以穿过细绳的小孔。在形态方面，虽然王京遗址曾发现外部雕上十二生肖像的特殊权，但是大部分仍然是和天官寺址中出土的直方角形模样相似，偶尔也会有下端突起的权。

250. 鎏金佛立像 Gilt-bronze Standing Buddha
天官寺址 H5.1厘米

251. 半切偏口瓶 Flattened Bottle in Half
天官寺址 H12.3厘米

荪谷洞、勿川里遗址 | Songokdong·Mulcheolli Archaeological Site
（庆尚北道庆州市荪谷洞、勿川里 | 史迹第430号 | 三国　统一新罗时代）

位于庆州普门地区北侧小山上的荪谷洞、勿川里遗址，作为从三国时代开始大量生产陶器和木炭的大规模生产遗址，发现了与陶窑相关的采土场、手工作坊、建筑遗址等设施，还出土有烧窑的垫具和陶拍等多种多样的生产工具，为研究新罗陶器生产的窑业技术史研究提供了重要的资料。

发掘的55座陶窑，均为东西向，集中排列在凸出的丘陵南坡上。通过相互叠压的陶窑遗迹可以得知，它们存在时间上的先后关系，显示出随着时代的变迁陶窑在结构上发生了变化。

制作陶器的作坊和居住址以及仓库等，大部分都在丘陵顶部。在作坊遗迹中，发现了陶器成型时必需的黏土堆以及辘轳的位置，建筑址则根据居住、贮藏、祭祀等用途分为础石建筑、爪棚式建筑、竖穴式建筑等多种形态。

除此之外，在丘陵顶部还发现了包括积石木椁墓在内的多种形式的墓葬，由此可知，在生产集团内部根据人们身份的高低，墓葬形式也各不相同。

荪谷洞、勿川里遗址不仅可复原供给新罗王京的陶器生产的整个过程，同时还出土了反映遗址生活状态的遗迹和遗物，具有重要的学术价值。

The archaeological site in Songokdong and Mulcheolli was related with the mass production of pottery and charcoal throughout the Three Kingdoms and United Silla periods.

The findings from the site included 55 kilns and their related facilities, including clay-gathering sites and workshops. Owing to the extensive range of the discovery, which includes tools as well as specific earthenware vessels, experts are now able to restore the entire process of pottery making as it was developed in Silla.

The latest excavation project conducted on the site included a survey of the graves scattered in the area, exhibiting a diversity of styles according to the social status potters in Silla's hierarchical society. The relics are expected to provide comprehensive information about Silla pottery and the potters' way of life.

252. 陶窑址分布情况 A Group of Potteries Kilns

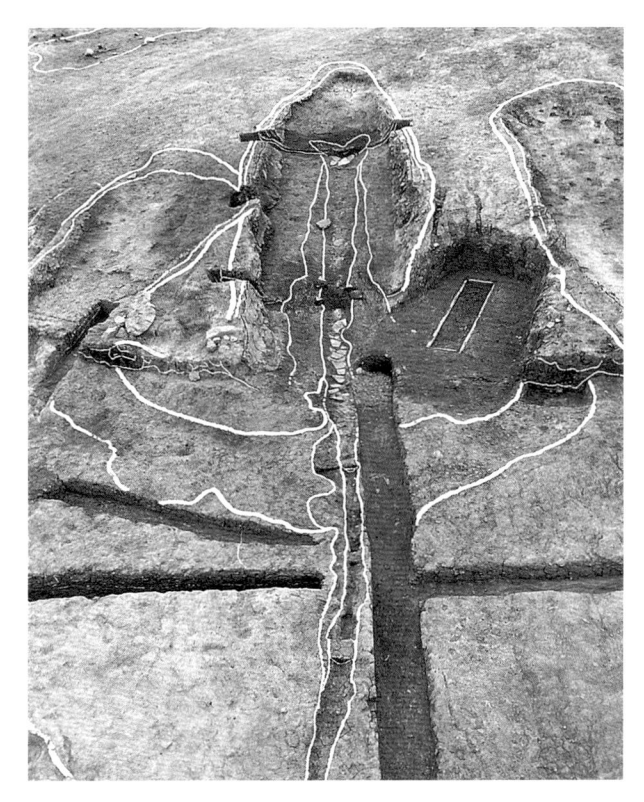

253. 陶窑址 Earthenware Kiln

254. 陶窑址 Earthenware Kiln

255. 瓦窑址 Tile Kiln

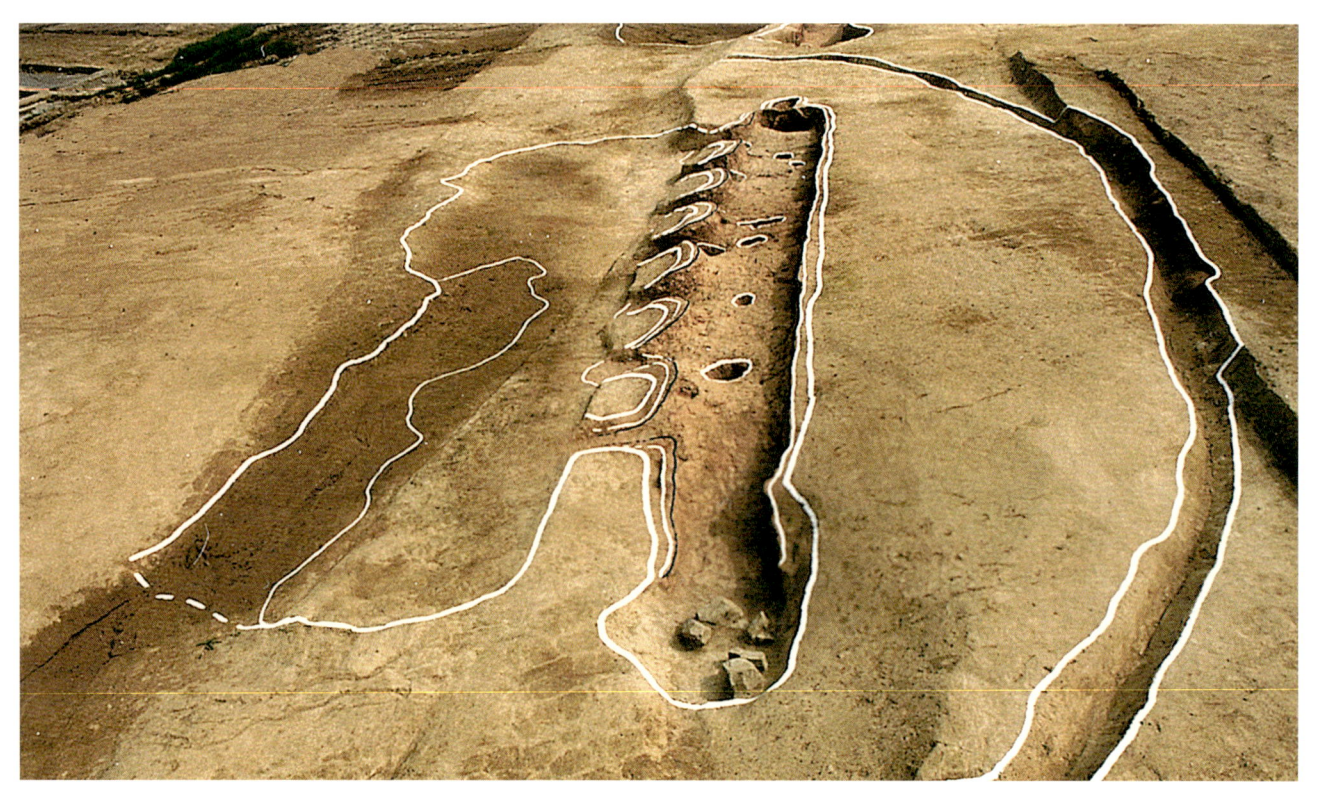

256. 木炭窑址 Charcoal Kiln

257. 石筑遗迹 Stone Construction

258. 作坊、民居、采土场叠压打破情况 Overlapping Pits of Workshops, Houses and Clay-gathering Sites

陶俑

陶俑有的单独使用，有的黏贴在其他陶器上。它们一般作为陪葬用品或祭祀用品使用，三国时期在新罗尤为盛行。苏谷洞、勿川里作为新罗陶器的大规模生产遗址，伴随其他遗物一起，也出土了大批陶俑。这些陶俑中，既有被捆绑的囚犯、演奏乐器的艺伎像、身背箭筒的猎人和相爱的恋人等人物题材，也有虎、犬、马、蛇、蛙、龟、鸟等动物题材，使我们体会到新罗人那精炼的感觉和技艺。这些陶俑既有黏在杯盖之上的，也有黏在陶壶肩上的，还有黏在器台之上的。它们表现了打猎或歌舞等特定的主题或动作，比如蛇衔蛙等主题含有富饶与辟邪的意义，推测其应用于祭仪用酒器、水器及装种子的器皿之上。

259. 陶俑　Clay Figurines
　　 苏谷洞、勿川里

260. 弹琴陶俑 Gum Player
 苏谷洞、勿川里 H3.3厘米

261. 吹笛陶俑 Piper
 苏谷洞、勿川里 H4厘米

262~266. 人物陶俑 People
 苏谷洞、勿川里 H4厘米

267、268. 罪囚陶俑 Prisoner
 苏谷洞、勿川里 H3.5厘米

269. 动物陶俑 Animals
　　 荪谷洞、勿川里

270. 蛇形陶俑 Snakes
　　 荪谷洞、勿川里

271. 鸟形陶俑 Birds
　　 荪谷洞、勿川里

272. 龟形陶俑 Turtle
　　 苏谷洞、勿川里 H3.6厘米

273. 虎形陶俑 Tiger
　　 苏谷洞、勿川里 L14厘米

274. 马形陶俑 Horse
　　 苏谷洞、勿川里 H9.9厘米

275. 马形陶俑 Horse
　　 苏谷洞、勿川里 H5厘米

276. 犬形陶俑 Dog
　　 苏谷洞、勿川里 H2厘米

277. 蛇形陶俑 Snake
　　 苏谷洞、勿川里 L6.8厘米

278. 鸭形陶俑 Duck
　　 苏谷洞、勿川里 H2.8厘米

279. 烧废陶器 Ill-fired Potteries
 苏谷洞、勿川里 D25厘米

280. 陶器生产工具 Pottery Production Tools
 苏谷洞、勿川里

窑具

将大批陶器放入窑炉中烧制时，为了防止它们因为受热融化而相互粘连，匠人们使用了多种多样的支垫烧工具和材料。像这样，在陶器和窑炉底之间放置的工具称为支烧具；将陶器堆积在一起烧制时，为防止陶器互相挤压而放置在陶器之间的工具，称为垫具。作为支烧具除了将陶器片铺在窑底之外，还有使用高足托座和王冠形托座的。作为垫具有长鼓形、环形、纺轮形和瓶形等。正是因为这些工具，陶器避免了与窑底或其他叠烧陶器发生粘连以及倾斜碰倒的现象，使陶器在烧制过程中受热均匀。支烧具的使用大约在6世纪左右开始并普遍化，主要发现于三国时代都城周边的窑址中。

281. 窑具、陶器 Stand and Pottery
 苏谷洞、勿川里 窑具 H5.2厘米

282. 角杯、角杯台 Horn-shaped Cup with Stand
 苏谷洞、勿川里 角杯台 H17厘米

Gaya 伽倻

伽倻（加耶，伽耶，Gaya）是公元前后至6世纪后半位于古代国家新罗和百济之间的政治集团，其维持联盟体制，又被称为驾洛国。公元前后随着铁器文化的普及，位于南部落海岸的这一集团开始以小国为单位合并了诸多小国，3世纪左右形成了相互联盟关系，统称其为弁韩（《三国志·魏书·东夷传》）。

伽倻前期是以临海的金海地区（今庆尚南道市金海市）的金官伽倻（42~532年）为中心的联盟，后期是以内陆的高灵地区（今庆尚南道高灵郡）的大伽倻（42~562年）为中心的联盟。以5世纪末为界限，伽倻联盟划分为前期和后期。

伽倻地区以丰富的铁矿资源为基础，成为连接乐浪和倭的海上交易中介地区。乐浪地区和中原器物的输入等因素使伽倻具有较高的文化水平。但是伽倻内部的各小国由于没有形成统一的国家，因此各自独立的小国联盟体制一直维持着。

5世纪初由于高句丽好太王（韩国学界称为"广开土王"）对伽倻地区进行征伐，伽倻逐渐依附于新罗。5世纪以后随着大伽倻联盟的形成，向中国南朝的萧齐政权派遣使者等原因，使伽倻在朝鲜半岛的三国（高句丽、百济、新罗）关系中扮演重要的政治变量。但是伽倻对百济战争的失利使其丧失了对倭交易权，其势力也随之急剧衰落。前期伽倻联盟的小国大部分附属于新罗，并在562年（新罗真兴王二十三年）新罗对大伽倻的征伐中最终消亡。

流传下来的关于伽倻的记录不多，因此伽倻的历史需要通过考古发掘来发现。伽倻文化最大的特征是其墓葬形式的变化：公元1~2世纪为木棺墓，3~4世纪为木椁墓，5世纪的大型封土石椁墓是伽倻代表性的墓葬形制。出土遗物包括各种铁器及大量陶器等，而且与新罗一样保存了人殉习俗，延续到6世纪前期。酋长级大型墓葬的修建地区如釜山、金海、咸安、固城、高灵、陕川等伽倻故地今天依然保存了大量的石椁墓。

Gaya (伽倻, 加耶, 伽耶) is an alliance of city-states, which existed between the two ancient countries in the Korean Peninsula Silla (新罗) and Baekje (百济) till the late 6th century, and it is also called Karagkug (驾洛国). The groups in the southern coast of Korea started to be integrated into small countries before and after Christ, and they were called Byeonhan (弁韩) [The Eastern Barbarian (东夷) Chronicle of Book of Wei (魏书), "Samgukji (三国志)"] as a generic term forming a mutual alliance around the third century. The history of Gaya is divided into the former part and the latter part before and after the late 5th century.

The former and latter part stands for the era, where the Gaya alliance developed with Geumgwan Gaya (金官伽倻) (42~532 A.D.) in the coastal region Gimhae (金海) and DaeGaya (大伽倻) (42~562 A.D.) in the inland area Goryeong (高灵), as the center, respectively.

Gaya established a very advanced culture due to the cultural import from Naklang (乐浪) and China as it became an intermediary of marine trade bridging Naklang and Japan (倭). But, it was maintained as an alliance of small countries with an independent power in that its unitary integration was not done.

Gaya became politically under Silla as Goguryeo's King Kwanggaeto (广开土) went on a conquest of it in the early 5th century. It dispatched an envoy to Qi (齐) of Southern Dynasty (南朝) in China forming the DaeGaya (大伽倻) alliance; it acted as a big political variable in the relationships among the three countries (i.e. Goguryeo, Baekje and Silla). However, it lost the sole right of trade with Japan (倭) and declined rapidly in that it was defeated in the war by Baekje. As small countries constituting the former Gaya alliance were subjugated one after another by Silla. Finally, it went out of existence due to Silla's conquest of DaeGaya (大伽倻) in the 23rd reign of King JinHeung (真兴) (562).

The history of Gaya, whose records are rarely handed down, is identified by archaeological excavations. The representative burial systems showing the characteristics of Gaya best are wooden coffin tomb (木棺墓) from the first to the second century, wooden outer coffin tomb (木椁墓) from the third to the fourth century, and stone outer coffin tomb (石椁墓) sealed off with large earth mounds and in the fifth century. At these tombs. all sorts of ironware and many various earthenware were excavated as grave goods. Like Silla, Gaya maintained a peculiar custom, the burial of the living with the dead, till the early 6th century. Large tombs under which the head was buried were constructed in Busan (釜山), Gimhae (金海), Haman (咸安), Goseong (固城), Goryeong (高灵), and Hapcheon (陕川). There are still a lot of stone chamber tombs in the ancient territories of Gaya.

伽倻文化 | The culture of Gaya

位于洛东江中下游，弁韩故地的伽倻国，以丰富的铁资源为基础，逐渐发展成为古代国际贸易的中心。伽倻国初期以庆尚南道金海地区的金官伽倻为中心，后期以庆尚北道高灵地区的大伽倻为中心。伽倻维持联盟体制的同时，保持地区性文化特征，相互之间交流不断。

通过发掘和调查发现的伽倻文化遗存，有各种形制的墓葬和山城。它们不仅反映了伽倻不同地区的文化特色，也展示了被认为与新罗和百济有密且关系的遗物。同时作为名副其实的铁器王国，出土了包括马具、武器和农具在内的大量铁器，还发现了大量有助于研究古代行政文书的记录材料——木简，因而备受学术界关注。

An ancient confederation of Korean chiefdoms located in the south of the Korean Peninsula, Gaya grew to be a regional trade hub thanks to rich iron deposits and an advanced iron culture. Gaya chiefdoms established their own unique culture by maintaining close ties with each other.

The archaeological remains of Gaya excavated so far consist largely of tombs, fortifications and reservoir facilities. Excavations of these vestiges have revealed a great variety of tomb structures, from which artifacts unearthed offer important clues to the relationship between neighboring chiefdoms and kingdoms. And the superb iron products such as horse trappings including harnesses, weapons, and farming tools represent a fine source of knowledge about ancient Korean society. The wooden strips (mokgan) used by the Gaya people as a writing material and excavations from Seongsansanseong Fortress are particularly highly regarded as an important source of knowledge concerning the record-based administration of ancient Korea.

松岘洞古墓群 | Songhyeondong Tomb Complex
（庆尚南道昌宁郡昌宁邑松岘里 | 史迹第81号 | 三国时代）

松岘洞古墓群和校洞古墓群、桂城古墓群、灵山古墓群，都是非火伽倻的故都——昌宁地区的代表性古墓群。在23座大中型古墓中，最近发掘的6、7号墓是由直径达到21米的两座封土墓组成，彼此连接为一座葫芦形墓葬。就其修筑过程而言，应是首先修筑6号墓，然后修筑7号墓。它们是在5世纪末至6世纪初建成的横口式石室墓，其特征是以石室为中心，封土在其四周呈放射状堆积。

石室长约8.5米，底部宽1.4~1.8米，墓室顶部宽约1米，平面形态呈长方形，剖面为梯形。在石室内部有一石棺台，长3.3米，宽1.5~1.6米，有一大型木棺置于其上，棺台与横口之间的地面上，按斜线方向，铺着一层方材是其重要特征。

在6、7号墓石室内，出土了各种陶器和金属遗物、木制遗物。在超过500件的陶器中，有带盖豆形器之类的小型陶器，特别的是，它们是装在筐里出土的。金属类遗物出土有鞍桥包片、云珠、杏叶、金耳环、银质腰带装饰、三叶纹环头大刀和箭镞等，共有100多件。木器类既有大型木棺，也有各种漆器和异型木制品、马鞍、箩筐等遗物。其中7号墓中的木棺呈独木舟状，用樟木制成，这种树木生长于济州岛、日本、中国台湾、中国大陆和印度尼西亚等地。

The Songhyeondong Tomb Complex is one of several sites containing the tomb of the ruling class of a Gaya chiefdom that was centered around the area now known as Changnyeong. The tomb complex consists of 23 tombs, all of which are situated on the slopes of Hwawangsan Mountain. Among them, archaeologists are particularly interested in tombs #6 and #7, as they form a distinctive gourd shape with two earthen mounds - each of which measures 21 meters in diameter - that are joined with each other. They found that tomb #6 was the first of the two tomb to have been built.

Built in the period between the late 5th and early 6th century, in the style consisting of a stone chamber with a horizontal entrance, the tombs feature a huge mound piled up in a radial pattern. The excavation of the stone burial chamber produced over 600 items of pottery and mental and wooden object. The wooden coffin discovered at tomb #7 is 3.3 meters long and is made of camphor wood carved in the shape of a boat.

283. 6、7号墓全景 View of Tomb #6 and #7

284. 松岘洞古墓群远景 View of Tomb Complex

285. 7号墓石室内部 Stone Chamber of Tomb #7

286. 清洗后的7号墓木棺 Wooden Coffin from Tomb #7

287. 7号墓在木棺清理后，遗物出土状态 Remains from Tomb #7

288. 7号墓木棺旁箭镞群
Arrows near Wooden Coffin in Tomb #7

289. 7号墓石室内部遗物出土状态
Remains in Tomb #7

290. 三叶纹环头大刀 Sword with Ring Pommel
松岘洞 L40厘米

三叶纹环头大刀

在三国时代，用金银华丽地装饰的大刀并不是为了砍击而制作的实用品，而是主人高贵身份与地位的象征物。这类大刀的刀柄末端，一般都附有一个环柄，因此被称为"环头大刀"。

在同时期的高句丽流行三叶纹环头大刀，百济流行龙纹环头大刀和三叶纹环头大刀，新罗则流行龙纹环头大刀、三叶环头大刀以及三累环头大刀。其中，龙纹大刀在6世纪的百济和新罗代表着最高的规格。

松岘洞出土的环头大刀，被称为三叶纹环头大刀，因其刀柄末端圆环中有三叶纹装饰而得名。其刀柄用银制作而成，表面装饰鱼鳞纹。这种形制的环头大刀在天马冢、金冠冢、福泉洞10号墓、福泉洞11号墓、义城郡鹤尾里均有发现，年代大约在5世纪末到6世纪初。

291. 金制耳环 Gold Earrings
   松岘洞 L10厘米

292. 银制腰带装饰 Silver Buckles
   松岘洞 W4厘米

293. 松岘洞出土马具 Horse Harness
    松岘洞

294. 鞍桥饰 Saddle Ornament
松岘洞 L20厘米

纵马驰骋时，为了保持骑手的稳定要使用马鞍，马鞍有前后鞍桥，鞍桥表面常以金属片装饰。这种装饰板或以一块金属板剪成，或用两块板材分别制成以对称形式黏贴在鞍桥上。中间部分用带扣连接，为此在两侧钻有两个对称小孔。为防止马鞍从马背滑落或倾斜，用带扣连接皮绳分别系在马的胸前和臀部。在松岘洞周围还出土了金铜透雕鞍桥的下部和黑漆马鞍桥。皇南大冢南墓、大邱内唐洞55号墓中都出土有类似的鞍桥饰。

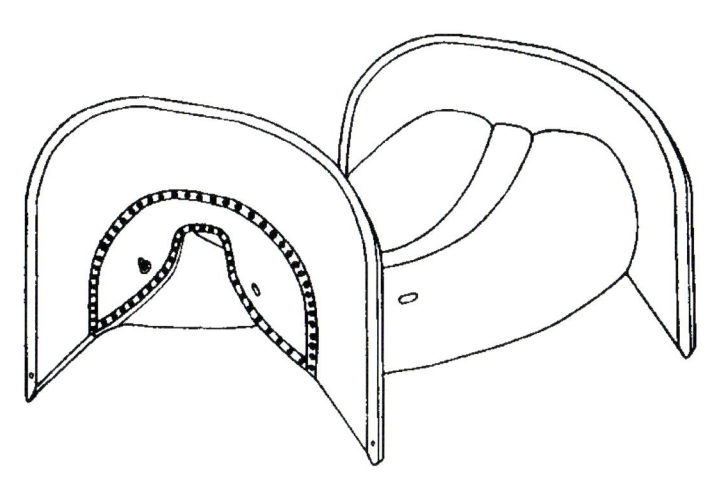

295. 马鞍示意图 Restoration of Saddle
(出处:《考古学事典》，国立文化财研究所)

296. 云珠 Harness Fittings for Crossbelt
松岘洞 H15厘米

297. 云珠 Harness Fittings for Crossbelt
松岘洞 大型 D15厘米

298. 杏叶 Horse Strap Pendants
松岘洞 W20厘米

299. 鎏金透雕马鞍桥前轮 Saddle Ornament
松岘洞 W25厘米

300. 鎏金透雕马鞍桥后轮 Saddle Ornament
松岘洞 W27.8厘米

301. 木制区划板 Wooden Vessel
    松岘洞 L20厘米

302. 杯状木器 Wooden Vessels
    松岘洞 大型 H17.4厘米

304. 侧面 Side of Fan Grip

303. 扇柄 Fan Grip
松岘洞 L23厘米

305. 棒状菱纹漆器 Bar-shaped Lacquer Ware
松岘洞 L107厘米

306、307. 棒状菱纹漆器细部
Detail of Bar-shaped Lacquer Ware

171

308. 长颈壶 Jar with Long Neck
松岘洞 H30厘米

309. 豆形器、红陶钵 Mounted Dishes and Bowls
　　 松岘洞 红陶钵 H10厘米

310. 有盖豆形器 Mounted Dishes with Cover
　　 松岘洞 H10厘米

311. 圈足长颈壶 Mounted Jars with Long Neck
　　 松岘洞 H30厘米

312. 双耳高圈足盏 Bowls With Handles
　　 松岘洞 H15厘米

内山里古墓群 | Naesalli Tomb Complex
（庆尚南道固城郡东海面内山里 | 史迹第120号 | 三国时代）

　　内山里古墓群，是三国时代小伽倻统治阶级的中心墓地之一，65座大中型墓葬密集地分布在在南海沿岸赤浦湾一带低矮的丘陵地区。

　　墓葬的中央以竖穴式石椁或横穴式石室作为主椁，在其周围排列数个小型石椁和瓮棺，形成多椁式结构。多椁墓既具有多次追加葬[①]特点，又反映了血缘共同体的社会面貌，内山里古墓群公认具有代表性。固城的松鹤洞古墓群、粟垈里古墓群、莲塘里古墓群也反映了这一墓制特点。

　　曾经以荣山江流域为中心广泛流行的坟丘墓，在固城这一遥远的南海沿岸出现，证明了两地在当时有过频繁的文化交流，从而受到学术界关注。

　　在出土遗物中，既有三角形透雕高脚杯、折沿壶等代表庆尚南道西部伽倻后期风格的陶器，也有璎珞装饰高脚壶等新罗风格陶器和广口带孔小壶等百济陶器，此外还发现了倭系陶器、马镫。据此，我们可以了解6世纪上半叶，曾经筑造了内山里古墓的人群以近海的地理优势为基础，从多个角度实施了极其活跃的对外交流活动。

　　The Naesalli Tomb Complex is one of several cemeteries built for the ruling class of a Gaya chiefdom centered around today's Goseong area in Gyeongnam. Consisting of 65 mid - and large - sized tombs, the complex is located on a gentle hill on the southern coast.

　　The structure of the tombs is characterized by a main stone burial chamber with a vertical or tunnel entrance that is surrounded by a number of stone cists and earthenware jar coffins of smaller size. The multi-chamber tomb, reflecting an ancient society based on blood ties, show common features with the ancient tombs in Naesalli and other archaeological remains located in the area.

　　The findings from this site include a large number of relics from Baekje and Wae (today's Japan), revealing that Gaya Chiefdoms were actively engaged in international exchange, thus making the most of their strategic geological location and marine products.

---

① 类似于江南土墩墓的葬制。

313. 内山里古墓群远景 View of Naesalli Tomb Complex

314. 内山里8号墓 Tomb #8

315. 8号墓遗物出土状态 Remains in Tomb #8

316. 内山里34号墓 Tomb #34

317. 34号墓遗物出土状态 Remains in Tomb #34

318. 34号墓主椁 Coffin of Tomb #34

319. 玻璃珠 Glass Beads
内山里 曲玉 L3厘米

320. 玻璃珠 Detail of Glass Beads

321. 耳饰 Earrings
内山里 D2.5~3.5厘米

322. 镯子 Bracelets
内山里 D7~8厘米

325. 铁镞 Iron Arrowheads
内山里 L13~15厘米

323. 铁矛、铁镦 Iron Spearhead, Iron Ferrule
内山里 铁矛 L39.5厘米

324. 铁矛细部 Detail of Spearhead

326. 铁斧 Iron Axes
内山里 大型 L18~20厘米

327. 铁镰 Iron Sickle
内山里 L18厘米

328. 铁环 Iron Ring
内山里 D7.1厘米

329. 大刀 Iron Sword
内山里 L74厘米

330. 内山里出土马具 Horse Harness
内山里

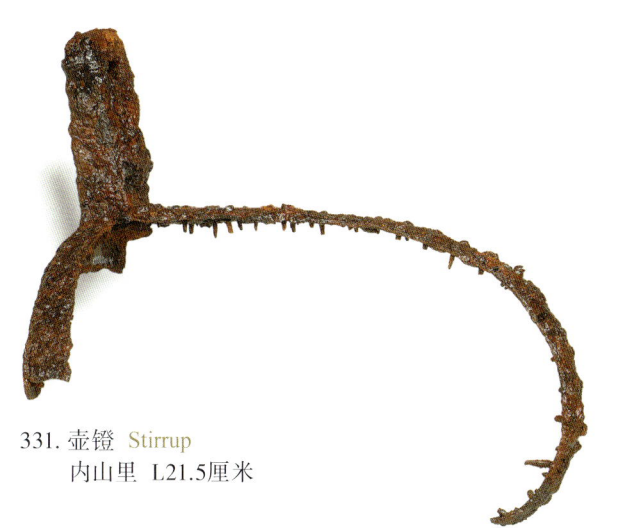

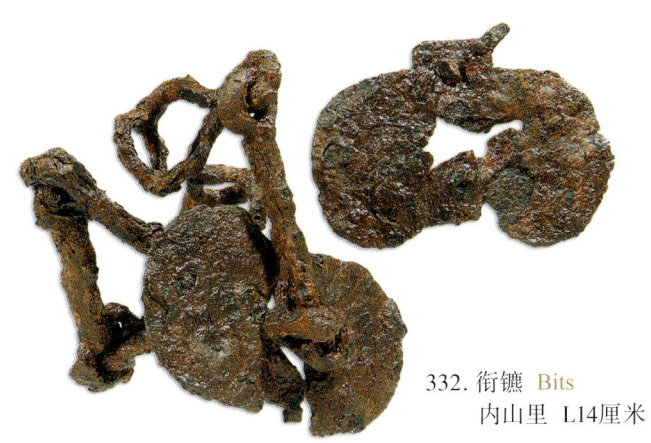

331. 壶镫 Stirrup
内山里 L21.5厘米

332. 衔镳 Bits
内山里 L14厘米

333. 青铜銮铃 Horse Bells
内山里 大型 D5.2厘米

334. 云珠 Harness Fittings for Crossbelt
内山里 大型 W9厘米

335. 带盖陶器 Potteries with Cover
　　 内山里 W12~13.5厘米

336. 单耳附碗 Bowls with Handle
　　 内山里 H9.2~9.4厘米

337. 单耳附碗 Bowls with Handle
　　 内山里 H9.7厘米

338. 广口带孔小壶 Jars with Hole
　　 内山里 H12厘米

339. 折沿壶 Wide-mouthed Jars
     内山里 H14.6厘米

340. 圈足直口壶 Mounted Jar
     内山里 H20.8厘米

341. 璎珞装饰圈足壶 Mounted Jar
     内山里 H42.6厘米

城山山城 | Seongsansanseong Fortress
（庆尚南道咸安郡伽倻邑广井里｜史迹第67号｜三国时代）

虽然城山山城被认为是以咸安郡为中心的阿罗伽倻的政治军事据点，然而从城的筑造方法和木简墨书的内容来看，实际上它是与新罗有关的6世纪中叶的山城。在遗址周围，分布着咸安郡道项里、末山里古墓群（史迹第84、85号）等阿罗伽倻的酋长级大型墓葬。

山城围绕鸟南山顶而建，周长为1.4公里，具有山脊式构造，其外墙底部以剖面呈三角形建材进行加固，是内外夹筑式石城。这样的筑城技法，被认为与新罗有密切关系，这种技法在报恩郡三年山城、庆州明活山城都有发现。另一方面，《日本书纪》19卷"钦明天皇二十二年（561年）条"中记载，新罗为了对抗日本，在阿罗的波斯山上修筑了山城，这一记录为深入研究筑城的年代，提供了重要的线索。

在2002年开始启动的对东门址周边池塘的发掘中，确定这里曾经多次修建，是带有石筑护岸和木柱设施的大型池塘。在这里出土了可以了解古代文书行政的木简和相当于卷轴式文书书签的题签轴等大量的木质遗物，这些遗物也是可以了解古代植被情况的有机遗物。虽然我们目前仅收集到了160余枚木简，但是考虑到在韩国总共只发现了400余枚木简的情况，其数量已经是非常多了。尤其值得一提的是，城山山城出土的木简，为了解新罗的地方统治体系和财政运营结构，提供了极其重要的线索，因此被学术界评价为重要的文献资料。

The remaining fortified walls which constitute Seongsansanseong Fortress were built in the 6th century on Gaya territory, an area which is today known as Haman. Around the east gate of the fortress are the vestiges of a large reservoir that was reconstructed several times with stone revetments and wooden columns. Excavation work on the site has produced a range of relics including wooden strips used as a writing material and a wooden piece used as a bookmark for a paper scroll.

Historians are particularly interested in the wooden strips–approximately 160 items have been discovered so far–as they contain records that important clues concerning Silla's system of local government and financial administration.

342. 城山山城远景 View of Seongsansanseong Fortress

343. 城山山城全景 View of Seongsansanseong Fortress

344. 东城墙周围贮水设施（三维） Reservoir near Eastern Fortress Wall

345. 东城墙周围木简集中出土地 Disclosure of Wooden Strips

346. 贮水池木柱设施 Wooden Pillar of Reservoir

347. 清理贮水池内木简的场面 Wooden Strips in Reservoir

348. 龟甲出土状态 Snapping Turtle Bones

349. 木简 Wooden Strips
　　 城山山城

350. 2006年出土木简红外线照片 Infrared Photography of Wooden Strips

城山山城木简和题签轴

在古代东亚，纸张没有发明之前直至纸张发明了很长一段时间内，人们是在削好的木片上，或用笔留下墨迹，或用刀刻上内容，称之为木简。在使用木简时，大体上要将完整的内容尽量记在同一枚木简之上，因此不仅要使用木简的正反面，而且要使用可能的各个侧面。木简作为货物标签或证明身份的通行证等，是与人的活动有关的记录工具，因此被广泛使用。韩国已经出土的400余枚木简，来自全国14个遗址，其中可以确认字迹的有250余枚。目前为止，城山山城是发现木简最多的遗址，其中也包含了可以插在卷轴形文书内，起索引作用的题签轴。题签轴有相当于头部的"题签"和支撑文书起到"芯"作用的轴构成。板状头部上，可以书写文书、记录、典籍等的内容或名称。在城山山城出土的题签轴，一般呈现出比日本题签轴更古老的形态，为我们研究古代韩日两国之间的文字文化交流，提供了重要的资料。

351. 题签轴 Wooden Strips for Bookmark
城山山城 L20厘米

352. 笔、书刀 Brush, Eraser Knife
城山山城 笔 L18.7厘米 刀 L19厘米

353. 城山山城出土木棒 Beetles
城山山城

354. 木制容器 Wooden Vessels
城山山城 大型 L43厘米

355. 长颈壶 Jar with Long Neck
城山山城 H30厘米

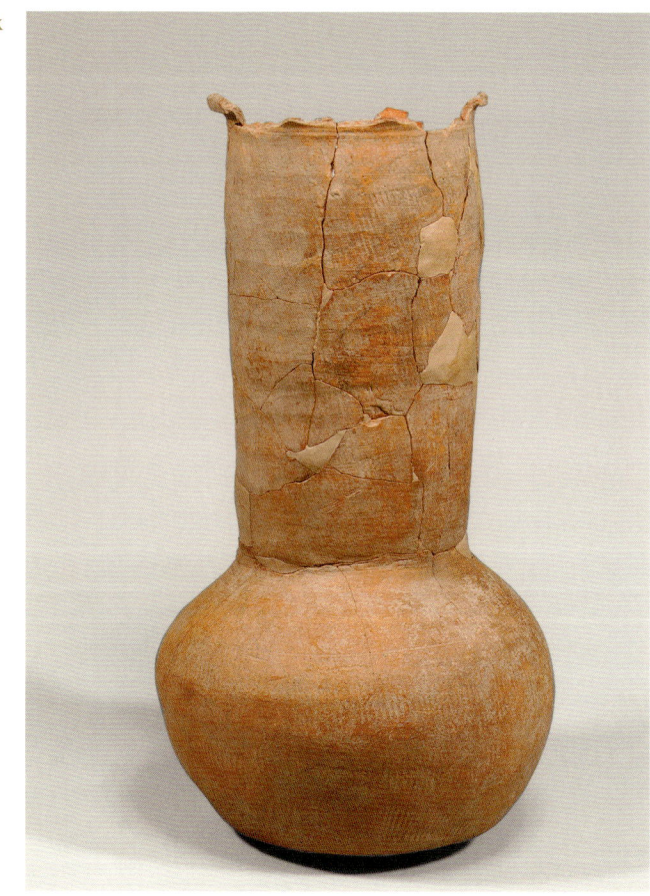

356. 封泥 Seal
城山山城 W5厘米

Goryeo 高丽

高丽是在统一了后三国（统一新罗、后高句丽、后百济）的分裂局面后形成的王朝，它承袭了高句丽的传统并实行北方政策，同时对辽金等北方民族采取了具体的军事性措施。它还采取积极的对内政策，与统一新罗相比社会呈现出更加繁荣的面貌。

建国初期经过定宗—光宗—成宗三朝，强化了王权并确立了中央集权，国家体制发展得更加完善。由于与契丹的战争，高丽王朝经历了全国性的灾难，在击退契丹后，高丽与宋、辽、金一起形成了东北亚地区多元政治秩序。同时，其文化也在不断发展，形成了以高丽青瓷为代表的贵族文化。

不久之后，高丽贵族文化先后经历了李资谦的叛乱和妙清的西京迁都运动，国家从此开始接连不断的内部冲突。这样的冲突最后以武臣政变而结尾并导致了以贵族为中心的政治体制的崩溃。武臣政权时期由于持续的贵族斗争和农民起义等因素，高丽王室的权威逐步衰落，到13世纪，由于与蒙古的战争，首都甚至还迁到了江都（江华岛）。

江都曾经作为高丽王朝的首都达39年（1232~1270年），虽然是为了避开蒙古而被迫迁都，但是江都依然形成了宫城—中城—外城的都城体制，同时和故都开京（开城，今朝鲜开城市）一样，具有行使各种职能的官府机构。

在江都还确认了从国王到一般贵族等各阶层的墓葬，其中硕陵、坤陵、嘉陵和陵内里石室墓的发掘为了解这一时期高丽王陵的全貌提供了重要材料。另一方面，统一新罗时期创建的实相寺作为禅宗九山禅门的祖庭在高丽时代最为繁盛，通过发掘我们厘清了既保持传统又不失变化的寺院布局，以高丽九层木塔为代表的众多建筑遗址为我们了解实相寺全盛时期的面貌提供了很大的帮助。

Goryeo (高丽) is a country which united the later three kingdoms Unified Silla(统一新罗), Later Goguryeo (后高句丽) and Later Baekje (后百济). It was inspired by Goguryeo's spirit and wired in pushing a northward policy. At the same time, it had taken specific military measures to respond to northern races such as Liao（辽）and Jin（金）.It had also adopted positive domestic policy.Compared to Unified Silla（统一新罗）, it showed a picture of more developed country.

In the early days, Goryeo strengthened royal authority and established a centralized authoritarian rule going through the reign of three kings King Jeongjong (定宗), King Gwangjong (光宗) and King Seongjong (成宗); it developed into a stable country. Goryeo had national difficulties such as Khitan (契丹). However, it overcame all of them and grew into a central country in the pluralistic order of East Asia composed of Goryeo, Song (宋), Khitan (契丹) and Jurchen (女真).Its overcoming of the invasions by foreign countries was sublimated into the cultural development; formed a sophisticated noble culture which is represented by Goryeo celadon (高丽瓷器).

After that time, the inner conflict of Goryeo's aristocracy which continued to prosper which had been going on ever since the establishment of Goryeo came to the surface due to Lee Ja-Gyeom's (李资谦) rebellion and Myocheong's (妙清) movement to transfer the capital in Seogyeong (西京). This conflict resulted in military official's coup (武臣政变), and hence, the political system which centered on the existing aristocrats collapsed. During the regime of military officers (武臣政变), a continuous power struggle and peasants' revolts caused Goryeo royal family's authority to be lost. The capital was transferred to Gangdo (江都) [(Gangwha Island (江华岛)] in the 13th century.

Gangdo (江都) acted as the capital of Goryeo for 39 years (1232~1270). It had a system of capital city composed of royal palace (宫城), middle castle (中城) and outer castle (外城), although it was a transferred capital. Its various government offices (官府) played the same identical roles as ones of the former capital Gaegyeong (开京).

There have been identified tombs of various classes from a king to general aristocrats in Gangdo (江都). Excavated and investigated were Seongneung (硕陵), Golleung (坤陵), Gareung (嘉陵) and Neungnaeri's (陵内里) stone chamber tomb (石室墓) among them. The excavating investigations supplied research for examining archetype (e.g. structural feature, etc.) of those days's royal tombs. Silsang (实相) Buddhist Temple, known as being founded in the period of Unified Silla, is the the first Buddhist temple of Nine Mountain Zen School (九山禅门) of Zen (禅宗), and it flourished most vigorously in the Goryeo period. The excavating investigation of Silsang Buddhist Temple shed light on the aspect of the site layout of the temple which has changed while maintaining its congregation for a long time. In addition, many building sites including a wooden pagoda site enable us to look into the florescence of Silsang Buddhist Temple.

高丽文化 | The Culture of Goryeo

建都于开京的高丽王朝，曾经迁都江华岛，坚持了39年。今天留给我们的遗产是与高丽王室相关的宫城、王陵、寺院等江都时代的遗迹。在江华岛的王陵级墓葬中，硕陵、坤陵、嘉陵和陵内里石室墓已经完成调查和发掘，为我们从墓葬结构入手了解和研究这一时期高丽王陵全貌提供了重要资料。另一方面，相传建于统一新罗时代的实相寺，作为禅宗九山禅门中最早创立的寺院，在高丽时代香火最盛。通过对实相寺的发掘与调查，我们了解了在漫长岁月中在保持寺院传统同时又不失变化的实相寺布局特点。其中，高丽木塔遗址为首的众多建筑遗址，为了解实相寺极盛时期的面貌提供了依据。

In early 13th century, the Goryeo dynasty had moved its capital from Gaegyeong to Ganghwado island. By the time the Goryeo rulers returned to the capital city proper after a hiatus of 39 years, they had left in the island palace buildings, royal tombs and government-sponsored temples. Archaeologist have recently excavated some of the Goryeo tombs in Ganghwado island, such as Seongneung, Golleung, Gareung and the Neungnacri Stone-chamber Tomb, collecting materials that help to define the characteristic features of Goryeo royal tombs and deepen our knowledge a period of relative darkness.

A recent archaeological investigation into Silsangsa, a temple established during the United Silla period as the first of the Nine Schools of Korean Seon(or Zen) Buddhism, which had its heyday in the following Goryeo period, also produced valuable sources of historical knowledge. The excavations revealed that the temple continued to grow as considerable change occurred in the architectural layout, and helped to create a comprehensive picture of the temple and its main buildings, including a wooden pagoda, in their most prosperous years.

江华高丽王陵 | Goryeo Royal Tombs in Ganghwa

[仁川广域市江华郡良道面 | 硕陵（史迹第369号）、坤陵（史迹第371号）、嘉陵（史迹第370号）、陵内里石室墓（纪念物第28号）| 高丽时代]

高丽王朝在高宗十九年（1232年）从开京迁都江华岛，到元宗十一年（1270年）还都之时，江华岛作为临时首都历经39年。这里分布的王陵、王妃陵各有两座，以及大臣许有全墓等大量江都时代的王陵级古墓。在2001年对硕陵、2004年对坤陵和嘉陵、2006年对陵内里石室墓进行发掘与调查，使我们对江华岛高丽王陵的面貌有了很大程度的了解。

上述王陵均为横口式石室墓，在石室入口处使用整齐的长条石构筑了门柱和门槛，在石室地面中央安置了棺台，并在周围垫以砖块。同时以三块长条石构筑墓室顶部，其上盖以8~12块护石并以此形成封土，再在护石外层围以雕栏，其间配以石兽，是这一类墓葬的特征。

最近调查了陵内里石室墓，已经确认了护石围起的封土、外围的雕栏及石兽以及曲墙式的围墙，墓室上部结构的完全复原因此成为可能。

另一方面，在坤陵和陵内里石室墓中，我们找到了位于陵前的应是举行祭祀仪式的建筑遗址。其中，坤陵的建筑遗址为三间，位于正中的御间前方连接着带有石阶的突起部分，使得建筑整体呈"丁"字形。

虽然墓葬都曾遭到多次盗掘，但是这里仍然出土了金属、玉器装饰、青瓷和瓦件等大量遗物。其中，陵内里石室墓中发现的镇坛具、嘉陵的中国唐宋时期铜钱和玉器颇受瞩目，在坤陵和硕陵中也大量出土了三足香炉和使用反镶嵌技法的唐草纹瓶盖等青瓷精品。

Ganghwado Island which is the temporary capital of the Goryeo dynasty between 1232 and 1270 contains a number of royal Goryeo tombs. An extensive project has been conducted recently on most of these tombs, revealing some characteristic features of Goryeo's royal tombs.

All of the royal tombs of Goryeo on the island to have been excavated of late feature a stone chamber with horizontal entrance complete with door posts and doorsill built with well-trimmed stones, and a ceiling finished with three large square stone. The mound is protected by stones encircling its base, and the entire tomb mound is enclosed by stone railings with stone guardian animals erected between railings.

Archaeologists discovered a large amount of precious metal and jade ornaments, celadon vessel, and roof tiles of fine quality.

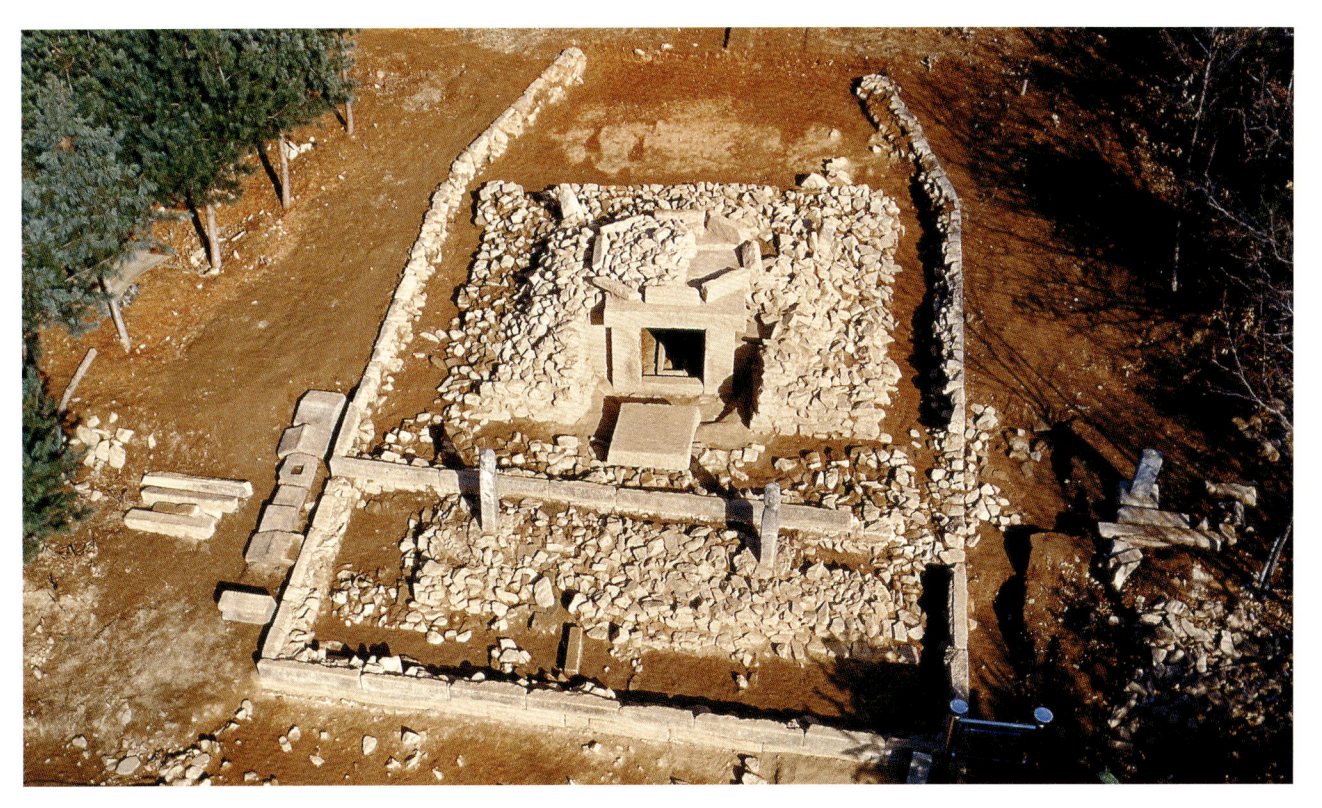

357. 嘉陵发掘后全景 View of Gareung Tomb

358. 嘉陵石室 Stone Chamber of Gareung Tomb

359. 坤陵发掘后全景 View of Golleung Tomb

360. 坤陵石室 Stone Chamber of Golleung Tomb

361. 陵内里石室墓全景 View of Neungnaeri Stone-chamber Tomb

362. 陵内里石室墓上部构筑物 Neungnaeri Stone-chamber Tomb

363. 石兽 Stone Image of Animal

江都时代

高宗十九年（1232年）高丽王室迁都江华岛，到元宗十一年（1270年）王室还都为止，高丽王室都城滞留江华的这段时期被称为江都时代。在江都时代，高丽设置了大藏都监，持续刻造八万大藏经，同时还在此地建立了禅源寺等寺庙。现在在江华岛仍然保留了高丽的宫殿和衙署，以及熙宗的硕陵、高宗的洪陵和一系列的王陵级别的墓葬，传承着那段历史。

364. 江华硕陵 Seongneung Tomb in Ganghwado

开京的高丽王陵

　　高丽王陵，除在江华岛有2座，还有3座位置不明外，其余大部分都被认定在开城一带。朝鲜政府已经将恭愍王玄陵、太祖显陵和高丽七陵群指定为国家文化遗产。高丽王陵大体是有着平顶结构的单间石室墓。在石室地面中央设置棺台，其上放置木棺，四壁和天井画有壁画，共确认了7座。

　　显陵是太祖和第一位王后神惠王后柳氏合葬的陵墓，据载曾经多次迁葬。所以，今天王陵所在的开城市开丰郡解线里万寿山是否为太祖最初埋葬之地，至今并不明确。1992年，朝鲜政府曾经对显陵进行了发掘，发现该陵为没有墓道的单间石室墓。在石室东墙上有梅、翠竹和青龙；西墙上有松、梅与白虎；北墙上有玄武；天井上画有八颗星辰。这次发掘之前进行的显陵改建工程中，在封土以北5米处，发现了被推测为王建的座像。发掘清理后，将雕有十二生肖像的原来的屏风石放置在王陵内保存，并树立了"高丽太祖王建王陵改建碑"。

　　恭愍王陵——玄陵被指定为国宝级文化财39号，其中也包括鲁国公主死后恭愍王直接建造的王妃陵——正陵。位于开城市开丰郡解线里正陵洞凤鸣山麓之上。恭愍王玄陵的墙壁上，每面有4个生肖像，三面共有十二生肖像壁画，和屏风石上的十二生肖像相似，据说是恭愍王亲自画上去的。在天井上画有太阳、北斗七星和三台星，另外在东壁上画了一个大门，在下面挖了一个四方形缺口作为连接正陵的通道。

　　位于太祖显陵西侧的高丽七陵群，在朝鲜被指定为史迹54号，墓主虽然没有被确定，但是据说其中六处是王陵级墓葬。

365. 高丽太祖显陵 Hyeolleung Tomb

366. 高丽恭愍王玄陵长明灯 Stone Lantern before Hyeolleung Tomb of King Gongmin

367. 高丽恭愍王玄陵和鲁国公主正陵 Hyeolleung and Jeongneung Tomb

368. 装饰品 Ornaments
    江华嘉陵

369. 蝶形装饰 Butterfly-shaped Ornament
    江华嘉陵 W2.3厘米

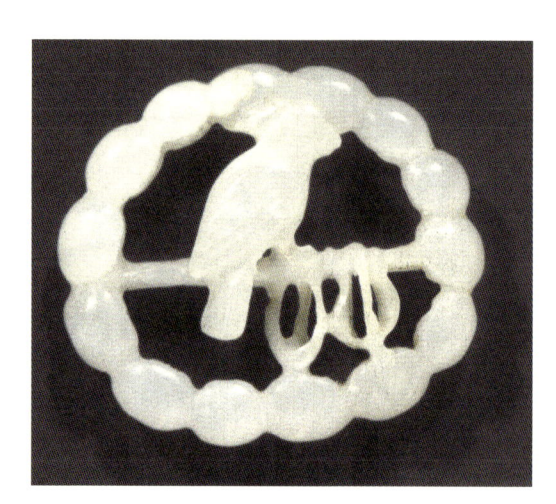

370. 鸟形装饰 Bird-shaped Ornament
    江华嘉陵 W2.8厘米

371. 青瓷 Celadons
江华坤陵

坤陵出土青瓷

坤陵是高丽王朝江都时期于1239年去世的康宗妃元德太后的陵墓，其中发掘出土了6件青瓷，有3件为花边折沿青瓷盘，1件兽形三足香炉，还有1件是在上面和侧面采用阴刻技法装饰花草和牡丹的瓶盖，最后1件是白土地青釉花的以反镶嵌技法画入简单唐草纹的瓶盖。这些青瓷在窑中烧制的时候，采用了高级用品专用的硅石垫具，胎土和釉色的选用也比较讲究，均是高丽时代不可多得的精品。

坤陵出土青瓷和1237年埋葬在江华岛的熙宗硕陵中出土的青瓷一起，向世人展示了高丽王室迁都江华岛之后的青瓷消费情况，同时这些遗物也是充分展示13世纪中叶高丽青瓷发展水平的珍贵资料。

372. 青瓷盖 Lid, Celadon
江华坤陵 D6.3厘米

373. 兽目纹瓦当 Roof-end Tiles
江华坤陵 瓦当 D15.5厘米

374. 石人 Funerary sculptures of the Tomb
江华坤陵 H49厘米

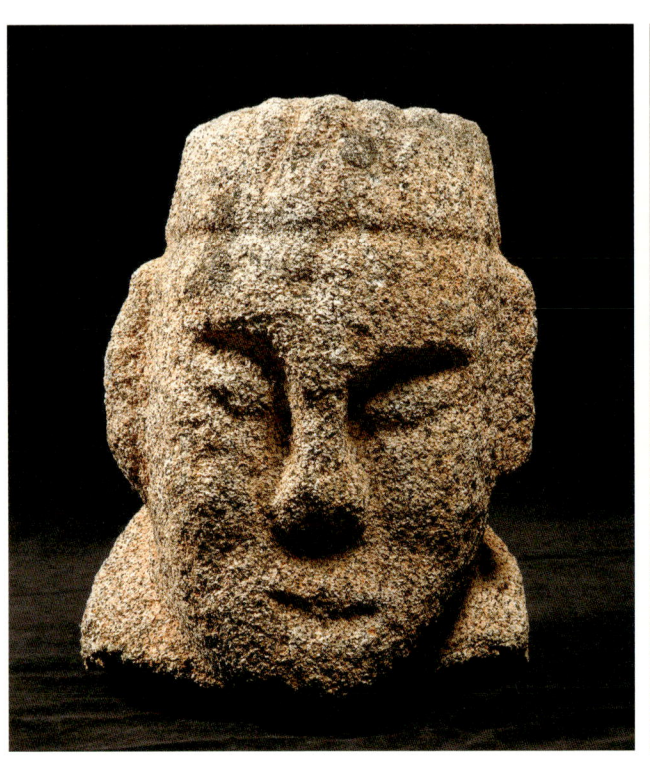

375. 凤凰纹装饰 Phoenix-shaped Ornament
江华陵内里 W3厘米

376. 凤凰纹装饰背面
Backside of Phoenix-shaped Ornament

377. 玉珠 Beads
江华陵内里 D0.3厘米

378. 地镇具 Buried Ceremonial Protective Objects
江华陵内里 大型 H26厘米

205

实相寺 | Silsangsa Temple
（全罗北道南原市山内面立石里 | 史迹第309号 | 统一新罗时代至今）

实相寺是新罗兴德王三年（828年）洪陟国师在智异山天王峰西侧创建的寺院，它是禅宗的九山禅门中最早建立的寺院。高丽时代宝月和尚曾经大规模重建，虽然在朝鲜时代寺院势力一度极为衰微，但是以肃宗十六年（1690年）修建大寂光殿等36栋建筑为契机，再度实现了中兴。但是由于高宗二十年（1883年）儒生们的放火事件，该寺再度受到打击，此后经月松大师再建才延续香火至今。

实相寺内不仅有宝光殿、药师殿、冥府殿等佛殿和僧房，而且附有百丈庵、药水庵等数间小庵。在寺内有三层石塔、石灯、浮屠、铁佛、香炉和佛画等，其中国宝级文物1件，宝物级文物11件以及其他文物若干。

从1996年开始，通过8次发掘调查，对寺院的变化情况已经有了大致了解。在统一新罗时期创建的寺院，石塔基址之间，中门址和金堂址处于一条直线上，讲堂遗址避开了寺内北侧的丘陵向东延伸，翼廊遗址也仅在讲堂东侧有发现，因地制宜安排寺内建筑的位置是这一时期寺院的特点。以后历经高丽和朝鲜时代，实相寺向东大幅扩张，并在此建立了曾经见证实相寺极盛时期的以面阔7间、进深7间的高丽木塔为首的众多建筑。

在实相寺先后出土了9世纪创建时代的以绳纹瓶为代表的众多遗物，其中有莲花纹瓦当、葡萄唐草纹板瓦瓦当、越窑青瓷、施釉的建材构建莲峰和脊兽。

Located on the western slopes of the Cheonwandbong Peak of Jirisan Mountain, Silsangsa Temple was established in 828 and became the first of the Nine Schools of Korean Zen Buddhism. The temple underwent considerable renovation during the Goryeo period.

Silsangsa Temple has preserved quite a large amount of precious cultural object such as a stone lantern, stupa, iron Buddha, incense burner and altar painting, one of which has been designated as a National Treasure and 11 of which have been designated as Treasure. A total of eight excavation projects have been conducted at the temple since 1996, enabling historians to identify the many changes which the temple underwent according to distinct period. The temple sanctuary was expanded to the east during its heyday in the Goryeo period, with the construction of large buildings including a huge wooden pagoda measuring seven-by-seven kan (kan refers to a bay situated between two columns).

379. 实相寺全景 View of Silsangsa Temple

380. 实相寺木塔立体复原图 Presumed Elevation of Wooden Pagoda

381. 木塔址 Wooden Pagoda Site

382. 附属建筑遗址 Annex Site

实相寺出土瓦

在实相寺出土了大量从新罗到朝鲜时代的瓦当。统一新罗时代的瓦当中虽然没有发现流行于以庆州为中心地区的花纹十分华丽的瓦当,但是作为这一时期瓦当中一个重要特征的重瓣式样瓦当有所发现。在实相寺创建时期,作为地方式样,大量采用了带有多重花瓣的瓦当。板瓦瓦当也采用了与中央有所不同的地方式葡萄唐草纹式样,其下方还采用了简略的纹饰进行了装饰。

在实相寺极盛的高丽时代,其筒瓦瓦当图案开始转变为单纯的宝相花纹,如莲花纹采用平面式或半球形子房图案。同时在花瓣部,选择了没有凹凸起伏的平面形莲花花瓣,兽目纹也在同一时期出现。在板瓦瓦当中,采用了多种多样的花纹图案,风格开始变得华丽,常见花草纹、莲花唐草纹、双鸟纹、唐草纹、兽目纹、兽面纹等纹饰。兽面纹在稳定的构图中蕴藏了极其精巧的图案。另外,我们推测相比于制作时费时费工的兽面纹图案,简单省事的兽目纹要更为流行。

进入朝鲜时代,连接技法和在瓦当内侧衬布等制作方法出现了变化,板瓦瓦当瓦面形态出现了向左右隆起的三角形的变化。莲花纹出现了单纯化趋势,表现得更为直接,重瓣也仅以阳刻的线条刻画而已。此外,刻有"康熙二十年"、"康熙二十一年"之类铭文的瓦当,为确定遗址年代提供了决定性的资料,这些与实相寺重修记录保持了惊人的一致。

383. 兽面纹瓦 Roof-end Tile
实相寺 W17厘米

384. 兽面纹瓦 Roof-end Tile
实相寺 W23.8厘米

385. 兽面纹瓦 Roof-end Tile
实相寺 W17.8厘米

386. 宝相花纹筒瓦瓦当、莲花纹筒瓦瓦当 Roof-end Tiles
实相寺 D15~17厘米

387. 莲花纹筒瓦瓦当 Roof-end Tiles
实相寺 D15~17厘米

388. 花草纹板瓦瓦当 Roof-end Tile
实相寺 W30厘米

389. 忍冬莲花板瓦瓦当 Roof-end Tile
实相寺 W30厘米

390. 双鸟纹板瓦瓦当 Roof-end Tile
实相寺 W35厘米

391. 兽面纹板瓦瓦当 Roof-end Tile
实相寺 W30厘米

392. 莲花纹筒瓦瓦当 Roof-end Tiles
    实相寺 D15~17厘米 统一新罗

393. 葡萄唐草纹板瓦瓦当 Roof-end Tiles
    实相寺 W29~30厘米 统一新罗

394. 葡萄唐草纹板瓦瓦当底面 Bottom Roof-end Tile
    实相寺 W29~30厘米 统一新罗

395. 铭文板瓦瓦当 Roof-end Tiles
实相寺 W27厘米 朝鲜时代

思○
○养大夫社教
片 有宗
大化 士如○
别座信宽
供泰主○○

396. 铭文板瓦瓦当 Roof-end Tiles
实相寺 W18.5厘米 朝鲜时代

四月 日
康熙二十一年壬戌
化士 杀净 比互
刑坐法抱 北○
○○○○莫比
○○干○正比
布施○王下○○土丙
○○施主○○比
沙○ 主思 ○
　　　良西

397. 铭文板瓦瓦当 Roof-end Tile
实相寺 W31厘米 朝鲜时代

公平已巳皿
施主金自坚
韩石老
主应淮○○
○月岑比
座天玉比丘
冲洽比丘

213

398. 瓷器 Ceramics
实相寺

实相寺出土瓷器

　　实相寺出土的瓷器种类多样，有青瓷、白瓷、粉青砂器以及唐宋瓷器和日本的瓷器等，出土情况按时代不同有所差异。创建期的统一新罗末期到高丽时期，以青瓷为主，其中莲峰瓦等青瓷制成的建筑材料引人注目。同时，还出土了这一时期的唐代越窑青瓷碗、邢窑白瓷和被推测为宋代建窑碗的黑釉盏和钧窑系的色釉瓷器等中国瓷器。但只出土了极少数高丽末期到朝鲜前期的青瓷和粉青砂器。到了17世纪后期，白瓷数量开始增加，这一时期白瓷被认定为是附近窑内生产的瓷器，其图案也是极为简单的铁画白瓷。这些不同时期瓷器的出土，真实地反映了实相寺香火的兴衰变化。

399. 青瓷铁画长鼓 Drum, Celadon
实相寺 灯笼颈 L14.5厘米

400、401. 唐宋瓷器 Chinese Ceramics
实相寺

402. 罗汉像 Image of Buddhist Saint
实相寺 H22.4厘米

403. 陶器 Potteries
实相寺

404. 虎子 Chamber Pot
实相寺 H21厘米

405. 石制有盖壶 Stone Jar with Cover
实相寺 H11厘米

Joseon 朝鮮

朝鲜从1392年太祖李成桂建国开始，到1910年纯宗逊位为止，共有27位国王前后继承大统，是国祚长达519年的王朝。从继承古朝鲜的意味出发，国号定为"朝鲜"，遂建都汉阳。这里农业发达，交通便利，同时也是不可多得的军事要塞。汉阳城周长17公里，其内有景福宫在内的宫殿（阙）、宗庙、社稷、官衙、市场和学校。其与位于平原地区的中国都城不同，充分利用了风水地理特点，规划了独特的都城形制。

朝鲜王朝的政治制度，是以儒教和两班为中心的中央集权体制；外交政策为事大交邻主义；文化上主张崇儒排佛；经济上采取了农本民生主义。

朝鲜前期，由于有着稳定的政治基础，出现了社会安定、学术发达的局面。

中期，先后爆发了1592年的壬辰倭乱、1627年的丁卯胡乱和1636年的丙子胡乱等三大战争。在此期间，佛国寺和景福宫在内的诸多文化遗产或被毁损殆尽，或被掠夺一空。

后期，由于势道政治（门阀政治），除了社会动荡不安之外，西洋列强的浸透带来的危机意识日趋高涨。高宗时（1863~1907年），朝鲜再建了壬辰倭乱时罹于战火的景福宫，之后移驾昌德宫。景福宫的重建工程，能再现光化门前六曹大街在内的汉阳旧貌，并由此确立朝鲜王朝的权威。

进入20世纪90年代以来，韩国政府不仅对朝鲜正宫——景福宫，而且对昌庆宫、庆熙宫等宫殿进行了复原工程，开始了对景福宫的发掘调查工作。目前，在景福宫已经完成了对寝殿、东宫、兴礼门、泰元殿和光化门等地区的发掘调查工作。同期，我们确认了景福宫内的各个殿台楼阁的位置和布局，由此确保了复原整修中必要的考证资料的准确性。同时，各类遗物的出土，也提供了多种多样的研究资料。

2005年，洛山寺因一场山火毁于一旦，我们制定了以发掘调查报告为基础的复原计划，并由此进行了两年多的发掘调查。作为结果，我们明确认识到，即便是在儒教为中心的朝鲜，洛山寺在世祖时代，仍保持香火中兴的事实；在确认了全体伽蓝排列构造的同时，也为恢复洛山寺的原貌，提供了有力的线索。

Joseon is a country which was founded by King Taejo (太祖), Seong-Gye Lee, and went out of existence in the King Soonjong (纯宗) era. It was a country governed by 27 kings for 519 years. Joseon (朝鲜) is chosen as the name of the country to the effect that it succeeds Gojoseon (古朝鲜). It decided as its capital city Hanyang (汉阳), which had a high productive capacity of agricultural farm and was an important military place. A castle, 17 km in circumference, was built in a ring in Hanyang. Including Gyeongbokgung (景福宫), constructed were a palace, Royal Ancestral Shrine (宗庙), Sajik (社稷), government offices (官衙), markets and schools in the castle. Contrary to China's cities located in plains, the structure of Hanyang was planned by making the most of its characteristics from a perspective of divination by the configuration of the ground (风水地理).

The system of government at which Joseon aimed was a Confucian yangban-oriented centralism. Joseon adopted "the principle of submission to strong countries and friendship with neighboring countries (事大交邻主义)", "the principle of pro-Confucianism and anti-Buddhism (崇儒排佛主义)", and "the priority principle of agriculture and people's lives (农本民生主义)" as a diplomatic policy, a cultural policy, and an economic policy, respectively. In its early years, Joseon developed fields of study by stabilizing the society based on a solid base of political support.

In the middle of the Joseon era, there were three large wars: the Imjin War (壬辰倭乱) (1592), the First Manchu Invasion of Korea (丁卯胡乱) (1627), and the Second Manchu Invasion of Korea (丙子胡乱) (1636). A lot of cultural assets [e.g. Bulguk (佛国) Buddhist Temple, Gyeongbokgung (景福宫), etc.] were destroyed or plundered during the wars.

In the latter part of the Joseon era, locally its society was extremely volatile under the government by a family in power, and internationally it was invaded by Western powers; there was a gradual upsurge of consciousness of crisis. King Gojong (高宗) (1863~1907) moved to Changdeokgung (昌德宫) to reconstruct Gyeongbokgung (景福宫), destroyed during the Imjin War (壬辰倭乱). The reconstruction of Gyeongbokgung was a long-cherished project to restore the structure of Hanyang including the Yukcho (六曹) street in front of Gwanghwamun (光化门) and to recover the identity of the Joseon Dynasty.

The excavating investigation of Gyeongbokgung was started to be conducted in earnest while the restoration projects of palaces such as Changdeokgung (昌德宫) and Gyeonghuigung (庆熙宫) including Joseon's main palace Gyeongbokgung (景福宫) were being conducted after the 1990s. So far, conducted were the excavating works of Chimjeon (寝殿 the hall containing the king's bedchamber), Donggung (东宫 the palace of the crown prince), Hengnyeymun (兴礼门), Taeweonjeon (泰元殿) and the Gwanghwamun (光化门) rage sphere in Gyeongbokgung. At that time, we obtained accurate historical materials necessary to the restoration and maintenance by confirming the location and arrangement of each royal palace (殿阁). The excavated relics supplied various research materials.

Devised was the restoration plan of Naksan (洛山) Buddhist Temple, destroyed by fire in 2005, based on the excavating investigation of it. The investigation was done for 2 years. As a result, it was confirmed that the temple was revived and flourished during the reign of King Sejo (世祖) of the beginning of the Joseon era. We established the foundation of the restoration of Naksan (洛山) Buddhist Temple as the whole arrangement of Dangwu (堂宇 large and small buildings) in it was identified.

朝鲜文化 | The Culture of Joseon

  景福宫被称为北阙，作为朝鲜时期五大宫殿之一，始建于太祖三年（1394年）。它虽然在壬辰倭乱中被烧毁，但是在高宗时代被重建。日本帝国主义殖民占领期间，不少殿阁被强行拆除，代之以朝鲜总督府等与殖民统治密切相关的建筑。最近，为了恢复和修缮被毁损的景福宫，韩国进行了长期的发掘与调查工作，为恢复景福宫原貌迈出了关键的一步。另一方面，最近发生的火灾使洛山寺的圆通宝殿和铜钟受到了极大的破坏，我们启动了发掘和调查工作。作为这些工作的成果，洛山寺从创建期的统一新罗到朝鲜时代为止的大量珍贵考古遗物被一一确认，为再次认识洛山寺的悠久历史和原貌提供了契机。

The construction of Gyeongbokgung Palace(also known as Bukgwol, which literally means "North Palace"), one of the five royal palaces of Joseon erected in the capital, began in 1394, the 3rd year of king Taejo's reign. Most of these original buildings were burnt down during the Imjin Wars which broke out as a result of the Japanese invasion of 1592, and it was only in the 19th century when Joseon was under the rule of king Gojong that the palace was fully restored, only to be severely disrupted and run down again by Japanese imperialists in the subsequent period of Japanese colonial rule.

Currently, the palace is undergoing extensive, long-term excavations and restoration work.

The latest archaeological achievements of the excavations include the discovery of the original location and size of important palace buildings.

Another important excavation project has begun at Naksansa Temple, which suffered the loss of two of its most precious cultural assets, the temple bell and the main prayer hall, in a mountain fire in 2005. The excavation, conducted as part of the effort to restore the historic temple, produced a large amount of relics raging from United Silla, when the temple is known to have been established, through to Goryeo and Joseon.

景福宫 | Gyeongbokgung Palace
（首尔特别市钟路区 | 史迹第117号 | 朝鲜时代）

景福宫作为朝鲜王朝五大宫殿的正宫，从太祖三年（1394年）12月开始修建，到第二年9月为止，主要宫殿初具规模。从2004年开始，为了恢复和修缮工作，我们开始对景福宫旧址进行调查和发掘，查明了包括了烧厨房址[①]和兴福殿址在内的咸和堂、缉敬堂等廊庑址的准确位置和规模。同时，我们还确认了与《北阙图形》和《宫阙志》等文献记录不一致的地方，以及一些仅凭记录难以推定的高宗之前的建筑遗迹。

烧厨房是准备宫中御用饮食的地方，又叫作水剌间（御厨），位于康宁殿东侧、慈敬殿和东宫之间。此外，还确认了为国王准备御膳的内烧厨房、为供奉历代国君肖像的真殿准备祭品的外烧厨房以及为宫廷准备饮料和茶点等零食的福会堂遗址和附属廊庑址以及相关设施。

另外，也详细调查了用来召开内阁会议或接见外国使节的兴福殿址及附属的9座廊庑遗址和现在仍残存的咸和堂、缉敬堂的7座廊庑遗址。

从出土遗物的角度来看，我们收集到了包括龙纹板瓦在内的青瓦、凤凰纹筒瓦等多种多样的朝鲜时代砖瓦类遗物以及署有"密阳长兴库"、"仁寿府"、"内赡"等官署名称的粉青砂器，雕有"福"、"寿"等字样的青花白瓷与各式各样的金属遗物。以上收集到的大量珍贵遗物，能够帮助我们了解朝鲜王朝宫廷生活的真实面貌。

The main and largest of the five royal palaces of the Joseon dynasty, the construction of Gyeongbokgung Palace began in the 12th month of 1394, with its major place buildings completed in the 9th month of the following year. The palace was also known as Bukgwol ("The Northern Palace"), as it was built as the northern end of the capital. Extensive excavation and restoration work has been conducted since 2004.

The recent excavation of the palace revealed the exact location and sizes of important palace buildings of galleries, including the Sojubang ("Cooking and Beverage Room") or palace kitchen, the Heungbokjeon ("The Hall of Prosperity and Fortune") which was used for cabinet meeting and the reception of foreign envoys, and the Heungbokjeon and Jipgyeondang Hall. The excavation also disclosed the structural remains of many other buildings that have existed only on paper since the complete destruction of the palace complex during the Japanese invasion (Imjin War) of the late 16th century, as well as remains from the Goryeo period and other artifacts that offer important clues about the court life of Joseon.

---

① 烧厨房为固有名词，指御膳房。

406. 景福宫远景 View of Gyeongbokgung Palace

庆会楼与龙

　　庆会楼是国家喜庆之时朝鲜国王与大臣们相聚宴饮的重要场所,有时也用于接待外交使节,进行经筵和祈雨祭祀等其他活动。初建景福宫时,人们在西侧低湿地带开凿了一个池塘,并在池内修建了一个小阁楼。太宗十二年(1412年),曾任过工曹判书的朴子青奉命,将池塘扩大到今日规模,并在此处重筑了一所楼台,取名"庆会"。此后,庆会楼在世宗十一年(1429年)时重修,成宗六年(1475年)又进行过大规模修缮;宣祖二十五年(1592年)壬辰倭乱时,被火焚毁,仅剩石柱残留,高宗四年(1867年)重建景福宫时被复原。

　　根据载有庆会楼建筑设计思想的《庆会楼全图》,庆会楼为了压制火灾,是根据《周易》原理,按照三十六宫之形式修造的。从位于池塘中央位置、方方正正的形态到内外柱子的数量和形态、内部空间结构的排列与组合等,均立足于《周易》的基本原理。从此庆会楼成为水的象征,起到了扬水德而抑火邪的作用。

　　从这样的寓意出发,当时在池塘中投入了两条铜龙的记录,就显得十分有趣了。据说,景福宫在创建之后,因为经常失火大量建筑被焚毁,所以在景福宫内有必要扬水德而抑火邪。事实上,在1997年11月的庆会楼池塘疏浚工程中,铜龙的现身证实了这个记录。当时,在庆会楼北侧的荷香亭前的池塘底部泥土中,发现了一具受损的铜龙,龙身首分离,横卧于一块被巨石压住的长方形石板之上。庆会楼之龙,从具有完整形态的右爪可知,是具有五趾的五爪龙,由此可以推测,这条龙是根据庆会楼的建筑设计要求精心制作的。

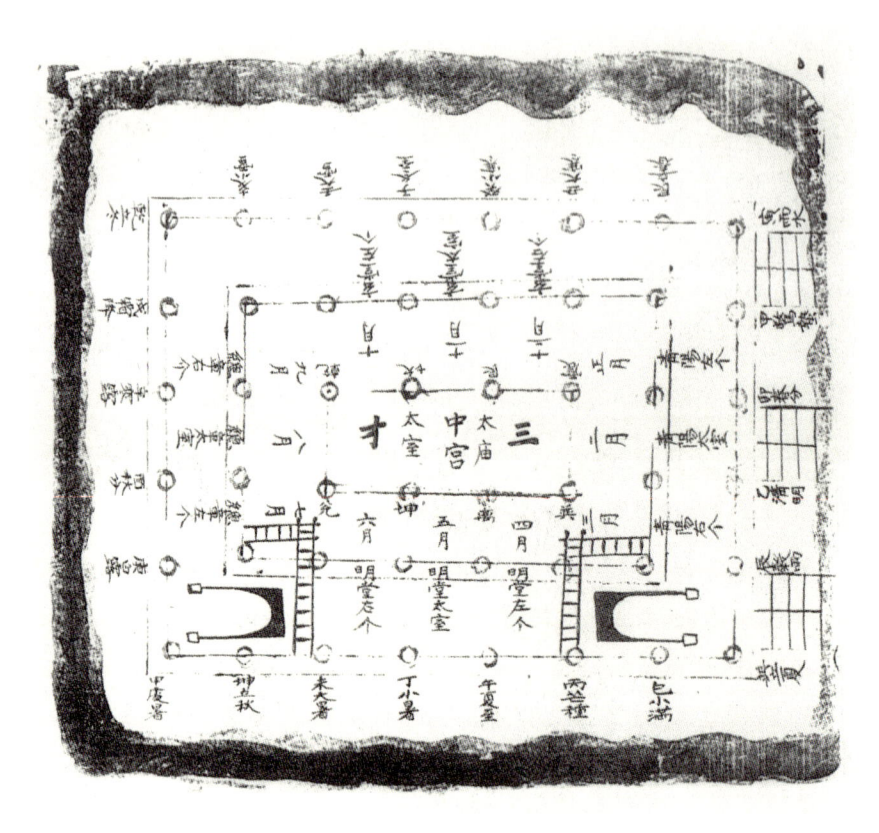

407. 庆会楼三十六宫地图　Blueprint of Gyeonghoeru Pavilion
　　　现存于国立中央图书馆

408. 庆会楼全景 View of Gyeonghoeru Pavilion

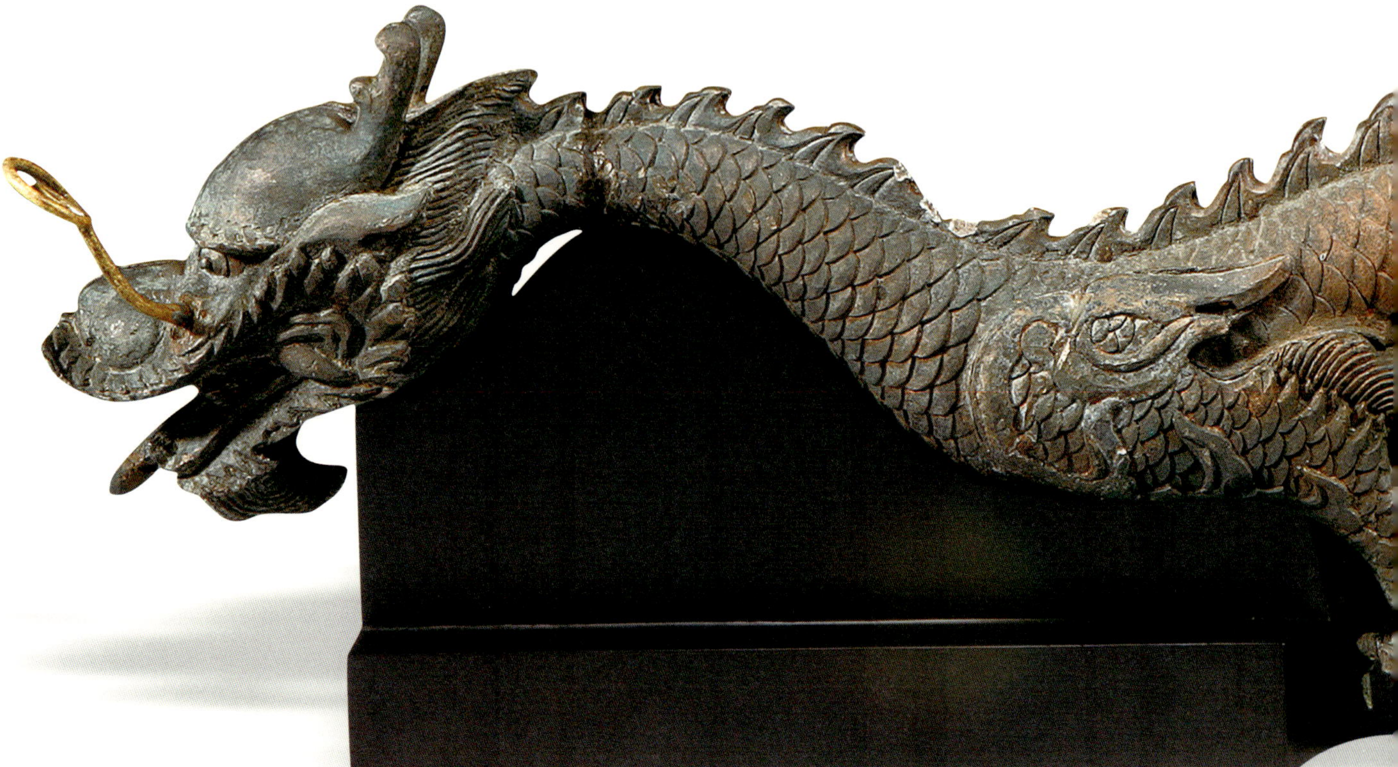

409. 龙 Figure of Dragon
景福宫庆会楼 L200厘米

《北阙图形》

《北阙图形》大约是高宗年间制成的一种建筑图，它记录了北阙即景福宫原貌。在《北阙图形》中，不仅记录了全部建筑的排列位置，而且详细地记载了各个宫殿楼阁的名称、规模及其用途，在探寻景福宫原貌的过程中，此图形可以提供最详细的资料，因而受到了重视。通过发掘调查确认的各遗迹与《北阙图形》大致一致，不过我们也发现两者在建筑的间数、位置及建筑的间距等方面有着一定的差异。

在烧厨房遗址调查中，显示出水井和库房的位置与《北阙图形》并不一致，外烧厨房与南外廊庑的次间缺少了4间，被记录为13间半的外烧厨房东外廊庑的间数实际上是16间半。在兴福殿遗址中，发现了《北阙图形》中没有记录的一座门址；咸和堂和缉敬堂南廊庑的位置和间数，以及缉敬堂东廊庑的间数等都发现与《北阙图形》有不同之处。除此之外，还发现了《北阙图形》中没有标出的建筑遗址、大门遗址、围墙等，并发现了可以用来推测《北阙图形》制成之前景福宫原貌的一些早期建筑遗址。

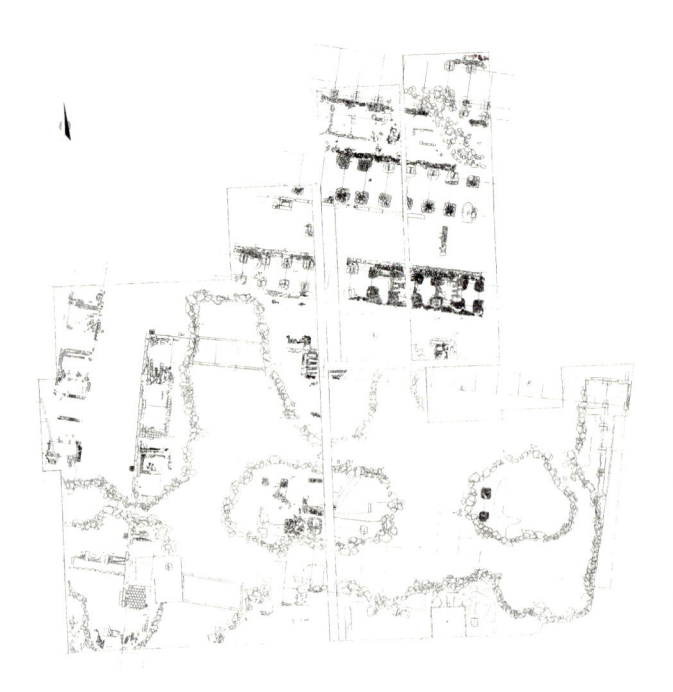

410. 兴福殿址发掘遗迹平面图　Drawing of Heungbokjeon Site

411. 烧厨房址发掘遗迹平面图　Drawing of Sojubang Site

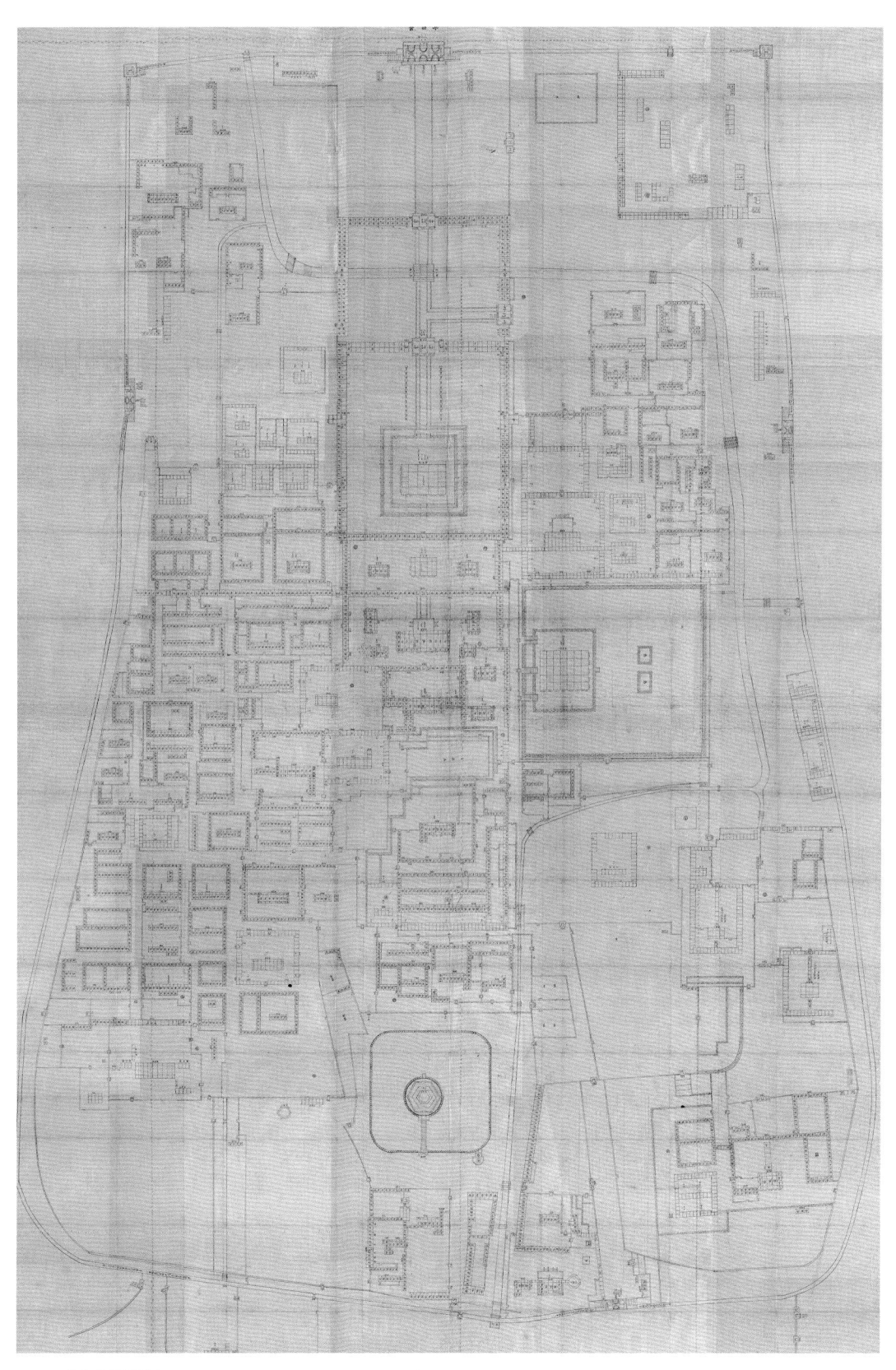

412.《北阙图形》 Diagram of Bukgwol, Gyeongbokgung Palace
284厘米×432厘米 现存于国立古宫博物馆

413. 景福宫烧厨房址、福会堂址 Sojubang and Bokhoedang Site, Gyeongbokgung Palace

414. 咸和堂、缉敬堂廊庑址 Site of Hamhwadang and Jipgyeongdang Halls, Gyeongbokgung Palace

415. 兴福殿 Heongbokjeon, Gyeongbokgung Palace

416. 兴福殿址 Heongbokjeon Site, Gyeongbokgung Palace

417. 瓷器 Ceramics
　　 景福宫烧厨房址

418. 石制盖 Stone Cover
　　 景福宫烧厨房址 D10.5厘米

419. 青花白瓷勺 Spoons, White Porcelain
　　 景福宫烧厨房址 L13.3厘米

烧厨房遗址出土的瓷器

景福宫烧厨房遗址出土的瓷器共有280余件,其中绝大部分为粉青砂器和白瓷,同时有极少量青瓷伴随其中。烧厨房遗址中出土的粉青砂器中,部分制品上留有产地和使用机构名称等铭文。可以确认的铭文有"蔚山仁寿府"、"密阳长兴库"、"内赡"等字样。其中"蔚山"和"密阳"是进贡地区的名称,而担当世子教育的"仁寿府"和管理宫内土特产等贡品的"内赡寺"则是官署名称。

白瓷有碟、盏、盖等,形式多样。没有花纹的制品最多,但也有刻印着"天"、"玄"等铭文,或刻有"웃소션"等字样的韩语古文。出土的少量青花白瓷中,在内壁底部有"福"、"寿"等字样,在外壁上绘有菊花、牡丹等花草花纹的情况也比较多见。除此之外,还出土有内部画有鸟纹图案的瓷勺残片。

420. 粉青砂碟 Dishes, Buncheong Ware
景福宫烧厨房址

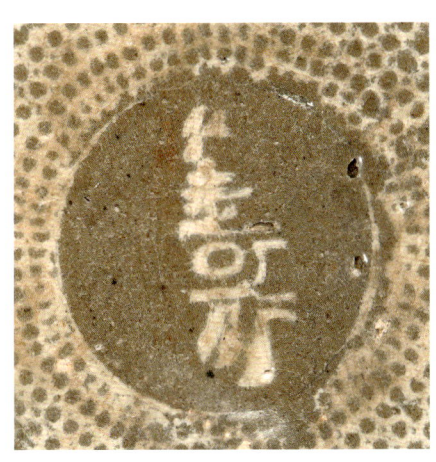

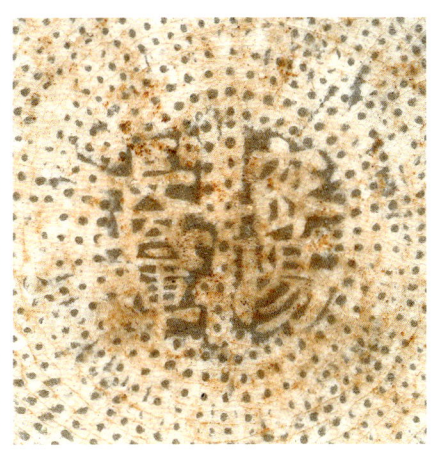

421. "仁寿府"铭   422. "密阳长兴库"铭   423. "内赡"铭

424. 兴福殿址出土瓷器 Ceramics
　　 景福宫兴福殿址

杂像

在朝鲜时代，人们制作出各种各样的动物像，排列成组，放置在建筑物的飞檐屋脊末端作为装饰，称为杂像(即中国的脊兽)。杂像在宋代从中国传入，在壬辰倭乱之后，以宫殿建筑物为中心广泛流行。在与王室有关的寺院之中，屋脊也开始出现。一般而言，从排在最前面的仙人开始，大约有十余种杂像，在朝鲜时代，从瓦匠中已经分离出了杂像匠人，专门烧制各种杂像。从功能上讲，杂像既可以增加建筑的威严，又包含了镇火避邪的意味。

在中国杂像通常是中国古代神话中出现的动物，并且都被认为是吉祥的化身。古代中国杂像往往根据宫殿的等级来决定其排列的数量和大小，其数量通常是单数。但在韩国排列时并不严格。

同时韩国杂像的名字通常会贯以《西游记》中人物的名称，戴着帽子放在最前面的人物模像是大唐师傅，是唐代的高僧，法号三藏法师。此外还有孙行者(孙悟空)、猪八戒和被称作同样名字的杂像。

425. 大唐师父杂像 Decorative Roof Tile
景福宫烧厨房址 H32.1厘米

426. 烧厨房址出土瓦当、青瓦 Roof Tiles
景福宫烧厨房址 筒瓦 L39.5厘米

427. 青瓦 Roof Tiles
　　景福宫咸和堂、缉敬堂 板瓦 W13.5厘米

428. 瓦当 Roof-end Tiles
　　景福宫烧厨房址 大型 L38.5厘米

429. 黄瓦、青瓦 Roof Tiles
景福宫兴福殿址 板瓦 W15厘米

青瓦、黄瓦

  青色瓦片在《朝鲜王朝实录》中被记录为"青瓦"，在世宗时代已经在重要的正殿建筑开始使用。中国从明代开始皇室已经使用了青瓦，中国明清皇室为了表现皇家至高无上的权威与居于天地中央的象征意义，在使用瓦时以黄瓦为中心。朝鲜时代成宗以后开始广泛地使用青瓦，就连都城周边的寺庙也不例外。由于青瓦的烧制需要包括铅铁在内的多种材料，因此使用的经济负担也着实不小。故此，在壬辰倭乱之后，由于经济、政治上原因，青瓦的使用逐渐减少。

  另一方面，从光海君时代"王又令匠人赍千金，学燔黄瓦于京师"的记载来看，可以推测出壬辰倭乱之后，朝鲜已经开始正式烧制黄瓦。但是限于天子才有资格使用的等级规定和材料难以购买的问题，朝鲜时代没有形成广泛使用黄瓦的风俗。

洛山寺 | Naksansa Temple
(江原道襄阳郡降岘面前津里 | 市道有形文化财第35号 | 统一新罗至今)

2005年4月，发生在江原道的一场山火，席卷了号称韩国三大观音道场之一的洛山寺的主要殿宇。洛山寺铜钟（宝物第479号）和法堂——圆通宝殿遭受到了极大的破坏。这件憾事成就了洛山寺的复原整修计划。这个计划决定采用"以发掘调查得到的资料为基础进行复原"的原则，同年开始了对受灾地区进行的全面发掘工作。

由于洛山寺经历了无数次的火灾重建，高丽时代之前的结构，几乎没有踪迹可寻。然而，从寺庙各处大量出土的统一新罗时期到高丽、朝鲜时代的碎瓦和瓷器残片中，我们可以推测出仅留下文献记录传世，从创建时期（671年）开始，经高丽、朝鲜两朝传承至今的洛山寺的原貌。

通过遗迹的叠压打破关系，我们知道了圆通宝殿历经五次重修，特别是在出土了刻有"成化三年"（1467年）铭文的板瓦的烧土层中，出土了大量龙纹板瓦瓦当与凤纹筒瓦瓦当，更是让我们得以管窥朝鲜世祖时期洛山寺中兴的一面。

洛山寺的整体布局可分为三层：第一层是作为法堂的圆通宝殿；第二层以中庭为中心，左右有两座建筑基址，其南侧有一座东西向的建筑基址；其下的第三层，发现设置有一座与出入设施相关的建筑遗址。这样的寺院布局，因与《洛山寺图》极为相似而受到瞩目。此画为韩国杰出画家金弘道（1745~？）于1778年受正祖大王御命饱览金刚山和"关东八景"之后而作。

A huge mountain fire broke out in Gangwon-do in April 2005, devastating Naksansa, one of the three main temples in Korea dedicated to Avalokitesvara. The fire devoured, among other things, two of the temple's most precious treasure, its bell (designated as Treasure #479) and the main prayer hall, Wontong Bojeon ("Avalokitesvara's Treasure Hall").

A restoration project conducted in the wake of the disaster revealed a valuable source of knowledge concerning the development of the temple from its establishment in 671 right through the Goryeo and Joseon periods to the present day. Historians are particularly interested by the fact that the original layout of Naksansa Temple unearthed by the excavation is remarkably similar to the temple painted in 1778 by the great court painter Kim Hongdo, who traveled around the Eight Scenic Sight of Gwandong-including the Diamond Mountains (Geumgangsan)- at the behest of King Jeongjo.

430. 洛山寺发掘现场全景 View of Naksansa Temple Site

431. 圆通宝殿 Wontong Bojeon in Naksansa Temple Site

洛山寺的创建传说

作为关东八景之一的洛山寺以秀丽风景而著称,是新罗义湘大师创建的寺庙。据说,义湘听到观音菩萨在东海现身的消息,沐浴斋戒之后,在海边石崖绝壁上整整祈祷了七天,最后一天结束祈祷之后,他在凌晨将蒲团投入了大海。这个时候,一条苍龙从天而降将他带到了绝壁岩洞中。在岩洞中经过长时间的祈祷,从天上落下了一串水晶念珠,义湘手捧念珠走出岩洞,随后又从海龙手中得到了如意珠。然而义湘认为自己没能亲自拜谒到观音菩萨是由于自己诚意不足,于是在沐浴斋戒之后,再次坐到石崖绝壁,更虔诚地进行了七昼夜的祈祷,但是观音菩萨依旧没有现身。对此,义湘大师伤心欲绝,在万念俱灰之下纵身跳入大海,就在这个时候,身穿白裳的观音菩萨赶来,托起坠向大海的义湘,走进了岩洞。昏厥的义湘大师慢慢醒来之后,知道了自己躺在岩洞内。观音菩萨告诉义湘大师:"后山之巅,必有双胎之笋破土而出,汝建伽蓝之刹,当在此。"随后,观音菩萨消失。义湘大师走出岩洞之后,按照观音菩萨的吩咐,到后山果然见到了双胎之笋破土而出。他就在这个地方建立了寺庙,在寺内供奉了观音菩萨像和从海龙那里得到的水晶念珠和如意珠。竹笋在建立寺院的时候忽然消失,盛传这个竹子就是观音菩萨暂时变化而成的观音竹。义湘大师在新罗文武王十一年(671年),借用观音菩萨所在圣地——普陀洛迦山的名称,将这个寺院命名为洛山寺[①]。

后来,据说元晓大师在去洛山寺亲谒观音菩萨的路上见到了化身为村姑的观音菩萨,但是没能认出观音菩萨显圣。在以后的日子里,他经常以佛心不足而后悔不迭。观音菩萨为了再次给元晓启示,再次变成小鸟,人们将这种鸟称为观音鸟,小鸟曾经落过的松树,被人们亲切地称为观音松。

432. "洛山寺"铭
Rubbed Copy of the Roof Tile

---

① 见于(高丽)一然著,李丙焘译注:《三国遗事·洛山二大圣》,明文堂,1992年。

433. "洛山寺"铭板瓦 Roof Tile
洛山寺 L11.2厘米

434. 洛山寺远景 View of Naksansa Temple

古画中的洛山寺

因为观看东海日出久负盛名的洛山寺建于671年。据说，是为了参拜观音菩萨真身而来的新罗高僧义湘大师创建。洛山寺，其名源于观音菩萨常驻说法的普陀洛迦山，它既是关东八景之一，也是金刚山游览的最后一站旅程。

洛山寺所在的关东地区的名胜图也是在这个时期创作的。高丽末期文人安轴（1282～1348年）曾经说过："某人自枫岳归，赠予关东图屏一，跋《金刚山诗》而回之。"如果考虑到这是一幅屏风的话，洛山寺也在其中的可能性是非常高的。另外，朝鲜初期的代表画家安坚（1418～1452年），也曾有以洛山寺为主题的创作作品的记录，有确切画名的洛山寺绘画作品的记录，可以追溯到朝鲜初期。担任过江原道三陟府使的闵仁伯，在1610年还曾经制作过四幅关东图屏。此外，郑歚（1676～1759年）、许佖（1709～1761年)、金弘道（1745～?）、金允谦（1711～1775年）、金夏钟（1793～?）金有声（1725～?）等朝鲜画家，纷纷把洛山寺作为作品的主题，他们的洛山寺图从眺望洛山寺的视角，大致可以分为三大类型构图。

涧松美术馆和国立中央博物馆收藏的郑歚的《洛山寺图》中，近景处两块突兀而起的巨岩对峙而立，其间奔流不息的波涛，对观音窟的生动描绘，聚在一起观赏日出的文人骚客以及寺院建筑的构成，显示出统一的构图。鲜文大学博物馆保存的许佖的《洛山寺图》明显是受到了郑歚的影响，与郑歚一样，在东南方向，将洛山寺和日出景观分别置于左右两侧，形成了基本构图。另外，已经成为金弘道代表作的《洛山寺图》上，对从进入洛山寺的拱形石门到寺院的全体寺院的布局，做了比郑歚和许佖的作品更为细致的描绘。

如果说，郑歚、许佖和金弘道的《洛山寺图》从画面左侧鸟瞰洛山寺全景，从右侧描绘了旭日喷薄而出的壮观场面的话，金夏钟的《洛山寺图》则与郑歚和许佖作品角度迥然相异，即从洛山寺后山之巅，呈一条直线远眺洛山寺与日出。因此，不是画面的右侧，而是独具匠心地将日出与沧海放在了构图的上端，洛山寺则放置在了在构图的下端。

除此之外，也有一些从其他视角构思的作品。奎章阁收藏的《关东十景帖》中的《洛山寺图》，日本清见寺收藏的金有声的《洛山寺图》，私人收藏的金允谦的《洛山寺图》都是这类作品。这些作品全都选择了从大海方向，或正或近似正面眺望洛山寺的视角，形成了群山环抱洛山寺的有趣构图。

435. 郑歚 《洛山寺图》 Painting of Naksansa Temple
18世纪 纸本水墨 22厘米×63厘米 现存于国立中央博物馆

436. 金夏钟 《洛山寺图》（出于《海山图帖》） Painting of Naksansa Temple
1815年 绢本淡彩 29.7厘米×43.4厘米 现存于国立中央博物馆

洛山寺的瓦

洛山寺在义湘大师创建之后，先后历经新罗末期的社会动荡、高丽时期的蒙古战争、朝鲜王朝的壬辰倭乱、现代的朝鲜战争的破坏，在多舛的命运中，洛山寺虽经多次重建，却依然保持了它的雄姿。因为这样的原因，经过一次次的重建和复原，我们很难在洛山寺找到高丽时代之前的遗址。但是，即便是在这样的情况下，也有大量的砖瓦按照新罗、高丽、朝鲜和现代的层位顺序出土，为瓦的编年研究，提供了极其重要的资料。尤其是从高丽时代开始到朝鲜时代的筒瓦瓦当与板瓦瓦当的成套出土，引起了人们极大兴趣。按时间顺序分别是莲花纹筒板瓦瓦当、兽目纹筒板瓦瓦当、凤凰纹筒瓦瓦当、龙纹板瓦瓦当、莲纹筒瓦瓦当、"皇帝万岁"铭文板瓦瓦当，"梵"铭文筒瓦瓦当、迦陵频加纹板瓦瓦当依次出土。

其中，凤纹筒瓦瓦当与龙纹板瓦瓦当在圆通宝殿烧土层中大量出现，在这些烧土之上发现了莲花纹瓦当和"皇帝万岁"铭文瓦。在朝鲜初期和王室保持了相当密切关系的桧岩寺遗址中，也出土了同一主题的凤凰纹、龙纹和"皇帝万岁"铭瓦。从瓦当与板瓦片连接部分按90°的角度咬合在一起，并且瓦当背面没有布痕等来判断，其制作期应当在高丽时代末期朝鲜时代初期。同时，在出土的瓦片中又有刻有"成化三年"（1467年，朝鲜世祖十三年）等铭文的板瓦瓦当，这些信息为推测其制作年代提供了依据。尤其值得一提的是，通过这次发掘调查，发现了刻有"洛山寺"的高丽时期板瓦残片，说明在高丽时代也已经沿用"洛山寺"这一名称了。

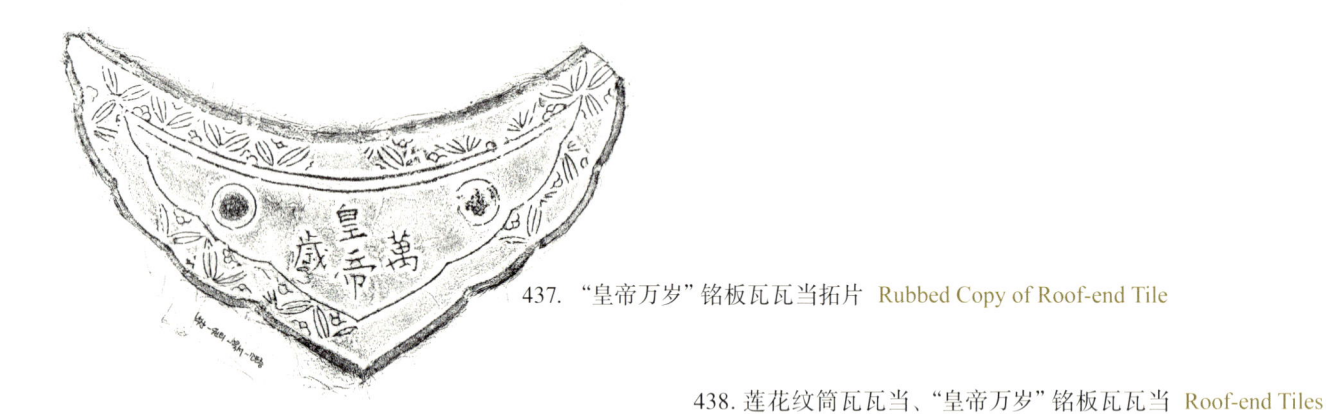

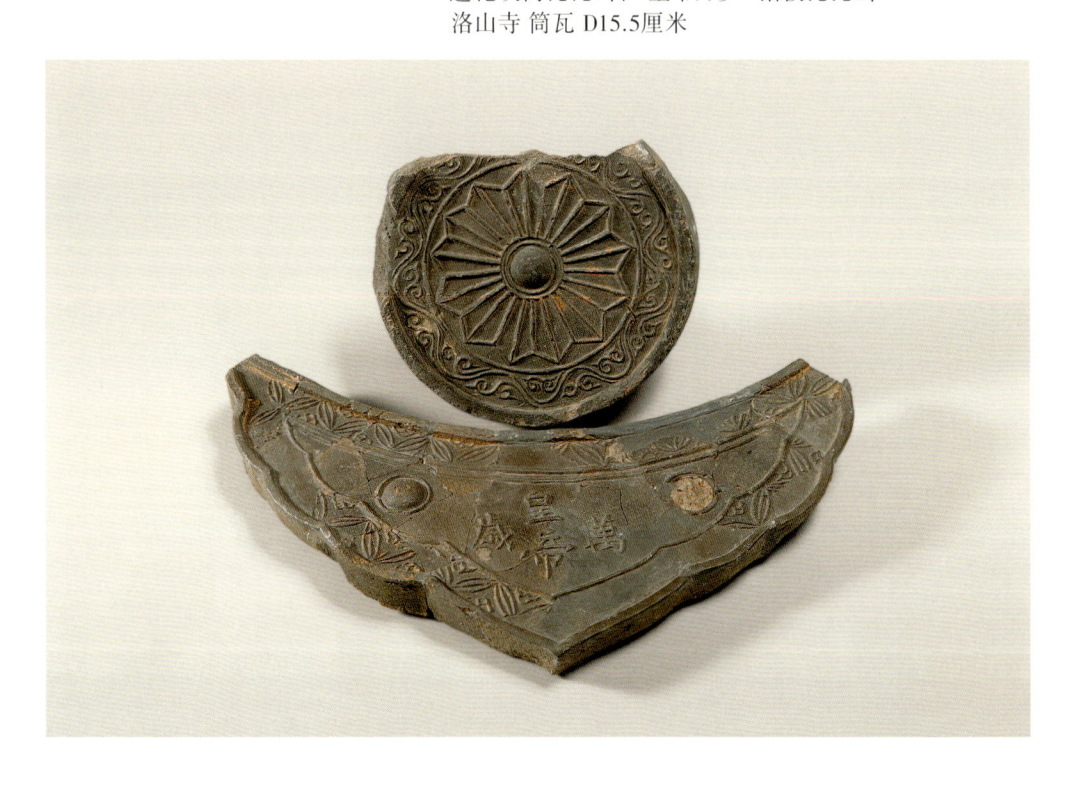

437. "皇帝万岁"铭板瓦瓦当拓片　Rubbed Copy of Roof-end Tile

438. 莲花纹筒瓦瓦当、"皇帝万岁"铭板瓦瓦当　Roof-end Tiles
洛山寺　筒瓦 D15.5厘米

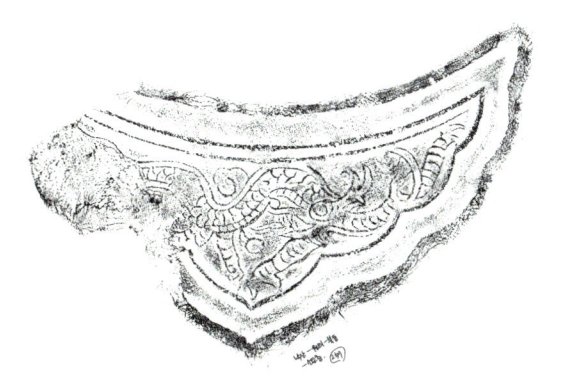

439. 龙纹板瓦瓦当拓片 Rubbed Copy of Roof-end Tile

440. 凤凰纹筒瓦瓦当、龙纹板瓦瓦当
Roof-end Tiles
洛山寺 筒瓦 D17厘米

441. "梵"字纹筒瓦瓦当、迦陵频伽纹板瓦瓦当 Roof-end Tiles
洛山寺 筒瓦 D16厘米

442. 迦陵频伽纹板瓦瓦当 Roof-end Tiles
洛山寺 W17厘米

243

443. 莲花纹瓦当 Roof-end Tiles
洛山寺 筒瓦 D14.5厘米 统一新罗

444. 兽目纹瓦当 Roof-end Tiles
洛山寺 筒瓦 D16厘米 高丽

Appendix 附录

国立文化财研究所
在韩国田野考古学史上的成长足迹

国立文化财研究所研究企划科科长（原国立庆州文化财研究所所长）　池炳穆

（一）

不知不觉中，在这片热土上，我们用考古学的方法进行遗迹发掘工作已有百年历史[1]。然而，即便是简陋如此的初期田野考古面貌，也不是产生于我们手下，不过是在旧韩末的混乱时期和主权被剥夺的纷杂状况下，所形成的悲痛史的一个剪影。毋庸置疑，位于东北亚一隅小国的历史和文化遗产能够被西方世界正式接受和承认[2]，也只是因为它们迎合了当时帝国主义势力膨胀的时代潮流而已。

从日本强占期的遗址调查内容来看[3]，其间发掘了大量的古墓，其中包括1909年最早发掘的庆州西岳洞石枕冢（最早发掘新罗石室墓）、1911年发掘的皇南洞剑冢（皇南洞100号墓）以及东川洞、普门洞一带的古墓群等。在这些发掘中，最引人注目的是在1921年8月24日庆州市的个人住宅重建工程中，路西洞积石木椁墓的发现。这座墓葬中出土有一顶金冠，迄今仍以金冠冢之名被视为新罗古墓中最负盛名的古墓。其后，举世闻名的金铃冢、饰履冢、瑞凤冢等大型积石木椁墓陆续被发掘。另外，在庆尚南道昌宁郡等地进行的大规模发掘调查，不仅称不上学术性发掘，简直就是盗墓者的盛宴[4]。所以，当时进行的所谓调查并非是在考古学这一近代学科的框架内进行的，称其为寻宝并不过分。尤其是当时的发掘报告等学术资料几乎荡然无存；大多数的遗物，没有准确记录出土位置或相互关系，仅记录为"传〇〇〇"出土等。上述事实，如实地反映了当时的调查是怎样进行的。

即便是在这样的乱世漩涡中，1915年建成的朝鲜总督府博物馆还是通过设立近代博物馆，开始建设出土遗物的收藏体系。到全境解放为止，这样的收藏机构逐渐扩张，在庆州和扶余设分馆，在开城和平壤设府立博物馆等，日后它们就成为了国立博物馆的基础。同时，即使在盗墓和文物走私频繁的社会背景下，为了以法律形式保护文化遗产，朝鲜总督府还是制定和颁布了《古坟级宝物保护规则（1916）》。之后，又颁布了《朝鲜宝物古迹名胜天然纪念物保存令（1933）》和

---

[1] 众所周知，韩国的考古发掘发端于1906年日本人今西龙主持的皇南洞南冢和东川洞北山古墓的发掘工作。
[2] 虽然曾经有过简单介绍的短篇文字，但是韩国历史和文化正式被世界所了解的契机可以说是世界贸易博览会等处的宣传。另外，韩国开始正式制作图书杂志、介绍韩国的历史和文化。
[3] 虽然当时将这种调查称为"考古学式（发掘）调查"，但是存在着很多问题，所以在此使用"遗址调查"这样的用语。对这一时期的发掘调查内容，下面两篇文章将介绍得更为详细。早乙女雅博：《新罗考古学调查100年研究》，《朝鲜史研究会论文集》第三十九集，2001年；车顺喆：《对日帝强占期的新罗古墓调查研究成果的考察》，《文化财》第三十九号，2006年，第95～130页。
[4] 国立文化财研究所：《小仓（おぐらじょう）系列（collection）韩国文化财——日本东京国立博物馆所藏》，2005年。

《朝鲜宝物古迹名胜天然纪念物保存令试行规则（1933）》，对其进行了补充和完善[1]。这些法律文书在解放后，仍作为韩国文化遗产保护的核心法规使用了相当长的时间，直到1962年才改为《文化财保护法》，并沿用至今。

　　解放后，遗址发掘工作也深受南北分裂的折磨，在三八线两侧，双方以互不相同的方式进行考古发掘。与较为活跃的朝鲜文化遗产调查不同，韩国并没有取得相应进展。直到1946年，由国立博物馆主持了一座古墓的发掘，才完成了依靠我们韩国人的双手独立进行的首次发掘。在这次调查中取得的意外成果对当时的考古学界来说真可谓是实实在在的鼓舞。通过对这座名为"壶杅冢"[2]的古墓进行发掘，韩国的田野考古史进入了一个新时代。此后虽然又进行过几次连续发掘，但是随着"朝鲜战争"拉开帷幕，韩国的发掘调查工作也不可避免地陷入了停滞状态。在这种历史背景下，韩国考古初创期的发掘调查工作形成了这样的格局：在国立博物馆主导下，由在国外学习过考古学的学者供职的大学承担相当一部分的发掘任务。这种局面的形成，可以说是日本强占时期接受过考古学专门训练的韩国人几乎绝迹造成的必然现象。

　　上述原因引发的人才断档，在1961年首尔大学设立了考古人类学系之后，才打开了新局面，然而专业人才在数量上仍难以满足韩国考古学发掘的需要。随着20世纪60年代初之后的经济开发计划、70年代的"新乡村运动"（New Community Movement），发掘的量也相对增多，对专业发掘人才的需要也出现增长的趋势。当然，这时的人才供给结构是，跟通过学校的正规课程培养、具有考古学专业知识背景的所谓正规军相比，学习过类似课程的人员、通过现场实习或直接的现场体验从而承担工作的所谓杂牌军，更具有普遍性。1969年，在当时的文化财管理局内设置了文化财研究室，在考察其建立背景和人员构成时[3]，我们仍然可以嗅到一丝这样的时代气息。

　　在韩国的田野考古学史上有几种值得注意的情况，其中之一就是为了配合庆州开发计划，而对位于该地区名为"味邹王陵"的墓葬群进行的大规模发掘工作。在这次发掘中，几乎动员了国内所有有能力进行发掘的机构和人员参与其中，其规模和重要性在韩国田野考古学史上写下了浓墨重彩的一笔。在此之后，历次大规模发掘，大都采用与发掘"味邹王陵"墓葬群时相类似的、组成联合发掘团的方式。这是因为，当时为配合基础建设（城市规划或建设大坝等大规模国土开发计划）需要完成的发掘任务，无论让哪个机关的少数专业人员来担当，都会在各方面受到极大的限制。

　　这样，经历了六七十年代的发掘体验过渡期，20世纪80年代以后，很多大学的考古系都掀起了扩招的热潮，学生数量急剧膨胀。前一阶段的现场实践者们纷纷进入大学的正规考古学系供职，以扩大考古学队伍为己任，大力培养专业人才。这是目前扩充韩国考古发掘队伍最为切实有效的方法。尤其是1995年以后开始出现的"专门从事考古发掘的公司"，是韩国田野考古学史上具有转折性的大事件。这种"公司"的出现，其原因可归结为前面提及的过渡期所造成的特有现象。

---

[1] 和日本强占期的考古调查相关联，有下列文章可供参考：Pai, Hyung II, 2000, Constructing "Korean" Origins-A Critical Review of Archaeology, Historiography, and Racial Myth in Korean State-Formation Theories. Harvard University Asia Center: pp. 23~35.
[2] 在这个墓葬中出土的青铜盒，其底面有"乙卯年国岗上广开土地好太王壶杅十"字样的铭文，引起了人们的注意。与高句丽广开土大王有关联的遗物在新罗首都庆州的古墓中以陪葬品形式出土，这为解释当时（5世纪）的朝鲜半岛三国之间的关系提供了重要的线索。
[3] 金正基：《回顾谈》，《国立文化财研究所三十年史》，1999年。

（二）

如上所述，国立文化财研究所在韩国田野考古发展过程中的成长，以及迄今为止所进行的发掘工作及其影响是本文最为关注的核心。功过是非的评判不是本文要涉及的问题，把这个机会留给立场更为客观的评论者要好得多。

众所周知，国立文化财研究所当初成立的原因，有相当一部分是由于国家策划的发掘需要和以此为基础的需求。直到1975年，转变成文化财研究所这一独立的正式机构之前，存在着所谓"文化财研究室（文化财研究担当官室）"时期，它的最大职能在于发掘。如果我们简单回顾一下国立文化财研究所走到今天所经历的漫长旅程的话，以其组织变化和发掘活动面貌为中心进行考察，大致可以将其分为以下几个阶段。

（1）胎动期：1969年11月~1975年4月
（2）成长期：1975年4月~1989年12月
（3）扩张期：1990年1月~2006年12月
（4）转换期：2007年1月~现在

第一阶段

称为胎动期，以1969年为始，在（原）文化财管理局内，设立了文化财研究室，通过组织运营形式，正式开始执行发掘调查的职能。

当然在这一时期之前，不能说以（原）文化财管理局为中心的发掘机构，完全没有承担起发掘的职能。但是当时发掘现场的组成人员，主要是以外部有发掘经验的人为主体，再补充部分内部人员，最终形成综合调查团性质的队伍[1]。由于这样的内部情况，以及1968年以后急剧增加的直接调查的需求，要求增设全职发掘机构的呼声越来越高。增设机构后的第二年，即1970年实施的十五项全国性发掘调查中，文化财管理局承担了其中的五项，从中我们也不难斟酌出个中滋味。胎动期发掘调查的特点是在抢救性发掘和大型国策性发掘（国家框架下进行的发掘）中投入了相当多的人力物力。即，在建筑工地施工过程中或偶然发现遗址，文化财研究室团队马上投入人力进行抢救性发掘。因此，当时的调查人员可以说几乎将所有的时间都投入在地方，在全国范围内，形成了马不停蹄地走村串寨的局面。特别是为了对庆州地区进行正式的调查，我们组成了庆州古迹发掘调查团，长期在当地驻扎，开展重要的调查活动。至今仍被交口称赞的"天马冢和皇南大冢工程"就是在这一时期实施的。

---

[1] 以文化财管理局名义刊行的第一件古迹发掘调查报告是在1967年发行的，刊载了庆州芬皇寺石佛出土遗址的内容。这个调查在1965年12月以抢救性发掘的方式，由国立博物馆完成调查。第二次成果是1967年7月调查庆州皇吾里1号墓的报告，在这个报告书中，还增加了几座古墓调查内容，在1969年出版发行。皇吾里1号墓由金元龙主持发掘并编写了报告。除此之外，昌宁郡桂城的桂南古墓（1967年），庆州的龙江洞古墓、仁旺洞建筑物址、九黄洞废寺址、普门洞古墓、坊内里古墓（以上为1968年），安东的造塔里古墓，庆州的佛国寺、利见台址（以上为1969年）等，都是在文化财研究室设立之前，以文化财管理局的名义进行发掘调查的实例（参阅：国立文化财研究所：《全国文化遗迹发掘调查年表（增补版）》，2001年）。

第二阶段

相对于第一阶段,要承担多种多样的文化遗产的调查工作,文化财研究室更加注重综合性组织的建设,正式进入了飞跃阶段。这一阶段是成长为国立文化财研究所的时期。1975年4月17日,以当时的文化财研究担当官室为框架,在文化财管理局内任命了相当于三级公务员的学艺研究官——金正基博士为所长,由此"文化财研究所"正式诞生。

在这个机构内,除原有的遗址发掘职能外,增设了能行使美术史和建筑史相关调查职能的"美术工艺研究室";另外,为了对遗迹和出土遗物进行科学的保存处理,并承担发掘后的各项职能,又新设了"保存处理研究室"。除此之外,为能在全国范围内对正在消失的民俗、民间工艺等领域进行调研,还特别设立了"艺能民俗研究室"。至此,文化财研究所名副其实地成为了韩国国内唯一的综合性文化遗产研究机构。这样的框架在过去三十年中,一直作为国立文化财研究所的基本结构保持了下来。

作为第二阶段主要业务的发掘调查,和前一阶段不同地形成了部分性的二元化模式,即文化财研究所直接运营的调查和文化财管理局直接运营的调查。即便如此,文化财管理局所组成的调查团也有相当一部分人员是由文化财研究所的专业人员兼任的。这与进行水下发掘等情况时采取的措施颇为相似,调查团的组成人员更为广泛,需要囊括研究所之外的专业人员。承担李忠武公(李舜臣)海战战场发掘任务的"李忠武公海战遗物发掘调查团"、为打捞新安海底遗物而组成的"新安海底遗物博物馆调查团"均属此列。无论如何,这一时期的最重要特征之一就是国家长期学术发掘项目的正规化。这类发掘项目不是一两年就能完成的短期调查,而是要投入十几年时间和持续的财政预算才有可能完成的调查。值得一提的是,这种调查的对象往往是性质单一的遗址,相对于多个机关的联合调查,不如依靠某个特定机关进行持续调查,可以更有效率地获得全面的调查成果。庆州皇龙寺址(1976~1983年)和益山弥勒寺址发掘调查(1980~1996年)都属于这种情况。在当地组成的调查团,作为首尔本部美术工艺研究室下辖的发掘机构,十几年间无间断地执行了这些调查任务。这些发掘可以说是文化财研究所胎动期之后,最具有代表性的发掘调查活动,毫不过分地说,这是我们所的两大代表性成绩。当时这些调查团的成员们发挥了很大的作用,他们自己也很有自豪感。毋庸置疑,他们支撑起了韩国田野考古学史的一片天空。

要更好地承担如上文所述的那种长期的、大规模的发掘调查以及大大小小的学术发掘调查和抢救性发掘任务,迫切地需要将行使这一职能的人员从美术工艺研究室的职能中分离出来,建立更为有效的发掘调查体系。由此,1988年10月,分离出了"遗址调查研究室",掌管全国的发掘调查业务。但是,随着国土开发事业在全国范围如火如荼地进行,仅仅靠一个位于首尔的研究室开展的发掘是不够的,确切地说在很久以前,研究室的工作就已经达到了饱和状态。在这样的时代背景下,地方研究所的设置成了当务之急,经过长时间的讨论和要求,1990年1月,这个问题终于得到了解决。

第三阶段

在国立文化财研究所内部增设了地方研究所。这一阶段是对全国范围内的遗迹发掘调查进行得更为顺利的时期。这一时期,国立文化财研究所的发掘职能有所扩大,可以称之为扩张期。1990年1月,文化财研究所先后设立了三个地方研究所,即以庆尚北道地区为中心设立了庆州文化财研究所,主要负责调查新罗文化圈;以忠清道和全罗道为中心,设立了扶余文化财研究所,主要负责调查百济文化圈;以釜山、蔚山和庆尚南道地区为中心,设立了昌原文化财研究所,主要调查伽倻文化圈。因为庆州和扶余(益山)地区已经有了常驻调查团,我们只是在接收这个组织的基础上进行扩大和改编,并没有碰到多少困难,很顺利地完成了新的组织的建设。然而,在昌原地区设立研究所时,由于那里没有现成的调查团或长期工地,筹建工作经历了一些困难。

第三阶段最大特征是各研究所在不同的领域进行调查,并由此形成了各自不同的特色。随之而来的是,国立文化财研究所本部的遗址调查研究室的调查职能,也不得不进行调整。按地区范围确定的原有的遗址调查研究室的发掘工地,都转由各个地方研究所管理。这样,遗址调查研究室转变职能,确立了以首尔、京畿道、江原道地区和海外调查(中国和俄罗斯等)为中心的方针,在此基础上将工作范围扩展到编纂考古学辞典、对外交流和二次利用发掘资料进行研究等业务上。这样的变化,将国立文化财研究所的职能,从单纯地收集发掘现场第一手资料的局限中解放出来,通过对第二三手发掘资料的加工整理,更注重了研究功能的发挥,这一点在研究所功能的转变中具有非凡意义。

1995年,文化财研究所在整体上有一个小的变化,即研究所的正式名称改为"国立文化财研究所"。这并不是单纯地增加了"国立"二字的问题。由于文化财研究所从一开始就是作为国立机关出现的,其形象、组织、构造等并没有任何变化。但是给研究所的对外形象和对内部成员都带来了诸多变化[1]。另外,2005年11月,在罗州地区设立了国立罗州文化财研究所,正式启动了调查研究以全罗道为中心的"马韩文化圈"的职能[2]。

这一阶段被命名为"扩张期"的又一原因是,在同一时期,研究所在其他领域也有了很大的发展。即,承担古建筑的小组从美术工艺室分离出来,成为"建筑物研究室"(2003年),为应急修复和处理破损的文化遗产,在建立了"文化财综合医院"的同时,还设置了"复原研究室"(2006年),这些都是在这一时期所发生的事情。另外,为了对自然文化遗产进行调查和研究,还设立了"自然文化研究室"(2006年)。充实大批研究员的举动,也可以视为国立文化财研究所在这一阶段取得扩张性效果的代表性事件。

---

[1] 但是当时地方研究所并未更名,仍是国立文化财研究所翼下的"庆州(扶余、昌原)文化财研究所"。这些地方研究所加上"国立"的称号是在2005年以后。
[2] 2006年末以忠清北道为中心的"国立中原文化财研究所"设立于忠州。

最后阶段

可以认为是刚刚开始的阶段。即，2007年1月开始，国立文化财研究所转变为责任运营机关，将要面临新的挑战。此前都是应国家的要求安排预算和组织，此后则将依据研究所的实际运营状况和取得的成果来安排预算和组织，其面貌也焕然一新。虽然还有一些不尽如人意的地方，但是基本的框架和编制都已初具规模。尤其是在发掘部分，虽然还有必要在首尔和韩国中部地区继续承担调查任务，但是各地区调查任务的基本框架已经悄然形成。更为重要的是，虽然近40个专门从事发掘的公司已经活跃在各地，但是谁也无法否认，业已存在的国立文化财研究所的发掘职能和作用，在新的转型期里仍然发挥着作用。或许转型开始的时间并不长，虽然有些迟，但至少我们已经站在起跑线上了。

（三）

在前面，我们仅通过考古发掘这样一个侧面观察到的国立文化财研究所的面貌都非常富有活力。以小规模人员参与建成的小小研究室为起点，通过5个地方研究所和本部的遗址调查研究室获得的成果可谓数量不菲。尤其是，到目前为止，任何发掘机构都没有进行过如此大规模的长期调查，也正是因为国立文化财研究所这一机构的存在，才使大规模的长期调查成为现实。

到目前为止，国立文化财研究所经过38年的发掘工作，取得了约436项调查成果。如果将它们按文化圈分类的话，首尔、中部圈有107项；新罗文化圈有（庆尚北道和大邱市）139项；百济文化圈（忠清道和全罗道）有136项；伽倻文化圈（庆尚南道、釜山和蔚山）有52项。我们将通过各个文化圈的调查成果，仔细考察国立文化财研究所形成的田野发掘面貌。

对"新罗文化圈"——庆尚北道地区的调查，其实从很早就已经开始，与其他文化圈相比，它的绝对重要性不言而喻。在韩国这片土地上率先开展的考古发掘工作，正是从这里起步的。尤其是"新罗等于黄金之国"之说，将世人的目光充分地吸引到了这一地区的发掘工作中。因此，有关韩国田野考古学史的相当一部分内容都涉及这一地区也是必然的[1]。世人再次关注庆州地区发掘调查的主要契机是20世纪70年代开始的"庆州观光综合开发计划"。它是配合国家经济开发政策，对以历史遗迹为资源的观光景点进行开发。在这样的时代背景中，如果要选择开发对象的话，千年古都庆州是当仁不让的。为此，庆州地区被划分为几个史迹地区，有针对性的大规模整备计划悄然上马。作为这个项目的一环，为了发掘和规划味邹王陵地区（现大陵苑地区），在1973年文化财管理局设立了下辖临时组织——"味邹王陵地区发掘调查团"。这个机构的性质是上文所述的那种以文化财研究室为中心的现场派遣调查团。当时这个调查团的基本目标是——确保观光资源，将大

---

[1] 在此文化圈中，以庆州为中心的主要发掘成果，在尹文中有更为详细整理。尹根一：《国立庆州文化财研究所的32年足迹》，《新罗的千年气息，发掘调查史的32年》，2006年，第152~175页。

型古墓的内部结构向公众开放。因此，就在外形比较大的古墓中选择了一座进行发掘，这就是被称为"皇南大冢"的第98号古墓，其平面形态呈瓢形。但在当时，调查团还没有发掘这种大型古墓的经验，为了积累经验，通过发掘掌握此类古墓的结构特征，对与之相邻的第155号古墓（后称为"天马冢"）进行了先期的发掘和调查工作。在这次具有演练性质的发掘中，我们意外地收获了巨大成果，使人们对庆州地区古墓的关注达到了最高潮。以这些经验为基础，对皇南大冢南墓和北墓的调查才得以顺利地进行。但是，由于当时的人员素质和相关学术水平较低，其调查结果历经相当漫长的时间才被消化掉，甚至到了今天，相关的学术活动仍然在进行中。

从古墓调查开始，走上正轨的庆州地区发掘工作，与1975年文化财研究所的萌生同步，其范围也更加开阔了。从调查团的名称变化上我们可窥一斑，由原来的"味邹王陵地区发掘调查团"变更为"庆州古迹发掘调查团"，发掘对象的范围扩大到包括附近地区的庆州全境。在这样的情况下，开始了对雁鸭池、感恩寺等主要遗址的发掘，其中最引人注目的项目莫过对皇龙寺址的调查了。在新罗千年历史的鼎盛时期，打下三国统一基础的时代背景下，创建和经营的皇龙寺，我们不能将之视为单纯的寺院。可以说，皇龙寺是考察新罗文化精髓的宝库。这次调查中获得的资料，真可谓是打开新罗考古之谜的万能钥匙。现在，对其复原的争论又一次成为人们关注的焦点。

到庆州研究所成立之前的1989年为止，以文化财研究所庆州古迹发掘调查团的名义进行的调查大约有40次左右。对在新罗都城研究中相当重要的月城护城河、月精桥址、新罗王京遗址、月城东门址等遗址安排了发掘，当然对兴轮寺址、掘佛寺址、龙江洞古墓和明活山城等遗址也进行了调查。1990年，庆州文化财研究所设立，几乎全盘接收了庆州古迹发掘调查团既存的组织、职能和调查业务。按照年度计划继续发掘月城护城河和新罗王京等遗址，选定芬皇寺等遗址作为新的长期发掘对象并启动了调查工作。90年代中后期，随着国土建设事业的扩张，研究所进入了对临时性的抢救性发掘投入大量时间和人力的时期。现在，国立庆州文化财研究所开始对传·仁容寺址和因发现新四天王像砖瓦而备受瞩目的四天王寺址进行长期调查，同时对月城护城河进行长期年度调查。特别是对蓝泉地区的发掘调查，作为2007年开始的新罗古墓规划新事业的一环，自20世纪70年代中期以来的又一次对新罗古墓实施综合性大规模学术调查，受到了国内外的广泛关注。

国立文化财研究所对百济文化圈的调查工作开始于1971年实施的武宁王陵的发掘调查。称这次发掘为世纪性的重大考古发现也毫不过分，但是它仍然留下了几点遗憾，直到今天仍有新的研究在进行当中[①]。但在此后的一段时间内，文化财研究所在这一地区并没有进行调查工作。当时，这个地区的发掘工作主要是由大学的博物馆（国立忠南大学、国立全南大学和圆光大学）和国立博物馆来负责的。文化财研究所对这个地区的正规调查开始于1980年7月弥勒寺址的发掘工作。发掘工作一直持续到1996年，经历了17年的岁月。这在当时是韩国国内难得一见的先例，堪称发掘时间最长的纪录之一。它不仅揭示了三塔一金堂式的百济伽蓝结构，而且确认了一

---

① 国立扶余文化财研究所、国立公州博物馆：《武宁王陵和东亚文化》（武宁王陵发掘30周年纪念国际学术大会发表文章），2001年；国立公州博物馆：《武宁王陵——出土遗物分析报告书（Ⅰ）》，2005年；国立公州博物馆：《武宁王陵——出土遗物分析报告书（Ⅱ）》，2006年。

直延续到朝鲜中期的大量遗物的层位关系，这些成果使这次发掘成为这一地区考古的标志性工作。另外，1985年还开始了扶余扶苏山城的长期发掘工作，但是这次发掘工作并非常设性调查，它在一年之中仅调查2~6个月，直到2002年才告一段落，持续了较长的时间。即使这样，我们也收获了关于百济都城和防御体系的重要成果。此外，还有因出土了百济鎏金铜冠而闻名遐迩的益山笠店里古墓（1986年）、公州宋山里古墓（1988年）等调查工作也非常重要。对弥勒寺址的发掘工作，采用了在当地设置下属于文化财研究所的"弥勒寺址发掘调查团"专门进行常驻调查，余下的部分由首尔的文化财研究所的相关人员在调查期间以临时派遣的形式展开工作。从1989年9月开始，策划并实施了对益山王宫里遗址的长期发掘工作，对这个遗址的发掘至今仍在进行当中。它正在成为揭示百济末期百济中央政府对益山的经营情况的最佳资料。

1990年以后，发掘工作开始在"扶余文化财研究所"的名义下进行，既存的文化财研究所承担的长期发掘计划中的遗址属于当地范畴的都由它接手，调查的范围与原来相比呈现出了更多样化的特点。从史前时代遗址（扶余山直里支石墓）到历史时代寺址（扶余龙井里寺址、王兴寺址、实相寺、普愿寺址等）、王京遗址（扶余官北里遗址等），发掘工作或已经结束，或正在进行中。其中，对百济古墓的调查（扶余陵山里古墓、楮石里古墓、芝仙里古墓和舒川郡堂丁里古墓等）是扶余研究所成立以后投入了大量心血的地方。另外，对扶余官北里遗址的再调查，与过去的单纯发掘相比，更注重综合性，在扩大发掘的层面上更多地去查找百济王京的资料。国立扶余文化财研究所在1990年成立之后，到2007年4月为止，对30余处遗址进行了共100余次的发掘调查。

2005年10月，在全罗道罗州成立了国立罗州文化财研究所，是对"马韩文化圈"所属地方进行独立调查的主体。从行政区域上看，罗州研究所将全罗南北两道纳入其管辖范围。通过已经发掘的罗州新村里或伏岩里古墓的调查实例，国立文化财研究所从很早以前就已经意识到了对这一地区调查和研究的必要性。现在通过新建的罗州研究所，对罗州会津城、东谷里横山古墓、化丁里马山古墓的调查工作，可以按年度计划长期发掘，或以抢救性发掘的形式进行。相信随着新的调查成果的出现，这个地区必将受到更多的关注和期待。

对伽倻文化圈的调查晚于其他地区。文化财研究所对这一地区的直接或间接调查，最早始于昌原的城山贝冢。在昌原工业园区的建设过程中发现的这片遗址，是铁之王国——伽倻第一次在公众面前亮相。从1975年开始连续三年实施的对晋阳大坪里遗址的发掘，是对这一地区进行调查的开始。这次调查之后，文化财研究所在相当长一段时期没有对伽倻地区进行调查。大学博物馆（釜山大学、东亚大学等）和国立博物馆等机构承担了这一部分调查的主要任务。在这样的情况下，1990年，在昌原设立了新的地方文化财研究所。昌原文化财研究所和其他地方研究所一样，在一片空白的状态下开始，经历了很多的困难。由于找不到办公地点，研究所在名为"昌原之家"的昌原市所属设施的一角建立了临时性的简易房屋办公室，工作人员们在这样的简陋条件下工作了5年多的时间。在人员问题上，新设机构也应付得十分辛苦。在初创期的把握调查发掘框架上，经历了不少的磨难。

昌原文化财研究所成立后，第一件调查业务是建所同年年末开始的，对昌原加音丁洞古墓群的调查。以此为开端，研究所开始对咸安岩画贝冢、昌原凤林寺址、蔚山早日里古墓群和晋州南江史前遗址等形式多样的地区和遗址进行调查。昌原文化财研究所成立后，最受瞩目的成果，当属在被认为是古阿罗伽倻的中心地区的咸安地区所获得的考古学成果。昌原研究所自1991年成立开始，对坐拥咸安道项里、末山里古墓等重要遗址，其调查工作却没有活跃过的昌原地区，展开了正式的调查工作。与道项里古墓群相邻的、被推定为伽倻中心山城的城山山城，其调查工作从

1991年开始一直持续到现在。虽然我们没有得到确实的伽倻时期城池的资料,但是到目前为止在韩国出土的木简资料中,有相当部分是在这一单一的遗址中得以确认的[1]。对邻近的道项里、末山里古墓的调查会成为揭示伽倻真相的重要机会。在这些古墓群所在的陵山脚下,1992年在修建公寓的过程中,人们偶然发现的废弃古墓成为了伽倻考古学研究的重要成果。战马甲胄按原貌出土。铁的王国伽倻,还有高句丽古墓壁画中可以看到的战马甲胄原物,也在1500年后重见天日。刚刚建立的研究所就取得这样的成果,不得不说是极为幸运的事情。以此为契机,对于附近道项里古墓群的发掘,历经七年得以完成。通过这次调查,我们了解了伽倻时期主要墓制(木椁墓、石椁墓等)的发展演变。除此之外,固城郡内山里古墓群的调查,可以说揭示了"小伽倻文化"相关的情况,取得了重要成果,直到现在仍然在持续发掘。

伽倻文化圈中可称得上中心位置的是东部地区,即金海或高灵等地区,研究所对这些地区的调查可以说比较贫乏。虽说高灵有管辖区域权限问题[2],但对于金海地区的调查应该是必须要解决的重要课题。从2004年开始实施的昌宁松岘洞古墓的调查工作,为我们提供了展示5~6世纪新罗和伽倻关系的重要资料。尤其是7号墓中出土的樟脑木的木棺,其主要产地在朝鲜半岛南部海岸和日本列岛等地,它的出土对于研究当时各地之间的交流非常有用。国立昌原文化财研究所在没有坚实的基础、事前准备也不充分的情况下出发,其发掘调查工作虽身处逆境,但到目前为止,仍旧很好地维持了下来[3]。迄今为止,对30座遗址进行的60余次调查,就是他们功劳的证明。

如上所述,在地方设立文化财研究所之前,所有的文化财研究所的发掘项目,均由美术工艺研究室管理。即,从1975年初文化财研究所成立以后,到1988年遗址调查研究室分离出来,发掘调查业务由各室分别负责为止,美术工艺研究室是几乎要管理所有的发掘业务的主要部门。随之,到地方研究所产生之前,在全国实施的发掘调查中,文化财研究所担当的部分,都是从属于美术工艺室的专门人员以在当地组成现场调查团或是到当地出差的形式来完成的。因此,当时的调查条件并不是非常令人满意。以不足的人员调查分布在全国的业务,可以说业务负荷非常沉重。

到1990年之前的调查业务,在前面介绍各地区的调查业务中已经简单涉及,在此不再赘述,而是重点阐述其后的调查成果。在那之后的调查业务主要是在首尔、京畿道和江原等中部地区进行的。其中,与军事保护区域有关的京畿道和江原北部地区的调查,在文化财研究所的工作中占据重要的位置。坡州金坡里旧石器遗址、瑞谷里壁画古墓、涟川三串里遗址、襄阳柯坪里遗址和高城文岩里史前遗址等,可以作为中部地区调查工作的代表性遗址来列举。莞岛将岛清海镇遗址和罗州伏岩里古墓(1996~1998年)、新村里9号墓(1999年)等几个特例,虽属于遗址调查研究室持续发掘的调查对象,但是又属于地方研究所的管辖范围。另一方面,1977年新开始发掘的首尔风纳土城,作为可以揭示百济汉城期的中心遗址的考古资料得到了确认。同时,这个遗址的发掘也体现了开发与保存两种观念的尖锐对立。通过这些,我们才认识到建立长期且现实的遗址保存规划是多么重要。

---

[1] 截至2006年1月,韩国国内确认的有墨书的木简资料,总计252枚,其中,城山山城出土的占94枚〔国立昌原文化财研究所:《韩国的古代木简(修订版)》,2006年,第19页〕。

[2] 高灵在行政区域上,属于庆尚北道;在研究所的管辖范围上,属于国立庆州文化财研究所的控制范围。

[3] 国立昌原文化财研究所:《国立昌原文化财研究所15年的足迹》,2005年。国立昌原文化财研究所自2007年11月起改名为国立伽倻文化财研究所。

研究所的调查业务中,其共同点是:除了部分寺院遗址的发掘调查之外,调查对象主要集中于统一新罗时代以前的遗址。在这样的情况下,最近正在进行的朝鲜时代宫殿(昌德宫、锦川桥周边、景福宫烧厨房址和光化门地区等)或衙署遗址相关调查,以及江华岛高丽王陵相关调查,吸引了人们的视线。尤其是在江华岛地区展开的高丽王陵相关调查(硕陵、嘉陵、坤陵和陵内里古墓等),不仅将研究扩大到了在很长一段时间内韩国国内从未开拓、残留至今的领域——高丽时代墓制,而且会成为日后与朝鲜携手对开城等地的高丽王陵进行共同发掘或研究的开端。

另外,我们不再局限于韩国国内,而是提高了对国外遗址的关注,这一点无疑将成为研究所日后在发掘调查业务中迈上一个新台阶的重要契机。1990年以后,文化财研究所在俄罗斯等地进行的发掘调查,与其他机关所进行的单纯短期调查不同,是持续几十年的长期工作。调查后,即刻进行的后续步骤,通过撰写并发行调查报告书将期间的调查结果在国内展示和介绍[1],此举必将谱写国立文化财研究所发掘旅程的新篇章。

(四)

迄今为止,国立文化财研究所进行的发掘调查,是单一机关所能够实施的范围最大、持续时间最长的工作。尤其是在进行长达十几年以上持续调查的工作的时候,充分体现了国家研究机关的优点。这也是我们保存国立文化财研究所发掘调查功能的最主要理由。但是,我们也要注意到韩国国内发掘调查条件或情况,已经发生了极大的变化,而且变得更为复杂多样。如果满足于现有的成果和面貌的话,在未来续写国立文化财研究所的田野考古学史的进程中,毫无疑问必然会遭遇到无数无法预料的难关。将近40个的专门性发掘机构,在韩国的发掘机构构成图中占据了绝对重要的地位,在这样的现实情况下,国立文化财研究所原有的以发掘调查为主要任务的性质需要转变。作为韩国的文化财责任运营机关——国立文化财研究所的发掘将具有的另一面貌,现在正是精心做出策划的时候。

考古学的发掘不是以寻找那些华丽如金冠或足以刺激世人神经末梢引起瞩目的遗址为前提条件的,这一点非常明确。另外,为了满足现实的某种要求,不得不使用的某些不良手段,更是要杜绝的行为。在韩国田野考古学史中,我们国立文化财研究所将严守发掘调查的正道,并以此为我们自豪的根本。

---

[1] 国立文化财研究所:《韩俄共同发掘特别展——黑龙江、沿海州的神秘》,2006年。

The NRICH from the Perspective of Korea's Excavation History

Dr. Ji Byong-Mok (Director of the Planning and Coordination Division, NRICH)

1.

A century has passed since historical remains in Korea started to be dug out, introducing the study of archaeology, which was a new field in those days[①]. The early excavations were not carried out by the Korean people, however, reflecting the chaos and tumult of the later Joseon period and the nation's tragic loss of sovereignty. That the history and cultural heritage of a small East Asian country was actively introduced to the Western world is related to the expansion of imperialism at that time[②].

According to records of investigation of remains carried out in the period of Japanese colonial rule[③], a large number of ancient tombs were investigated: Seokchimchong Tomb (石枕冢) in Seoak-dong (西岳洞), Gyeongju (庆州), excavated in 1909 and recorded as the first excavation of a Silla stone-chamber tomb (石室墓); Geomchong Tomb (劍冢) in Hwangnam-dong (皇南洞) (Tomb No. 100), excavated in 1911; and ancient tombs around Dongcheon-dong (东川洞) and Bomun-dong (普门洞). Of these excavations, that attracting most attention was a wooden-coffin tomb with stone mound (积石木椁墓) discovered September 24, 1921 during extension work on a private house in Gyeongju. The tomb was named Geumgwanchong (金冠冢), meaning "gold crown tomb," for the gold crowns that were discovered inside it and is the most famous of the ancient tumuli of Silla. Afterwards, investigations of large wooden-coffin tombs with stone mound continued, including the well-known Geumnyeongchong Tomb (金铃塚), Singnichong Tomb (饰履冢) and Seobongchong Tomb (瑞凤冢). On the other hand, the extensive investigations that were carried out in Changnyeong (昌宁) were not academic projects, but rather had the nature of tomb robbery[④]. It can be said that excavations in the early days were not carried out within the framework of modern archaeology but remained at the level of treasure hunts. The state in which the

---

① It is known that these excavations were carried out in 1906 on Namchong Tomb (南冢) in Hwangnam-dong (皇南洞) and the Buksan Tombs in Dongcheon-dongs (东川洞) by a Japanese person named Imanishi Ryu (龙今西).

② Korean history and culture was introduced in a fragmentary manner. Full-scale introduction of Korean history and culture likely came when the country took part in world trade fairs. The following served as a momentum for introducing Korean culture directly to the world: full-scale production of a Korean bibliography, and academic introduction of the epigraph of King Gwanggaeto's (广开土) Tomb.

③ Here we use the term "investigation of remains" in that there are problems in expressing the investigations of those days as "archeological investigation" or "excavations." Excavations from that time are summarized will in the following books: Saotome Masahiro (雅博早乙女). 2001. The 100 years of an Archaeological Investigation of Silla. *Journal of Research of Joseon History*. p.39. Cha Soon-Cheol. 2006. Review on the Investigations of Silla's Ancient Tombs during the Period of Japanese Rule. *Munhwajae*, 39: pp.95~130.

④ National Research Institute of Cultural Heritage. 2005. *Korean Cultural Heritage of the Ogura Collection:* Tokyo National Museum. Possession.

early excavations were carried out is clearly indicated by the fact that very few academic materials such as investigation reports remain from those days, and that excavated relics were generally marked with the presumed place of origin only and no details on their provenance including exact place of discovery.

It was during such times that the Muscum of the Japanese Government-General of Korea was founded in 1915, a modern museum that established the foundation for a system of restoration and maintenance of excavated relics. Up till Korea's liberation in 1945 more modern museums were established in local areas including Gyeongju (庆州), Buyeo (扶余), Gaeseong (开城), and Pyeongyang (平壤), and were later turned into national museums. As tomb robbery and smuggling were frequent, the Regulations on Preservation of Treasures in Ancient Tombs (1916) were passed in 1916 for the protection of cultural heritage. This was supplemented by the Regulations on Preservation of Joseon's Treasures, Historical Remains, and Natural Monuments (1933) and the Directive on Enforcement of Regulations on Preservation of Joseon's Treasures, Historical Remains, and Natural Monuments[①]. These remained the legal base for preservation of cultural heritage for some time after Korea's liberation until the Cultural Properties Protection Law was enacted in 1962.

After liberation and national division, South Korea and North Korea carried out excavations in their own respective ways. While excavation of cultural heritage was relatively active in the North, the same could not be said for the South. The first proper excavation by South Korea was that of a tomb conducted by the National Museum in 1946. The excavation of the so-called "Houchong Tomb (壶杅塚)"[②] produced greater results than expected, which was greatly encouraging and enabled excavation work to enter a new phase. The tomb was excavated in several phases, but the work was suspended by the outbreak of the Korean War in 1950. In the initial stage, the work was led by the National Museum and carried out in part by university teams with researchers who had studied archaeology abroad. This was an inevitable consequence of the dearth of domestic researchers who had majored in archaeology since the colonial period.

The lack of professional experience in the field was somewhat appeased with the foundation of the Department of Archeological Anthropology at Seoul National University in 1961, but the number of archaeologists remained insufficient. However, as the number of excavations, continued to increase under the government's economic development plans in the early 1960s and the New Community (Saemaeul) Movement in the 1970s, the demand for archaeologists also grew accordingly. In those days, such demand was generally filled not so much by those who had majored in archaeology at university but by those who had completed similar short courses or by those who had gained field experience by participating in actual excavations. The establishment of the Cultural Heritage Research Office at the Cultural Heritage Bureau in 1969 and its organization[③] is closely related to the situation at that time.

---

① The following are related to archaeological investigations during the Japanese ruling era: Pai Hyung Il. 2000. *Constructing "Korean" Origins-A Critical Review of Archaeology, Historiography, and Racial Myth in Korean State-Formation Theories.* Harvard University Asia Center: pp.23~35.

② This tomb attracted attention in that the characters "乙卯年国岗上广开土地好太王壶杅十" were found inscribed on the bottom of an excavated bronze bowl. This means that a relic related to Goguryeo's King Gwanggaeto (广开土) was excavated as a buried object in an ancient tomb in Gyeongju, the capital of Silla, and as such it supplied important information on understanding the relationships among the three kingdoms in the 5th century A.D.

③ Kim Jeong-Ki. 1999. *Reminiscence: 30 Years of the National Research Institute of Cultural Heritage.*

Among the most significant excavations in Korea is the extensive investigation on the area around King Michu's (味邹) Tomb in Gyeongju (庆州), the necessity for which arose under the Gyeongju Development Plan. It is considered a landmark work in terms of scale and importance with all possible related institutions and human resources taking part. Thereafter, many large excavations were conducted in a similar manner with a combined team of workers. In those days no single institution had a sufficient number of professionals to deal on its own with excavations ensuing from development projects (large-scale land development plans, urban planning programs, and dam construction).

The experiences of the transitional phase in the 1960s to 1970s described above resulted in noticeable quantitative expansion at universities in the 1980s. That is, those who had gained on-site experience in the earlier stage entered official courses in archaeology at university, contributing not only to increasing the number of professional workers but also the training of new professionals. This served as the base for Korea's present supply of human resources in the excavation field. In particular, the appearance of specialized corporate bodies after 1995, resulting from the above transitional stage, proved to be a turning point in Korean excavations.

2.

The purpose of this article is to examine the role of the National Research Institute of Cultural Heritage (NRICH) and the excavations it has carried out so far in context of the above mentioned history. An evaluation of its achievements and mistakes will be left for another occasion and by one in a more objective position.

It is undeniable that the NRICH was established in large part to meet the demand for planned excavation projects, as mentioned above. This is because the major role of the so-called Cultural Heritage Research Office was to conduct excavations before it was transformed into the Research Institute of Cultural Heritage (RICH) in 1975. The history of the NRICH can be divided into the following four stages based on changes in its organization and excavation work.

1) Early Stage (胎动期): 1969.11~1975.4
2) Growth Stage (成长期): 1975.4~1989.12
3) Expansion Stage (扩散期): 1990.1~2006.12
4) Transformation Stage (转换期): 2007.1~Present

The early stage is the period when the Cultural Heritage Research Office, established under the former Cultural Heritage Bureau in 1969, was in charge of excavations. Originally, excavation work had been the responsibility of the Cultural Heritage Bureau. But in those days, the work was mainly carried out by outside professionals with the help of some within the organization; so the work was done by a combined research group[①]. The establishment of an organization in charge of excavation was called for by the internal situation and the necessity for direct excavations, which grew rapidly after 1968. That the Cultural Heritage Bureau conducted five out of fifteen excavations carried out on a nationwide scale in 1970 attests to the growing need. In this early stage, it is notable that many researchers from the Cultural Heritage Research Office went to work in emergency control and large-scale national excavations. That is, they were instantly dispatched to urgent investigations of remains found by chance or during construction work, and hence worked all over the country. A special team was formed for long-term sojourn in Gyeongju to take part in extensive excavations in the Gyeongju (庆州) area. This is when excavations of Cheonmachong Tomb (天马冢) Tomb and Hwangnam-daechong Tomb (皇南大冢) were carried out.

The growth stage refers to the period when the Cultural Heritage Research Office was turned into a comprehensive organization to enable work on diverse cultural heritage. The Research Institute of Cultural Heritage (RICH) was established April 17, 1975 on the foundations of the Cultural Heritage Research Office, and Dr. Kim Jeong-ki, a third-rank researcher in the Cultural Heritage Bureau, was appointed the first director.

In addition to its existing major function of conducting archaeological investigations, RICH became a more comprehensive organization with the establishment of Research Division of Art and Handicraft, which made investigations in the field of art history and architectural history, and the Research Division of Conservation, which took charge of preservation of the relics and sites after excavation. With the later establishment of the Research Division of Folk Art, which investigated the folk arts that are disappearing in Korea today, RICH became the sole comprehensive institute of cultural heritage in Korea. For 30 years this organization provided the basic framework for the NRICH.

At this stage, RICH worked under a dual system whereby it conducted its own excavations while others were conducted by the Cultural Heritage Bureau. However, researchers from RICH accounted for a large part of the excavation team for the latter. This is seen as a measure taken for projects such as marine excavations which require a larger investigation team including professionals from other institutes. Some major examples are the excavation team for Admiral Yi Sun-sin's naval war relics and that for the relics off the Sinan (新安) sea bed. This period was characterized by an increase in long-term national excavation projects. In this period, RICH carried out excavations that were conducted over more than ten years and required continued budget commitment. Such projects usually involved a single site, meaning continued investigation by one institute was more efficient in producing comprehensive results than investigation by a joint team from various institutes. The major projects from that time include excavations of Hwangnyongsa Temple site (皇龙寺址) in Gyeongju (1976~1983), and Mireuksa

---

① The first investigation report of a historical site (excavation) in the name of the Cultural Heritage Bureau was a report on the excavation of a stone Buddha at Bunhwangsa Temple (芬皇寺) in Gyeongju published in 1967. It was an emergency control excavation conducted by the National Museum in December 1965. The second report published was that on Hwango-ri (皇吾里) Tomb No. 1 in Gyeongju in July 1965. Together with the results of several other ancient tomb investigations, this report was published in 1969. Hwango-ri (皇吾里) Tomb No. 1 was investigated and reported by Kim Won-Ryong. The following were investigated by the Cultural Heritage Bureau: Gyeseong (桂城) Gyenam (桂南) Tombs in Changnyeong (昌宁) (1967), Yonggang-dong (龙江洞) Tombs in Gyeongju (1968), Inwang-dong (仁旺洞) building site (1968), Guhwang-dong (九黄洞) collapsed Buddhist temple site (1968), Bomun-dong (普门洞) Tombs (1968), Bangnae-ri (芳内里) Tombs (1968), Jotap-ri (造塔里) Tombs in Andong (安东) (1969), Chodang-dong (草堂洞) Tombs in Gangneung (江陵) (1969), Bulguksa Temple (佛国寺) (1969), and Igyeondaeji (利见台址) (1969). (See National Research Institute of Cultural Heritage. 2001. *A Chronology of Excavations by the National Research Institute of Cultural Heritage.* Revised Edition II).

Temple site (弥勒寺址) in Iksan (益山) (1980~1996). The team for these excavations was comprised of professionals from RICH's Research Division of Art and Handicraft, and the work was carried out over ten years. It can be said that these two have been RICH's most prominent excavations since its foundation. The members of the two excavation team had great pride in the crucial role they played in these projects, which are such a significant part of the history of archaeological excavation in Korea.

As the Research Division of Art and Handicraft conducted all large long-term excavations, academic excavations, and emergency control excavations, it became necessary to separate such excavation work from everyday business to increase operational efficiency. So in October 1988 the Research Division of Archaeology was created to take charge of excavation work across the country. With land development projects under way nationwide, however, and rising demand for excavations there were limits to the amount of work that a single office in Seoul could handle. Therefore, regional offices of RICH, the necessity of which had long been recognized, were finally established in January 1990.

The third stage is the period when RICH had the capacity to conduct excavation work across the country more smoothly thanks to the establishment of regional branches. This is the expansion stage, when RICH expanded its role in the conduction of excavation projects. RICH founded three regional offices in January 1990: (1) Gyeongju Research Institute of Cultural Heritage, in charge of the Silla cultural area in and around Gyeongsangbuk-do Province (庆尚北道); (2) Buyeo Research Institute of Cultural Heritage, in charge of the Baekje cultural area in and around Chungcheong-do Province (忠清道) and Jeolla-do Province (全罗道); and (3) Changwon Research Institute of Cultural Heritage, in charge of the Gaya cultural area in and around Busan (釜山), Ulsan (蔚山) and Gyeongsangnam-do Province (庆尚南道). The Gyeongju and Buyeo branches were established with little difficulty as excavation teams already resided in the area. However, the case was different in Changwon as there was no resident excavation team or excavation site already existing there.

The third stage was marked by the fact that each regional office began to take on a distinct character according to the excavation work it conducted. Accordingly, the role of the Research Division of Archaeology changed when authority for local investigations was transferred to the relevant regional office. The business undertaken by the office expanded to include not only excavations in Seoul, Gyeonggi-do Province (京畿道) and Gangwon-do Province (江原道), but also overseas excavations (China, Russia, etc.), publication of a dictionary of archaeology, international exchange, and secondary use of excavation materials, among other things. The change was significant in that it enabled the RICH to move beyond the simple collection of the primary materials from excavation sites to the creation of secondary and tertiary materials to carry out true research.

In 1995 a slight change was made when the official name of RICH was changed to the National Research Institute of Cultural Heritage (NRICH). The implications were greater than the simple addition of "National" to the name. While there was no change in its status, organization and structure as a national institute, the new name had a ripple effect on its members and its public image[1]. The NRICH established the Naju National Research Institute of Cultural Heritage in November 2005, and began excavation in the Mahan (马韩) cultural area in and around Jeolla-do[2].

This period is named the "expansion stage" also for the quantitative expansion within the NRICH. In 2003 the Research Division of Architecture, in charge of ancient architecture, was separated from the Research Division of Artistic Heritage (Art and Handicraft). The NRICH also decided on the establishment of a conservation office to take charge of restoration and maintenance of damaged cultural heritage, which led to the foundation of the Research Division of Conservation Science in 2006. That same year the Research Division of Natural Heritage was established and the number of staff was considerably increased, attesting to the expansion of the NRICH in this period.

The final stage began not so long ago. In January 2007, the NRICH was turned into a government agency responsible for its own management. The government-set budget and organization made under the request of the NRICH changed considerably according to the management and achievements of NRICH. The changes fall short of satisfaction in many respects, but the framework for the desired basic structure and organization has been set. In particular, while it is absolutely necessary for the NRICH to be in charge of excavations in Seoul and the central area, the basic system for regional excavations is now in place. It cannot be denied that the NRICH has entered a stage of change in terms of its existing role in excavation works as around 40 excavation corporate bodies are currently in operation. It can be said that such change comes rather late if indeed they did not get under way quite some time ago.

3.

From the perspective of excavation, the NRICH has been considerably active. Beginning with a small office and a handful of researchers it has grown to comprise four regional offices in addition to the main office and its achievements over the years have been considerable. As a national institute the NRICH has been able to conduct large long-term excavations that could not be handled by any other excavation institute.

So far, the NRICH has conducted 436 excavations in some 38 years: 109 in Seoul and the central area, 139 in the Silla cultural area (Gyeongsangbuk-do and Daegu), 136 in the Baekje cultural area (Chungcheong-do and Jeolla-do), and 52 in the Gaya cultural area (Gyeongsangnam-do, Ulsan and Busan). This section will look at the results of the NRICH's excavations by area.

Excavations in the Silla cultural area in and around Gyeongsangbuk-do began quite early. This area accounts for a greater part of Korea's excavation history than any other region, with the country's first excavation being carried out here. The equation Silla=Golden Kingdom is enough to attract public attention to any excavation regarding Silla, and hence it is natural that many of the major finds and issues in Korea's excavation history originated in this area[3]. Particular attention was drawn to the excavation

---

[1] However, the district research institute remained "Gyeongju (Buyeo, Changwon) Research Institute of Cultural Heritage" under NRICH in those days. The word "National" was not added to the name of these institutes until 2005.
[2] In late 2006, the Jungwon National Research Institute of Cultural Heritage was established in Chungju (忠州).
[3] The achievements of major excavations in and around Gyeongju are well summarized well in the following: Yoon Geun-Il. 2006. "*32 years of Gyeongju National Research Institute of Cultural Heritage*", 32 Years of Excavating the 1000 Year History of Silla: pp.152~175.

of Gyeongju, the ancient Silla capital, because of the Gyeongju Comprehensive Tourism Development Plan of the 1970s. Under the name of economic development, plans were made to develop tourism products based on historical remains, and the 1000-year ancient capital of Gyeongju was chosen as the first location. Gyeongju was divided into several historical site zones (史迹地区) and wide-ranging restoration and maintenance plans were devised. As a part of such plans, the King Michu (味邹) Tomb Area Excavation Team was established as a temporary organization under the Cultural Heritage Bureau in 1973, in order to investigate and restore the area [present Daereungwon (大陵苑) area]. This team had the nature of an investigation team dispatched by the Cultural Heritage Research Office, as mentioned above. The team's basic objective was to turn the large ancient tumuli into tourist resources by opening up the inside for public viewing. The first tomb chosen for excavation was a large gourd-shaped tomb called Hwangnam-daechong (皇南大塚), or the Great Tomb of Hwangnam, classified as Tomb No. 98. However, as the team had no experience in excavating such a large tomb, it chose to work first on a smaller tomb nearby, Tomb No. 155 (later named Cheonmachong, or Tomb of the Heavenly Horse), in order to gain the necessary experience and identify the structure through a similar example. This preliminary excavation yielded unexpectedly good results, escalating interest in the ancient tombs of Gyeongju. Subsequent excavation of the South and North mounds of Hwangnam-daechong proceeded smoothly, thanks to the team's previous experience. It required a great deal of time to properly understand the results of the investigation due to the lack of experience on the part of the researchers and lack of related studies in those days. Related research activities are still under way.

Starting with the tombs, excavations expanded to the whole Gyeongju area, widening in scope in line with the foundation of RICH in 1975. The King Michu (味邹) Tomb Area Excavation Team was renamed the Historical Sites of Gyeongju Excavation Team and took charge of excavation work in Gyeongju and the vicinity. Some important sites were investigated at this time including Anapji Pond (雁鸭池), and Gameunsa Temple (感恩寺). The most important project, however, was the excavation of Hwangnyongsa Temple Site (皇龙寺址). Hwangnyongsa was a special temple in that it was built in the golden age of Silla, when the foundation for the unification of the three kingdoms was established and is a repository of the essence of Silla culture. The excavation was important as the materials obtained from it provide almost all the vital clues to unraveling archaeological questions regarding Silla. The issue now is restoration of the finds.

The Historical Sites of Gyeongju Excavation Team conducted around 40 excavations before 1990 when the Gyeongju Research Institute of Cultural Heritage was established. The team investigated not only remains essential to research of Silla's capital city (Weolseong moat (月城护城河), the site of Woljeong wooden bridge (月精桥址), Wanggyeong (王京), the site of the east gate of Weolsong (月城东门址)) but also Heungnyunsa Temple site (兴轮寺址), Gulbulsa Temple site (掘佛寺址), the Yonggang-dong (龙江洞) Tomb, and Myeonghwal-sanseong (明活), a mountain fortress. The team's organization, role and investigation projects were transferred to the Gyeongju office, which carried out annual excavation work on Weolseong moat and Wanggyeong, and selected new sites such as Bunhwangsa Temple (芬皇寺) for long-term excavation work. In the mid- to late-1990s, the institute had to invest much time and human resources into control excavations due to the expansion of the land development projects. Presently, the institute is conducting not only long-term investigations of the presumed Inyongsa Temple site (传·仁容寺址) and Sacheonwangsa Temple site (四天王寺址), which is creating excitement due to the discovery of Sacheonwangsangjeon (四天王像砖), a temple hall with images of the four heavenly kings, but is also continuing annual investigation of Weolseong most (月城护城河). In addition, another notable project is the excavation of the Jjoksaem area, part of the maintenance project of Silla's ancient tumuli which began in 2007, as it entails a comprehensive large-scale academic investigation of ancient Silla tumuli following the first carried out in the mid-1970s.

The beginning of the NRICH's excavation of the Baekje cultural area was the excavation of King Munyeong's (武宁) Tomb in 1971. The so-called excavation of the century was not completely satisfying, and new studies continue to be carried out to this date[①]. For some time afterwards, the NRICH did not do any excavation work in the area. In those days, the investigations were mainly carried out by university museums (e.g. Chungnam National University, Chonnam National University, Wonkwang University, etc.) and the National Museum. The NRICH resumed full-scale work in the area with the excavation of Mireuksa Temple Site (弥勒寺址), which began July 1980 and entailed 17 excavations of the site till 1996. The unprecedented project was one of the longest excavations in Korea. It not only revealed the basic layout of Baekjae's Buddhist temples [three pagodas and one main hall (3塔1金堂)] but also established the relationship of Baekje relic layers to the mid-Joseon era; in this sense, it played a landmark role in archaeological studies on this area. From 1985, the NRICH conducted annual excavations of Busosanseong (扶苏) mountain fortress in Buyeo (扶余). These were not concluded until 2002 as work was carried out only two to six months every year. Nevertheless, important results were yielded in shedding light on Baekje's capital and its defense system. Further, in 1986 the NRICH conducted excavations of the Ipjeom-ri (笠店里) Tomb in Iksan (益山), famous for the gold crown discovered there, and in 1988 the Songsan-ri (松山里) Tombs in Gongju (公州). For the excavation of Mireuksa Temple site (弥勒寺址), a permanent on-site team was formed, supplemented by researchers temporally dispatched to the site by RICH in Seoul. Annual excavations of the Wangung-ri (王宫里) site in Iksan (益山) began in September 1989 and are still under way. This site is anticipated to yield important materials shedding light on the management of Baekje's central government in the late-Baekje period.

When the Buyeo National Research Institute of Cultural Heritage was established in 1990 it took over excavation work in the Baekje cultural area and was able to widen the scope of its investigations. The institute completed or is conducting investigations on prehistoric remains such as Sanjik-ri (山直里) dolmens in Buyeo (扶余); Buddhist temple sites such as Yongjeongnisa Temple site (龙井里寺址) in Buyeo, Wangheungsa Temple site (王兴寺址), Silsangsa Temple (实相), and Bowonsa Temple site (普愿寺址); and ancient capitals such as the remains of Gwanbuk-ri (官北里) in Buyeo. Since its founding, the institute has concentrated on the excavation of ancient Baekje tombs including the Neungnae-ri (陵内里) Tombs in Buyeo, Jeoseok-ri (楮石里) Tombs, Jiseon-ri (芝仙里) Tombs, and Dangjeong-ri (堂丁里) Tombs in Seocheon (舒川). The re-investigation of the remains of Gwanbuk-ri (官北里) is a comprehensive and extended project in contrast to the previous fragmentary excavation and is anticipated to produce many findings that will shed light on the ancient capital of the Baekje Kingdom. From 1990

[①] Buyeo National Research Institute of Cultural Heritage and Gongju National Museum. 2001. *King Munyong's (武宁) Tomb and East Asian Culture*. Proceedings of the King Munyeong's Tomb Excavation Memorial International Conference. Gongju National Museum. 2005. *King Munyong's (武宁) Tomb: Report on Excavated Relics (I)*. Gongju National Museum. 2006. *King Munyong's (武宁) Tomb: Report on Excavated Relics (II)*.

to April 2007, the Buyeo National Research Institute of Cultural Heritage conducted 100 excavations of around 30 sites.

The Naju National Research Institute of Cultural Heritage has carried out excavations in the Mahan (马韩) cultural area since it was established in Naju (罗州), Jeollanam-do Province (全罗南道) in October 2005 to cover the Jeollanam-do and Jeollabuk-do (全罗北道) administrative district. The need for investigation of this area has been recognized since work on the tombs in Sinchon-ri (新村里) and Bogam-ri (伏岩里) in Naju (罗州). The institute is now conducting annual or emergency excavations of Hoejinseong (会津) Fortress in Naju (罗州), the tombs in Hoesan, Donggok-ri (东谷里), and the tombs in Hwajeong-ri (化丁里), Masan (马山), among others. There are great expectations for the results of these investigations.

Excavations in the Gaya cultural area began later than other areas. The first site investigated directly or indirectly by RICH was the Seongsan (城山) Shell Mound in Changwon (昌原), which began when the Changwon Industrial Complex was established. This project served as an opportunity to make known the true nature of the iron kingdom of Gaya for the first time. Three years later, in 1975, RICH conducted a full-scale excavation of the remains of Daepyeong-ri (大坪里) in Jinyang (晋阳), but for some time afterwards it conducted no further work in the Gaya area. In those days, excavations were generally carried out by university museums (e.g. Pusan National University, Dong-A University, etc.) and the National Museum. In 1990 the Changwon Research Institute of Cultural Heritage was established. Contrary to other regional offices, the Changwon branch suffered many difficulties as it did not have any existing permanent excavation sites or projects in progress. In addition, it did not have its own building, so for the first five years the staff occupied a temporary office built next to a facility called Changwon House. As a new organization it also suffered a lack of manpower, and hence experienced many difficulties in establishing the foundation for excavations in its area.

The first excavation carried out by the Changwon Research Institute of Cultural Heritage was the Gaeumjeong-dong (加音丁洞) Tombs in Changwon at the end of 1990. Following investigations were carried out on various sites such as the Rock Paintings and Shell Mound of Haman (咸安), Bongrimsa Temple site (凤林寺址) in Changwon, the Joil-ri (早日里) Tombs in Ulsan, and the prehistoric remains of Namgang River (南江) in Jinju (晋州). The Changwon office came under the spotlight with the results of the excavation in Haman, known as the center of Ara Gaya (阿罗伽倻). Despite the known existence of important sites in the Haman area such as the tombs of Dohang-ri (道项里) and Malsan-ri (末山里), no proper investigations had been made until the Changwon institute started a full-scale excavation in 1991. In addition, excavation of Seongsang-sanseong (城山), a mountain fortress near the Dohang-ri Tombs presumed to be the major Gaya fortress of its kind, has been under way since 1991. While the investigation has not produced much material on Gaya fortresses, it has uncovered a significantly large number of wooden tablets (木简) for a single site[①]. Excavations of the neighboring ancient tombs in Dohang-ri (道项里) and Malsan-ri (末山里) served as an opportunity to understand

---

① A total of 252 ink-inscribed wooden tablets have been found in Korea as of January 2006. Of them, 94 were excavated from the Seongsan (城山) mountain fortress site. (Changwon National Research Institute of Cultural Heritage. 2006. *Korea's Ancient Wooden Tablets*: 19.

the true nature of the Gaya confederacy. Emergency excavation of a collapsed ancient tomb (废古墓) found in what was presumed to be the slope of the tomb area during the construction work on an apartment in 1992 achieved great results that marked a new era in the archaeological study of Gaya. One of the major finds was a suit of horse armor (马甲), a discovery made 1,500 years later than the pictures of armor seen in the ancient tomb murals of Goguryeo in the territory of Gaya, which had an advanced iron culture. For a newly founded institute, such an important discovery was a stroke of fortune. This motivated the institute to conduct excavations of the Dohang-ri (道项里) Tombs over the next seven years, which yielded important research materials in studying development of the major burial systems such as the wooden chamber tomb (木椁墓), stone-lined tomb (石椁墓), and stone chamber tombs (石室墓) of the Gaya era. Further, annual excavations of the Naesan-ri (内山里) Tombs in Goseong (固城) have produced important results in putting together an accurate picture of the state of Sogaya (小伽郷).

The Changwon office has conducted few excavations in the eastern region [Gimhae (金海) and Goryeong (高灵)], the center of the Gaya cultural area, compared to other areas. Research in Goryeong may be limited due to administrative boundaries[①], but Gimhae (金海) will be an important area for future investigation. Excavation of the Songhyeon-dong (松岘洞) Tombs in Changnyeong (昌宁), conducted since 2004, is important in producing research materials showing the relationship between Silla and Gaya in the 5th and 6th centuries. Tomb Number No. 7 yielded a wooden coffin (木棺) made of camphor wood, and as it is known that such coffins were mainly produced on the south coast of the Korean Peninsula and in Japan the discovery provides interesting research material for studying the relationship between the two countries at the time. While the Changwon institute started excavation of the Gaya cultural area without a solid foundation and little advance preparation, its work continues unabated to the present[②] with a record of 60 excavations at 30 sites.

As mentioned above, all NRICH excavation projects were undertaken by the Research Division of Art and Handicraft before the regional branches were established. That is, the Research Division of Art and Handicraft was the division in charge of excavations from early 1975, when RICH was established, to 1988, when a separate Research Division of Archaeology was created. Hence, before the regional branches were established, researchers from this office were assigned as members of excavation teams organized for projects across the country or were dispatched to the site when needed. As this indicates, excavation conditions in those days were not so favorable, and to conduct projects nationwide with limited human resources would have been a considerable burden.

As the above reviews excavations conducted before 1990 by cultural area, the rest of this section will be devoted to the achievements of such excavations. After 1990, excavation efforts were concentrated on the central area including Seoul, Gyeonggi-do (京畿道) and Gangwon-do (江原道). Excavations of military sites in the three places were particularly important: the Geumpa-ri (金坡里) Paleolithic Site in Paju (坡州), Seogok-ri (瑞谷里) Mural Tombs, the remains of Samgot-ri (三串里) in Yeoncheon (涟

---

① Goryeong (高灵) belongs to the administrative district of Gyeongsangbuk-do. So, it is covered by the Gyeongju National Research Institute of Cultural Heritage.
② Changwon National Research Institute of Cultural Heritage. 2005. *The 15 Years of Changwon National Research Institute of Cultural Heritage.*

川), the remains of Gapyeong-ri (柯坪里) in Yangyang (襄阳), and the remains of Munam-ri (文岩里) in Goseong (高城). The remains of Jangdo Cheonghaejin (将岛 清海镇) on Wando Island (莞岛), the Bogam-ri (伏岩里) Tombs in Naju (罗州) (1996-1998), and Shinchon-ri (新村里) Tomb No. 9 (1999) are sites within the domain of regional offices that continued to be excavated by the Research Division of Archaeology. Meanwhile, in the excavation of Pungnap-toseong (风纳), an earthen wall fortress, which began in 1997, archaeological materials confirming that the fortress was a key facility of Baekje when its capital was located in Hanseong (present Seoul) continue to be found. At the same time, this site is representative of the severe conflict between the arguments for preservation against development. This serves to remind us of the importance of establishing and implementing realistic, long-term cultural heritage conservation plans.

Excepting excavations of some Buddhist temple sites, most of the excavation projects by the NRICH have been concentrated on remains predating the Unified Silla period. In this respect, recent investigations of Joseon period remains [around Geumcheon Bridge (锦川桥) in Changdeokgung Palace (昌德宫), the site of the royal kitchen (烧厨房址) in Gyeongbokgung Palace (景福宫), and the Gwanghwamun (光化门) area] are notably different. Also, excavations of Goryeo royal tombs [Seongneung (硕陵), Golleung (坤陵), Gareung (嘉陵) and the Neungnae-ri (陵内里) Tombs] on Gangwha Island (江华岛) are expected to open up a new area of study as the burial systems of Goryeo have remained an unexplored field so far and to pave the way for mutual excavation and study with North Korea of Goryeo royal tombs in Gaeseong (开城).

In addition, rising interest not only in domestic archaeological sites but also in overseas sites serves as momentum for widening the scope of excavation activity by the NRICH. While other institutes have conducted excavations in Russia on-and-off since 1990, the NRICH has done so steadily for over ten years. Through publication of a report following overseas excavation and then exhibition of the results at home[1], the NRICH is taking the next step forward in its archaeological excavations.

4.

The excavations conducted by the NRICH so far have been long-term continuous projects of the largest scale possible by a single institution. The status of the NRICH as a national institute is one factor that has enabled the investigation of many sites for over ten years. This is the first reason for NRICH maintaining its excavation function. However, the conditions and circumstances of excavations in Korea are extremely varied and complicated. Unexpected difficulties lie ahead if the NRICH proceeds only on the basis of its status and achievements so far. The NRICH has reached the point where new directions must be explored in terms of the nature and purpose of its excavations in a situation where around 40 specialized excavation organizations (corporate bodies) account for much of the country's excavation work. It is time to determine the nature of excavations by the NRICH as a

---

[1] National Research Institute of Cultural Heritage. 2006. *Korea-Russia Special Exhibition: The Amur, the Mystery of the Maritime Province.*

responsibility management institute.

Needless to say, archaeological excavations are not based on the premise of discovery of splendid relics such as golden crowns or approach to extraordinary sites that will attract the notice of the world. Furthermore, archaeological excavations should not be treated as or carried out as some kind of rite of passage in order to satisfy realistic demands. The NRICH takes pride in the fact that its excavations have been conducted without forgetting or overlooking these premises in Korea's excavation history.

韩国国立文化财研究所发掘年表
Chronicle of the Field Work of the NRICH

年 度	发掘遗址名	时 代
1966	庆州皇吾里30、60号墓	新罗
1968	庆州龙江洞古墓	统一新罗
	庆州仁旺洞建物址	统一新罗
	庆州九黄洞废寺址	新罗
	庆州普门洞古墓	统一新罗
	庆州芳内里古墓群	新罗
1969	江陵草堂洞古墓	新罗
	庆州佛国寺	统一新罗
	庆州望德寺址	统一新罗
	庆州芳内里古墓群	新罗
	安东造塔里古墓	三国
1970	庆州望德寺址	统一新罗
	庆州安溪里古墓	新罗
	江陵下诗洞古墓	三国
	骊州甫通里古墓	三国
	庆州佛国寺九品莲池	三国
1971	和顺青铜器遗址	青铜器
	广州仓谷里朝鲜墓	朝鲜
	公州武宁王陵	百济
1972	庆州兴轮寺址周边	新罗
	杨平两水里支石墓	青铜器
	居昌屯马里壁画古墓	高丽
1973	庆州天马冢	新罗
	大邱太平路支石墓群	青铜器
	庆州皇南大冢北墓	新罗
	李忠武公海战址	朝鲜
	庆州皇南大冢南墓	新罗
	安东马里新基古墓	三国
	庆州坤元寺址	统一新罗
1974	庆州皇南大冢南墓	新罗
	安东道谷里逸名寺址	朝鲜
	安东罗所里古墓	三国
	安东元浙江逸名寺址	三国
	李忠武公海战址	朝鲜
1975	长城德在里支石墓群	青铜器
	长城双熊里支石墓	青铜器
	首尔芳荑洞1号墓	三国
	安东宜村里支石墓、石室墓、石堆	青铜器至三国

（续表）

年　度	发掘遗址名	时　代
1975	安东陶山面石室墓	三国
	庆州皇南大冢南墓	新罗
1976	庆州金尺里古墓	新罗
	晋阳大坪里先史遗址	青铜器
	庆州雁鸭池	统一新罗
	庆州皇龙寺址	新罗
	李忠武公海战址	朝鲜
1977	李忠武公海战址	朝鲜
	新安海底遗物出土址	高丽
	晋阳大坪里先史遗址	青铜器
1978	庆州兴轮寺址塔址	新罗
	华城一里、元时里古墓	朝鲜
	荣州浮石寺安养门	高丽
	新安海底遗物出土址	高丽
	庆州金丈里新罗瓦窑址	新罗
1979	庆州皇龙寺址	新罗
	庆州芬皇寺门址	新罗
	新安海底遗物出土址	高丽
1980	扶余西腹寺址	百济
	扶余西腹寺址	百济
	庆州感恩寺址	统一新罗
	庆州皇龙寺址	新罗
	新安海底遗物出土址	高丽
	益山弥勒寺址	百济
1981	庆州皇龙寺址	新罗
	益山弥勒寺址	百济
	新安海底遗物出土址	高丽
	扶余扶苏山城军仓址	百济至朝鲜
	杨州杨州山城	三国至统一新罗
	山清江楼里先史遗址	青铜器
	庆州兴轮寺址周边	新罗
1982	庆州皇龙寺址	新罗
	新安海底遗物出土址	高丽
	春城新梅里古墓	三国
	益山弥勒寺址	百济
1983	扶余扶苏山城内穴居址	三国
	庆州皇龙寺址	新罗
	益山弥勒寺址	百济

（续表）

年 度	发掘遗址名	时 代
1983	新安海底遗物出土址	高丽
	杨州杨州山城	三国
1984	新安海底遗物出土址	高丽
	扶余扶苏山城内穴居址	三国
	和顺双峰寺大雄殿址	朝鲜
	首尔昌庆宫	朝鲜
	庆州仁旺洞月城护城河	新罗
1985	庆州皇龙寺址	统一新罗
	庆州仁旺洞月城护城河	新罗
	荣州飞凤山城	三国
	荣州顺兴邑内里壁画古墓	三国
	庆州掘佛寺址	统一新罗
	庆州远愿寺址外围	统一新罗
1986	扶余扶苏山城南门址	百济
	庆州龙江洞古墓	统一新罗
	庆州瞻星台西侧遗物包含层	统一新罗
	庆州皇龙寺址	统一新罗
	益山笠店里古墓	百济
1987	庆州拜里石佛立像周边	统一新罗
	庆州皇龙寺址	统一新罗
	益山弥勒寺址	百济
	春川清平寺影池和龙仁殿址	高丽
	荣州飞凤山城	三国
	庆州仁旺洞月城护城河	统一新罗
1988	扶余扶苏山城东门址	百济
	庆州仁旺洞月城护城河	统一新罗
	益山弥勒寺址	百济
	公州松山里古墓	百济
	蔚珍凤坪碑周边	新罗
1989	坡州金坡里旧石器遗址	旧石器
	莞岛清海镇法华寺址	统一新罗
	庆州普门洞明活山城	新罗
	益山王宫里遗址	百济
	庆州皇龙寺址	统一新罗
1990	莞岛清海镇法华寺址	统一新罗
	益山弥勒寺址	百济
	莞岛孤山尹善道遗址	朝鲜
	首尔景福宫内宫阙遗址	朝鲜

（续表）

年 度	发掘遗址名	时 代
1991	扶余山直里支石墓	青铜器
	庆州校洞财买井址	统一新罗
	咸安城山山城	三国
	庆州九黄洞王京遗址	统一新罗
	将岛清海镇遗址	统一新罗
	浦项冷水里古墓	新罗
	坡州冷坡里旧石器遗址	旧石器
	扶余芝仙里古墓	百济
	扶余楮石里砖椁墓	百济
	咸安道项里岩画遗址	青铜器至伽倻
	昌原加音丁洞贝冢	伽倻
	庆州仁旺洞月城护城河	新罗至统一新罗
	扶余龙井里寺址	百济
1992	坡州金坡里旧石器遗址	旧石器
	咸安城山山城	三国
	庆州九黄洞芬皇寺址	统一新罗
	清原米川里古墓群	三国
	咸安道项里马甲冢	伽倻
	扶余扶苏山城	百济
	庆州青令里废古墓	新罗
	庆州九黄洞王京遗址	统一新罗
	庆州仁旺洞月城护城河	新罗至统一新罗
	益山弥勒寺址	百济至朝鲜
	浦项冷水里古墓	新罗
	益山王宫里遗址	百济
	扶余龙井里寺址	百济
	浦项达田里支石墓群	青铜器
	庆州校洞财买井址	统一新罗
	将岛清海镇遗址	统一新罗
	庆州多山里支石墓	青铜器
1993	扶余扶苏山城	百济
	庆州城东洞殿廊址	新罗至统一新罗
	扶余旧衙里百济遗址	百济
	咸安道项里古墓群	伽倻
	涟川三串里积石冢	百济
	益山狮子庵	百济至统一新罗
	庆州校洞财买井址	青铜器至统一新罗
	庆州仁旺洞月城护城河	统一新罗

(续表)

年 度	发掘遗址名	时 代
1993	益山王宫里遗址	百济
	益山弥勒寺址	百济至朝鲜
	庆州乾川休息所新筑地基遗址	青铜器至新罗
1994	庆州皇城洞601-2番地遗址	新罗
	扶余圣兴山城周边古墓群	百济
	将岛清海镇遗址	统一新罗
	王宫里遗址	百济
	咸安道项里古墓群	伽倻
	庆州皇南洞建筑新筑地基内遗址	不详
	庆州千军洞垃圾埋立场地基内遗址	青铜器至新罗
	庆州九黄洞芬皇寺址	统一新罗
	高敞禅云寺东佛庵遗址	高丽至朝鲜
	益山弥勒寺址	百济至朝鲜
	庆州王京地区内煤气管道埋设地遗址	统一新罗
	首尔景福宫东宫址	朝鲜
	襄阳柯坪里先史遗址	新石器
1995	襄阳柯坪里先史遗址	新石器
	庆州九黄洞王京遗址	统一新罗
	庆州仁旺洞月城护城河	新罗
	益山王宫里遗址	百济
	庆州九黄洞芬皇寺址	统一新罗
	扶余扶苏山城	百济
1996	蔚山岩里遗址	三国
	罗州伏岩里3号墓	三国
	扶余扶苏山城	百济至统一新罗
	庆州芳内里道路扩改地区内遗址	统一新罗
	庆州天龙寺址	统一新罗
	南原实相寺境域内遗址	统一新罗
	将岛清海镇遗址	统一新罗
	高阳元堂洞胎碑石群	朝鲜
1997	将岛清海镇遗址	统一新罗
	首尔风纳洞公寓新筑地基内遗址	百济
	固城内山里古墓	伽倻
	南原实相寺境域内遗址	统一新罗
	庆州九黄洞王京遗址	统一新罗
1998	韩国传统文化学校新筑地基	不详
	庆州月山里货物停车场地基遗址	青铜器至统一新罗
	扶余韩国传统文化学校建盖地基内遗址	不详

（续表）

年 度	发掘遗址名	时 代
1998	庆州九黄洞王京遗址	统一新罗
	扶苏山城	百济
	南原实相寺境域内遗址	统一新罗
	高城文岩里先史遗址	新石器
	庆州月山里货物停车场地基遗址	青铜器至统一新罗
	潭阳潇洒园建筑址	朝鲜
	固城内山里古墓	伽倻
1999	南原实相寺遗址	统一新罗
	扶余宫南池	百济
	扶余扶苏山城	百济
	益山王宫里遗址	百济
	庆州九黄洞王京遗址	统一新罗
	扶余扶苏山城	百济
	扶余邑污水集管路埋设工程区域内遗址	不详
	江华谯楼墩台	朝鲜
	扶余宫南池	百济
	山清断俗寺址	三国
	南原实相寺遗址	统一新罗
	庆州推定鬼桥址遗址	新罗
	庆州黄龙寺址展示馆地基遗址	统一新罗
	扶余韩国传统文化学校建立地基内遗址	不详
	罗州新村里9号墓	三国
	庆州黄龙寺址展示馆地基遗址	统一新罗
	庆州仁旺洞月城护城河	新罗至统一新罗
	驻韩俄罗斯大使馆建设豫定地内遗址	朝鲜
	昌原吐月洞上南商业地基内遗址	先史
	将岛清海镇遗址	统一新罗
	昌原吐月洞上南商业地基内遗址	先史
2000	庆州赛马场预定地基	青铜器至朝鲜
	庆州推定鬼桥址	朝鲜
	庆州皇龙寺址展示馆地基	统一新罗
	庆州仁旺洞孝不孝遗址	统一新罗
	江华龙头墩炮台	朝鲜
	益山弥勒寺址西塔周边遗址	百济至朝鲜
	益山王宫里遗址	百济
	扶余百济历史再现地基内遗址	青铜器至朝鲜
	庆州仁洞里古墓	初期铁器
	固城松川里宋岛石棺墓	三韩

(续表)

年 度	发掘遗址名	时 代
2000	首尔风纳土城内未来村公寓重建地基内遗址	百济
	南原实相寺遗址	统一新罗
	扶余王兴寺址	百济
	首尔风纳土城外换银行公司公寓地基内遗址	百济
	庆州仁旺洞月城护城河	新罗
	庆州天官寺址	统一新罗
2001	江华高丽王陵(硕陵)基底部和周边遗址	高丽
	江华岛墩台	朝鲜
	首尔风纳洞154番地一圆停车场新筑地基遗址	百济
	首尔奥林匹克美术馆和雕刻公园新筑地基内	百济
	小延坪岛贝冢Ⅱ	新石器
	莞岛将岛清海镇遗址(10次)	统一新罗
	昌德宫锦川桥周边遗址	朝鲜
	南原实相寺遗址	统一新罗
	扶余官北里百济遗址	百济
	扶余宫南池	百济
	扶余扶苏山城	百济
	益山王宫里遗址	百济
	庆州九黄洞芬黄寺址	统一新罗
	庆州九黄洞王京遗址	统一新罗
	庆州九黄洞芬黄寺址	统一新罗
	庆州九黄洞王京遗址	统一新罗
	庆州仁旺洞月城护城河	新罗
	庆州天官寺址	统一新罗
	庆州皇南洞194-11、12番地	新罗
	庆州皇龙寺址展示馆地基	统一新罗
	庆州孝不孝桥址	统一新罗
	庆州市厅舍增筑地基	不详
2002	南原实相寺遗址	统一新罗
	扶余扶苏山城	百济
	益山王宫里遗址	百济
	首尔风纳洞三票产业社屋新筑地基内遗址	百济
	中部西海岸岛屿地区先史遗址(毛伊岛贝冢)	新石器
	高城文岩里先史遗址	新石器
	昌德宫锦川桥周边遗址	朝鲜
	庆州九黄洞王京遗址	统一新罗
	庆州仁容寺址	统一新罗
	庆州出土遗物保管栋建立地基	不详

（续表）

年 度	发掘遗址名	时 代
2002	庆州皇龙寺址展示馆地基	统一新罗
	庆州孝不孝桥址	统一新罗
2003	庆州南里寺址	统一新罗
	庆州芬皇寺	统一新罗
	庆州月城护城河	新罗
	庆州仁容寺址	统一新罗
	新罗王京遗址	新罗
	南原实相寺	统一新罗
	扶余官北里百济遗址(研究所院内)	百济
	扶余官北里百济遗址(推定王宫址)	百济
	扶余宫南池	百济
	扶余王兴寺址	百济
	扶余王兴寺址	百济
	益山王宫里五层石塔周边遗址	百济
	益山王宫里遗址	百济
	首尔风纳洞三表产业社屋新筑地基内遗址	百济
	中部西海岸岛屿地域(瓮津延坪岛喜鹊山贝冢)	新石器
	风纳土城	百济
2004	新罗王京遗址	统一新罗
	庆州月城护城河	新罗
	南原实相寺	统一新罗
	扶余加神里古墓抢救性发掘调查	百济
	扶余官北里百济遗址	百济
	观音寺址	百济
	扶余宫南池	百济
	扶余王兴寺址	百济
	益山王宫里遗址	百济
	益山王宫里整修预定地区内遗址	百济
	景福宫烧厨房址和兴福殿址	朝鲜
	江华高丽王陵(嘉陵、坤陵)	高丽
	昌庆宫西安门南侧休息所新筑地基内遗址	朝鲜
	风纳洞重建地基(336-1番地)内遗址	百济
	风纳洞重建地基(410番地)内遗址	百济
	风纳土城	百济
2005	昌宁松岘洞古墓群6、7号墓	三国
	芬皇寺	统一新罗
	传·仁容寺址	统一新罗
	皇南洞906-番地石室墓	统一新罗

（续表）

年 度	发掘遗址名	时 代
2005	月城护城河	新罗至统一新罗
	益山王宫里整修备预定区域内遗址	百济至高丽
	扶余王兴寺址	百济至高丽
	益山王宫里遗址	百济
	扶余军守里寺址	百济
	扶余官北里百济遗址	百济至朝鲜
2006	咸安城山山城	三国至统一新罗
	昌宁松岘洞古墓群17号墓和周边遗址	三国
	罗州横山里古墓	青铜器至三国
	罗州伏岩里古墓周边遗址	旧石器,三国至高丽
	罗州会津城	三国至朝鲜
	九黄洞新罗王京造林工程地基内遗址	统一新罗
	庆州天龙寺址三层石塔周边排水管道布置区域内遗址	统一新罗至高丽
	皇南洞123-3番地建筑遗址	统一新罗
	月城护城河	新罗至统一新罗
	芬皇寺	统一新罗
	四天王寺址	统一新罗
	瑞山普愿寺址	朝鲜
	扶余宫南池	百济
	益山王宫里遗址	百济
	益山王宫里整修预定区域内遗址	百济
	扶余军守里寺址	百济
	扶余王兴寺址	百济至高丽
2007	扶余王兴寺址	百济至高丽
	益山帝释寺址	百济至高丽
	瑞山普原寺址	高丽(推测)至朝鲜
	咸安城山山城	三国至统一新罗
	罗州会津城	朝鲜
	罗州五良洞陶窑址	三国
	罗州花亭里马山古墓	三国
	罗州大安里方头古墓	三国
	传·仁容寺址	统一新罗
	大邱东区不老洞古墓群内石椁墓	三国
	月城护城河	新罗至统一新罗
	列岩谷石佛坐像整修工程地区内遗址	统一新罗
	三陵溪石佛坐像整修工程地区内遗址	统一新罗
	庆州四天王寺址	统一新罗

（续表）

年 度	发掘遗址名	时 代
2007	新罗王京遗址	统一新罗
	芬皇寺	统一新罗
	庆州蓝泉地区遗址	新罗
	扶余官北里遗址	百济至朝鲜
	扶余军守里寺址	百济
	益山王宫里遗址	百济
	瑞山普愿寺址内自来水工程区域内遗址	朝鲜
	扶余陵山里寺址	百济至统一新罗
2008	咸安城山山城	三国至统一新罗
	昌宁述亭里东三层石塔整修工程地基内遗址	统一新罗
	益山帝释寺址	百济
	益山王宫里整修预定区域内遗址	百济
	罗州会津城	统一新罗至朝鲜
	罗州五良洞陶窑址	三国
	罗州伏岩里古墓周边遗址	三国至高丽
	忠州楼岩里古墓群	三国
	忠州塔坪里(中原京推定地)遗址	统一新罗
	传·仁容寺址	统一新罗
	庆州南里寺址东西塔址	统一新罗
	月城护城河	新罗至统一新罗
	四天王寺址	统一新罗
	新罗王京遗址	统一新罗
	益山王宫里遗址整修预定地区内遗址	百济
	扶余官北里百济遗址	百济至朝鲜
	扶余定林寺址整修工程地基内遗址	百济至朝鲜
2009	扶余王兴寺址	百济至朝鲜
	灵岩沃野里长洞古墓	三国
	罗州五良洞陶窑址	三国
	罗州伏岩里古墓群周边遗址	三国至高丽
	忠州塔坪里(中原京推定地)遗址	统一新罗
	忠州下九岩里古墓群	三国
	春川美军驻扎地区内遗址	统一新罗至高丽
	皇龙寺研究中心建立预定地基内遗址	统一新罗
	月城护城河	新罗至统一新罗
	四天王寺址	统一新罗
	芬皇寺	统一新罗
	新罗王京遗址	统一新罗

韩国 考古学重大发现（2002~2007）

图片目录索引 | Plates Index

首尔风纳土城
Pungnap Mud Fortress Wall in Seoul
国立文化财研究所

1. 风纳土城全景 / 17
   View of Pungnap Fortress
2. 南北道路 / 18
   North and South Road
3. 遗物出土状况 / 19
   Remains
4. 居住遗址 / 19
   Housing Site
5. 木筑井全景 / 20
   Wooden Well
6. 取水用陶器出土状况 / 20
   Pottery for Well-bucket
7. 井内部遗物出土状况 / 20
   Remains in the Well
8. 取水用陶器 / 21
   Pottery for Well-bucket
9. 取水用陶器 / 21
   Pottery for Well-bucket
10. 井内出土木制品 / 21
    Wooden Ware
11. 城墙剖面状态 / 22
    Section of Fortress Wall
12. 城墙出土陶器 / 22
    Potteries
13. 城壕出土陶器 / 22
    Potteries
14. 黑陶 / 23
    Black-polished Jar
15. 百济陶器 / 23
    Baekje Potteries
16. 风纳土城出土陶器 / 23
    Potteries
17. 瓦 / 24
    Roof Tiles
18. 瓦当 / 24
    Roof-end Tiles
19. 础石 / 25
    Cornerstone
20. 陶管 / 25
    Pipes
21. 陶管底面 / 25
    Bottom of the Pipe
22. 中国瓷器 / 26
    Chinese Ceramics
23. 石臼、网坠 / 26
    Stone Mortar, Fishing Net-sinkers
24. 网坠 / 26
    Fishing Net-sinkers
25. 鱼骨 / 27
    Fish Bones
26. 马骨 / 27
    Horse Bones
27. 牛骨 / 27
    Cattle Bones

扶余扶苏山城
Busosanseong Fortress in Buyeo
国立扶余文化财研究所

28. 扶苏山城远景 / 29
    View of Busosanseong Fortress
29. 城墙筑造状况 / 26
    Fortress Wall
30. 扶苏山城城墙 / 26
    Fortress Wall
31. 背光 / 30
    Aureole

278

Appendix 附录

32. 背光 / 30
Aureoles

33. 背光 / 30
Aureoles

34. 扶苏山城出土黑釉瓷器 / 31
Black-glazed Wares

35. "大通"铭板瓦 / 31
Roof Tile

36. "大通"铭板瓦细部 / 31
Detail of Roof Tile

扶余官北里遗址
Gwanbungni Baekje Archaeological Site in Buyeo

国立扶余文化财研究所

37. 莲池遗址 / 33
Pond Site

38. 官北里遗址全景 / 33
View of Gwanbungni Site

39. 官北里遗址大型建筑物址 / 34
Large Building Site

40. 大型建筑物复原图 / 34
Presumed Elevation of Large Building

41. 木椁仓库 / 35
Wooden Warehouse

42. 石椁仓库 / 35
Stone Warehouse

43. 土水道设施 / 35
Water Supply Facilities

44. 人面纹陶器 / 36
Pottery with Human Face Design

45. "下部乙瓦"铭 / 37

46. "前部乙瓦"铭 / 37

47. "午-斯"铭 / 37

48. "首府"铭 / 37

49. 戳印瓦 / 37
Roof Tiles

50. 瓦当 / 38
Roof-end Tiles

51. 瓦当 / 39
Roof-end Tiles

52. 唐瓦 / 39
Roof-end Tiles

53. 虎子 / 40
Chamber Pot

54. 虎子侧面 / 40
Side of Chamber Pot

55. 器座 / 41
Pottery Stand

56. "合"铭陶器 / 41
Pottery

57. "合"铭陶器内部 / 41
Inside of the Pottery

58. 官北里出土坩埚 / 42
Melting Pot

59. "官"铭坩埚细部 / 42
Detail of the Melting Pot

60. 开元通宝 / 42
Chinese Coin

61. 竹尺 / 43
Ruler

62. 竹尺细部 / 43
Detail of the Ruler

63. 木简 / 43
Wooden Strips

64. 背光 / 44
Aureole

65. 鎏金佛立像 / 45
Gilt-glazed Standing Buddha

66. 鎏金佛立像 / 45
Gilt-glazed Standing Buddha

279

扶余宫南池
Gungnamji Archaeological Site in Buyeo
国立扶余文化财研究所

67. 宫南池全景 / 47
View of Gungnamji Site

68. 蓄水槽遗迹 / 47
Water Tank

69. 草鞋 / 48
Straw Shoes

70. 宫南池出土陶器 / 49
Potteries

71. 锯痕 / 49
Traces of Sawing

72. 锯柄 / 49
Saw Grip

益山王宫里遗址
Wanggungni Archaeological Site in Iksan
国立扶余文化财研究所

73. 王宫里遗址全景 / 51
View of Wanggungni Site

74. 东墙残存状态 / 52
Eastern Wall

75. 大型建筑遗址 / 52
Large Building Site

76. 排水沟 / 53
Drainage

77. 车轮痕迹 / 53
Traces of Wagon Wheel

78. 厕所遗址 / 53
Toilet Room

79. 厕所示意图 / 53
Presumed Elevation of Toilet Room

80. 施釉陶器 / 54
Glazed Ware

81. 中国瓷片 / 54
Chinese Celadons

82. 烟囱帽（烟囱装饰陶器）/ 55
Chimney Head Cover

83. 灶形陶器 / 56
Cooking Stove-shaped Pottery

84. 虎子 / 56
Chamber Pot

85. 便器 / 56
Toilet

86. 陶器 / 57
Potteries

87. 有唇陶器 / 57
Pottery with Extended Rim

88. 瓶、盘 / 57
Bottle and Dish

89. 带流陶器 / 57
Bottle with Spout

90. "弥力寺"铭盖杯 / 57
Dish with Cover

91. "弥力寺"铭盖杯细部 / 57
Detail of the Cover

92. 玻璃 / 58
Glass

93. 玻璃坩埚 / 58
Melting Pot for Glass

94. 金坩埚、金箔 / 59
Melting Pot for Gold and Gold Foil

95. 金属坩埚 / 59
Melting Pot for Metal

96. 砥石 / 59
Grindstones

97. 牌形瓦制品 / 60
Tablet-shaped Earthenwares

98. 瓦当 / 60
Roof-end Tiles

99. 兽蹄形器足 / 61
Paw-shaped Pottery Leg

100. 造景石 / 61
Garden Stones

Appendix 附录

扶余王兴寺址
Wangheungsa Temple Site in Buyeo
国立扶余文化财研究所

- 101. 王兴寺址远景 / 63
  View of Wangheungsa Temple Site
- 102. "王兴"铭板瓦当 / 64
  Roof-end Tile
- 103. "王兴"铭板瓦当细部 / 64
  Detail of the Roof Tile
- 104. 莲花纹筒瓦当 / 64
  Roof-end Tiles
- 105. 鸱尾 / 65
  Ridge-end Tile
- 106. 板瓦当 / 65
  Roof Tiles
- 107. 鸱尾 / 65
  Ridge-end Tile

罗州伏岩里古墓群
Bogamni Tomb Complex in Naju
国立文化财研究所

- 108. 伏岩里3号墓 / 67
  Tomb #3 of Bogamni Tomb Complex
- 109. 鎏金饰履 / 68
  Gilt-bronze Shoe
- 110. 鎏金饰履底面 / 68
  Bottom of the Shoe
- 111. 鎏金饰履侧面 / 68
  Side of the Shoe
- 112. 冠饰 / 69
  Crown Ornament
- 113. 金制装饰 / 69
  Gold Ornaments
- 114. 石头枕 / 69
  Stone Headrests
- 115. 圭头大刀 / 70
  Sword
- 116. 三叶纹环头大刀 / 70
  Sword with Pommel
- 117. 三叶纹环头大刀、圭头大刀 / 70
  Swords
- 118. 马具 / 71
  Horse Harness
- 119. 壶镫 / 71
  Stirrup
- 120. 广口带孔小壶 / 72
  Jar with Hole
- 121. 盛有朱漆的陶器 / 72
  Pottery with Red-lacquer
- 122. 盛有朱漆的陶器 / 72
  Pottery with Red-lacquer

庆州新罗王京
Royal Capital of Silla in Gyeongju
国立庆州文化财研究所

- 123. 皇龙寺东侧王京地区 / 77
  East Side of Hwangnyongsa Temple
- 124. 东西大路 / 78
  East and South Main Road
- 125. 2号房屋 / 78
  House #2
- 126. 南北道路、大型排水道 / 78
  North and South Road, Large Drainage
- 127. 新罗王京推定复原图 / 79
  Presumed Reconstruction of Royal Capital of Silla
- 128. 兽面纹瓦 / 80
  Roof-end Tiles
- 129. 天马纹板瓦瓦当 / 80
  Roof-end Tile
- 130. 䰍棋瓦 / 80
  Roof-end Tile for Gable
- 131. 戳印纹陶盒 / 81
  Mounted Dish with Cover
- 132. 多棱纹瓶 / 81
  Bottle

133. 滑石印、陶印 / 81
Seals

134. 鎏金立佛 / 82
Gilt-bronze Standing Buddha

135. 鎏金菩萨立像 / 82
Gilt-bronze Standing Bodhisattva

136. 鎏金佛立像 / 83
Gilt-bronze Standing Buddha

137. 鎏金药师佛立像 / 83
Gilt-bronze Standing Buddha

138. 鎏金异形装饰 / 84
Gilt-bronze Ornament

139. 鎏金异形装饰细部 / 84
Detail of Gilt-bronze Ornament

140. 鎏金异形装饰细部 / 84
Detail of Gilt-bronze Ornament

141. 鎏金异形装饰细部 / 84
Detail of Gilt-bronze Ornament

142. 羊形玉饰和滑石制玉饰 / 85
Ornaments

143. 祖形石 / 85
Stone Phallus

144. 石权 / 85
Weights

庆州月城护城河
Wolseong Moat in Gyeongju
国立庆州文化财研究所

145. 月城护城河 / 87
Wolseong Moat

146. 月城全景 / 87
View of Wolseong

147. 木简 / 88
Wooden Strips

148. 鎏金装饰 / 89
Gilt-bronze Ornament

149. 鎏金装饰细部（正面）/ 89
Detail of Gilt-bronze Ornament

150. 鎏金装饰细部（反面）/ 89
Detail of Gilt-bronze Ornament

151. 陶器 / 90
Potteries

152. 绿釉盖 / 90
Green-glazed Cover

153. 鸭形陶器 / 91
Duck-shaped Pottery

154. 坩埚 / 91
Melting Pot

155. 陶球 / 91
Clay Balls

156. 渔网坠 / 91
Fishing Net-sinkers

庆州皇南洞遗址
Hwangnamdong Archaeological Site in Gyeongju
国立庆州文化财研究所

157. 月城周围大型建筑址 / 93
Large Building Site near Wolseong

158. 地镇具 / 94
Buried Ceremonial Protective Objects

159. 皇南洞遗址地镇具出土状况 / 94
Buried Ceremonial Protective Objects

160. 黄漆盒 / 95
Detail of Covered Bowl with Yellow-lacquer

161. 盛有黄漆的戳印纹盒（黄漆盒）/ 95
Covered Bowl with Yellow-lacquer

庆州皇龙寺址
Hwangnyongsa Temple Site in Gyeongju
国立庆州文化财研究所

162. 皇龙寺址全景 / 97
View of Hwangnyongsa Temple Site

163. 木塔中心础石 / 98
Foundation Stone of Wooden Pagoda

164. 中金堂佛座、木塔址 / 99
Central Golden Hall and Wooden Pagoda Site in Hwangnyongsa Temple Site

Appendix 附录

165. 鎏金佛立像 / 100
Gilt-bronze Standing Buddha

166. 鎏金透雕装饰 / 100
Gilt-bronze Ornaments

167. 鎏金板佛 / 101
Gilt-bronze Plate of Seated Buddha

168. 青铜佛头 / 101
Bronze Buddha Head

169. 鎏金凤凰装饰 / 102
Gilt-bronze Phoenix-shaped Ornament

170. 鎏金凤凰装饰背部细部图 / 102
Detail of Gilt-bronze Phoenix-shaped Ornament

171. 人物土偶装饰灯盏 / 103
Lamplight Cup

172. 镕范、钗 / 103
Moulds and Hairpin

173. 兽面纹瓦 / 104
Roof-end Tile

174. 龙头 / 104
Dragon Head

175. 砚台 / 105
Inkstone

庆州芬皇寺
Bunhwangsa Temple in Gyeongju
国立庆州文化财研究所

176. 芬皇寺全景 / 107
View of Bunhwangsa Temple

177. 芬皇寺仿砖石塔 / 108
Stone Pagoda in Bunhwangsa Temple

178. 九黄洞苑池 / 109
Garden Pond in Guhwangdong Site

179. 蜡石制菩萨像 / 110
Agalmatolite Bodhisattva

180. 鎏金佛立像 / 110
Gilt-bronze Standing Buddha

181. 鎏金板菩萨坐像 / 111
Gilt-bronze Plated of Seated Bodhisattva

182. 鎏金神将像 / 111
Gilt-bronze Buddhist Guardian

183. 狮子装饰青铜权 / 112
Bronze Weight

184. 狮子装饰青铜权细部 / 112
Detail of Bronze Weight

185. 狮子装饰青铜权细部 / 112
Detail of Bronze Weight

186. 狮子装饰青铜权细部 / 112
Detail of Bronze Weight

187. 葡萄鸟纹铜镜 / 113
Bronze Mirror

188. 勺范 / 113
Spoon Mould

189. 青铜容器 / 113
Gilt-bronze Bowls

190. 唐朝瓷器（青瓷贴花壶残片）/ 114
Chinese Ceramics

191. 青瓷碗 / 114
Bowl, Celadon

192. 唐朝陶瓷 / 114
Chinese Ceramics

193. 镇坛具 / 115
Buried Ceremonial Protective Objects

194. 镇坛具 / 115
Buried Ceremonial Protective Objects

195. 鸭形杯 / 116
Duck-shaped Cup

196. 虎子 / 117
Chamber Pot

197. 动物形陶器 / 117
Animal-shaped Pottery

198. 坩埚盖 / 117
Melting Pot Cover

199. 装饰品 / 117
Architectural Ornament

200. 棋盘砖 / 118
Brick of Baduk Board

283

201. 棋盘砖细部 / 118
Detail of Baduk Board

202. 鸱尾 / 119
Ridge-end Tile

203. 莲花纹砖 / 119
Brick

204. 瓦当 / 120
Roof-end Tiles

205. 创建期瓦当 / 121
Roof-end Tiles

206. 第一次重建期瓦当 / 121
Roof-end Tiles

207. 兽面纹瓦 / 122
Roof-end Tile

208. 兽面纹筒瓦瓦当 / 122
Roof-end Tile

209. 麒麟纹板瓦瓦当 / 122
Roof-end Tile

210. 飞天纹板瓦瓦当 / 122
Roof-end Tile

211. 龙纹板瓦瓦当 / 122
Roof-end Tile

212. 莲花纹筒瓦瓦当 / 123
Roof-end Tile

213. 莲花宝相花纹筒瓦瓦当 / 123
Roof-end Tile

214. 莲花纹筒瓦瓦当 / 123
Roof-end Tile

215. 莲花宝相花纹筒瓦瓦当 / 123
Roof-end Tile

216. 莲花纹筒瓦瓦当 / 123
Roof-end Tile

217. 双鸟纹筒瓦瓦当 / 123
Roof-end Tile

218. 狮子纹筒瓦瓦当 / 123
Roof-end Tile

219. 花草纹筒瓦瓦当 / 123
Roof-end Tile

庆州四天王寺址
Sacheonwangsa Temple Site in Gyeongju

国立庆州文化财研究所

220. 四天王寺远景 / 125
View of Sacheonwangsa Temple Site

221. 四天王寺全景 / 125
View of Sacheonwangsa Temple Site

222. 西塔址 / 126
Western Pagoda Site

223. 西塔址全景 / 127
View of Western Pagoda Site

224. 西塔台基细部 / 127
Stereobate of Western Pagoda

225. 四天王像绿釉壁砖 / 128
Green-glazed Brick of Buddhist Guardian

226. 四天王像绿釉壁砖 / 129
Green-glazed Brick of Buddhist Guardian

227. 四天王像绿釉壁砖示意图 / 130
Presumed Restoration of Buddhist Guardian
（姜友邦复原案）

228. 四天王像绿釉壁砖 / 131
Green-glazed Brick of Buddhist Guardian
（下半身）国立庆州博物馆藏（庆199）

229. 四天王像绿釉壁砖 / 132
Green-glazed Brick of Buddhist Guardian

230. 四天王像绿釉壁砖 / 132
Green-glazed Brick of Buddhist Guardian

231. 四天王像绿釉壁砖 / 132
Green-glazed Brick of Buddhist Guardian
国立中央博物馆藏（本馆12495）

232. 四天王像绿釉壁砖示意图 / 133
Presumed Restoration of Buddhist Guardian
（姜友邦复原案，左臂部分另有复原图）

233. 四天王像绿釉壁砖 / 134
Green-glazed Brick of Buddhist Guardian

234. 四天王像绿釉壁砖示意图 / 135
Presumed Restoration of Buddhist Guardian
国立中央博物馆简图

庆州传·仁容寺址
Inyongsa Temple Site(Alleged) in Gyeongju
国立庆州文化财研究所

235. 传·仁容寺址全景 / 137
View of Alleged Inyongsa Temple Site

236. 金堂遗址 / 137
Main Building of the Temple

237. 天龙八部像 / 138
Image of Eight Buddhist Guardians

238. 鎏金菩萨立像、鎏金佛立像 / 140
Gilt-bronze Standing Bodhisattva and Buddha

239. 龙头 / 141
Dragon Head

240. 小塔 / 141
Small Pagoda

241. 传·仁容寺址出土中国瓷器 / 141
Chinese Ceramics

242. 瓦 / 142
Roof-end Tiles

243. 鸱尾 / 143
Ridge-end Tile

244. 兽面纹瓦 / 143
Roof-end Tile

245. 施釉瓦片 / 143
Glazed Roof-end Tile

庆州天官寺址
Cheongwansa Temple Site in Gyeongju
国立庆州文化财研究所

246. 天官寺址全景 / 145
View of Cheongwansa Temple Site

247. 骑马人物形陶器出土状态 / 145
Disclosure of Remains

248. 骑马人物形陶器 / 146
Horse Rider-shaped Pottery

249. 权 / 147
Weights

250. 鎏金佛立像 / 147
Gilt-bronze Standing Buddha

251. 半切偏口瓶 / 147
Flattened Bottle in Half

庆州荪谷洞、勿川里遗址
Songokdong·Mulcheolli Archaeological Site in Gyeongju
国立庆州文化财研究所

252. 陶窑址分布情况 / 149
A Group of Potteries Kilns

253. 陶窑址 / 149
Earthenware Kiln

254. 陶窑址 / 149
Earthenware Kiln

255. 瓦窑址 / 150
Tile Kiln

256. 木炭窑址 / 150
Charcoal Kiln

257. 石筑遗迹 / 151
Stone Construction

258. 作坊、民居、采土场叠压打破情况 / 151
Overlapping Pits of Workshops, Houses and Clay-gathering Sites

259. 陶俑 / 152
Clay Figurines

260. 弹琴陶俑 / 153
Gum Player

261. 吹笛陶俑 / 153
Piper

262~263. 人物陶俑 / 153
People

264. 人物陶俑 / 153
People

265. 人物陶俑 / 153
People

266. 人物陶俑 / 153
People

韩国 考古学重大发现（2002~2007）

267. 罪囚陶俑 / 153
Prisoner

268. 罪囚陶俑 / 153
Prisoner

269. 动物陶俑 / 154
Animals

270. 蛇形陶俑 / 154
Snakes

271. 鸟形陶俑 / 154
Birds

272. 龟形陶俑 / 155
Turtle

273. 虎形陶俑 / 155
Tiger

274. 马形陶俑 / 155
Horse

275. 马形陶俑 / 155
Horse

276. 犬形陶俑 / 155
Dog

277. 蛇形陶俑 / 155
Snake

278. 鸭形陶俑 / 155
Duck

279. 烧废陶器 / 156
Ill-fired Potteries

280. 陶器生产工具 / 156
Pottery Production Tools

281. 窑具、陶器 / 156
Stand and Pottery

282. 角杯、角杯台 / 156
Horn-shaped Cup with Stand

| 昌宁松岘洞古墓群
Songhyeondong Tomb Complex in Changnyeong
国立昌原文化财研究所

283. 6、7号墓全景 / 161
View of Tomb #6 and #7

284. 松岘洞古墓群远景 / 161
View of Tomb Complex

285. 7号墓石室内部 / 162
Stone Chamber of Tomb #7

286. 清洗后的7号墓木棺 / 162
Wooden Coffin from Tomb #7

287. 7号墓在木棺清理后，遗物出土状态 / 163
Remains from Tomb #7

288. 7号墓木棺旁箭镞群 / 163
Arrows near Wooden Coffin in Tomb #7

289. 7号墓石室内部遗物出土状态 / 163
Remains in Tomb #7

290. 三叶纹环头大刀 / 164
Sword with Ring Pommel

291. 金制耳环 / 165
Gold Earrings

292. 银制腰带装饰 / 165
Silver Buckles

293. 松岘洞出土马具 / 166
Horse Harness

294. 鞍桥饰 / 167
Saddle Ornament

295. 马鞍示意图 / 167
Restoration of Saddle
（出处：《考古学事典》，国立文化财研究所）

296. 云珠 / 168
Harness Fittings for Crossbelt

297. 云珠 / 168
Harness Fittings for Crossbelt

298. 杏叶 / 168
Horse Strap Pendants

299. 鎏金透雕马鞍桥前轮 / 169
Saddle Ornament

300. 鎏金透雕马鞍桥后轮 / 169
Saddle Ornament

301. 木制区划板 / 170
Wooden Vessel

302. 杯状木器 / 170
Wooden Vessels

Appendix 附录

303. 扇柄 / 171
Fan Grip

304. 侧面 / 171
Side of Fan Grip

305. 棒状菱纹漆器 / 171
Bar-shaped Lacquer Ware

306、307. 棒状菱纹漆器细部 / 171
Detail of Bar-shaped Lacquer Ware

308. 长颈壶 / 172
Jar with Long Neck

309. 豆形器、红陶钵 / 173
Mounted Dishes and Bowls

310. 有盖豆形器 / 173
Mounted Dishes with Cover

311. 圈足长颈壶 / 173
Mounted Jars with Long Neck

312. 双耳高圈足盏 / 173
Bowls With Handles

固城内山里古墓群
Naesalli Tomb Complex in Goseong
国立昌原文化财研究所

313. 内山里古墓群远景 / 175
View of Naesalli Tomb Complex

314. 内山里8号墓 / 176
Tomb #8

315. 8号墓遗物出土状态 / 176
Remains in Tomb #8

316. 内山里34号墓 / 177
Tomb #34

317. 34号墓遗物出土状态 / 177
Remains in Tomb #34

318. 34号墓主椁 / 177
Coffin of Tomb #34

319. 玻璃珠 / 178
Glass Beads

320. 玻璃珠 / 178
Detail of Glass Beads

321. 耳饰 / 179
Earrings

322. 镯子 / 179
Bracelets

323. 铁矛、铁镈 / 180
Iron Spearhead, Iron Ferrule

324. 铁矛细部 / 180
Detail of Spearhead

325. 铁镞 / 180
Iron Arrowheads

326. 铁斧 / 181
Iron Axes

327. 铁镰 / 181
Iron Sickle

328. 铁环 / 181
Iron Ring

329. 大刀 / 181
Iron Sword

330. 内山里出土马具 / 182
Horse Harness

331. 壶镫 / 183
Stirrup

332. 衔镳 / 183
Bits

333. 青铜銮铃 / 183
Horse Bells

334. 云珠 / 183
Harness Fittings for Crossbelt

335. 带盖陶器 / 184
Potteries with Cover

336. 单耳附碗 / 184
Bowls with Handle

337. 单耳附碗 / 184
Bowls with Handle

338. 广口带孔小壶 / 184
Jars with Hole

339. 折沿壶 / 185
Wide-mouthed Jars

340. 圈足直口壶 / 185
Mounted Jar

341. 璎珞装饰圈足壶 / 185
Mounted Jar

咸安城山山城
Seongsansanseong Fortress in Haman
国立昌原文化财研究所

342. 城山山城远景 / 187
View of Seongsansanseong Fortress

343. 城山山城全景 / 187
View of Seongsansanseong Fortress

344. 东城墙周围贮水设施（三维）/ 188
Reservoir near Eastern Fortress Wall

345. 东城墙周围木简集中出土地 / 188
Disclosure of Wooden Strips

346. 贮水池木柱设施 / 189
Wooden Pillar of Reservoir

347. 清理贮水池内木简的场面 / 189
Wooden Strips in Reservoir

348. 龟甲出土状态 / 189
Snapping Turtle Bones

349. 木简 / 190
Wooden Strips

350. 2006年出土木简红外线照片 / 190
Infrared Photography of Wooden Strips

351. 题签轴 / 191
Wooden Strips for Bookmark

352. 笔、书刀 / 191
Brush, Eraser Knife

353. 城山山城出土木棒 / 191
Beetles

354. 木制容器 / 192
Wooden Vessels

355. 长颈壶 / 192
Jar with Long Neck

356. 封泥 / 192
Seal

江华高丽王陵
Goryeo Royal Tombs in Ganghwa
国立文化财研究所

357. 嘉陵发掘后全景 / 197
View of Gareung Tomb

358. 嘉陵石室 / 197
Stone Chamber of Gareung Tomb

359. 坤陵发掘后全景 / 198
View of Golleung Tomb

360. 坤陵石室 / 198
Stone Chamber of Golleung Tomb

361. 陵内里石室墓全景 / 199
View of Neungnaeri Stone-chamber Tomb

362. 陵内里石室墓上部构筑物 / 199
Neungnaeri Stone-chamber Tomb

363. 石兽 / 199
Stone Image of Animal

364. 江华硕陵 / 200
Seongneung Tomb in Ganghwado
存于国立中央博物馆，玻璃原版照片（中无38-07）

365. 高丽太祖显陵 / 201
Hyeolleung Tomb
存于国立中央博物馆，玻璃原版照片（无38-2）

366. 高丽恭愍王玄陵长明灯 / 201
Stone Lantern before Hyeolleung Tomb of King Gongmin
存于国立中央博物馆，玻璃原版照片（无957-05）

367. 高丽恭愍王玄陵和鲁国公主正陵 / 201
Hyeolleung and Jeongneung Tomb
存于国立中央博物馆，玻璃原版照片（D390003）

368. 装饰品 / 202
Ornaments

369. 蝶形装饰 / 202
Butterfly-shaped Ornament

370. 鸟形装饰 / 202
Bird-shaped Ornament

371. 青瓷 / 203
Celadons

372. 青瓷盖 / 203
Lid, Celadon

373. 兽目纹瓦当 / 204
Roof-end Tiles

374. 石人 / 204
Funerary Sculptures of the Tomb

375. 凤凰纹装饰 / 205
Phoenix-shaped Ornament

376. 凤凰纹装饰背面 / 205
Backside of Phoenix-shaped Ornament

377. 玉珠 / 205
Beads

378. 地镇具 / 205
Buried Ceremonial Protective Objects

南原市实相寺
Silsangsa Temple in Namwon
国立扶余文化财研究所

379. 实相寺全景 / 207
View of Silsangsa Temple

380. 实相寺木塔立体复原图 / 208
Presumed Elevation of Wooden Pagoda

381. 木塔址 / 209
Wooden Pagoda Site

382. 附属建筑遗址 / 209
Annex Site

383. 兽面纹瓦 / 210
Roof-end Tile

384. 兽面纹瓦 / 210
Roof-end Tile

385. 兽面纹瓦 / 210
Roof-end Tile

386. 宝相花纹筒瓦瓦当、莲花纹筒瓦瓦当 / 211
Roof-end Tiles

387. 莲花纹筒瓦瓦当 / 211
Roof-end Tiles

388. 花草纹板瓦瓦当 / 211
Roof-end Tile

389. 忍冬莲花板瓦瓦当 / 211
Roof-end Tile

390. 双鸟纹板瓦瓦当 / 211
Roof-end Tile

391. 兽面纹板瓦瓦当 / 211
Roof-end Tile

392. 莲花纹筒瓦瓦当 / 212
Roof-end Tiles

393. 葡萄唐草纹板瓦瓦当 / 212
Roof-end Tiles

394. 葡萄唐草纹板瓦瓦当底面 / 212
Bottom Roof-end Tile

395. 铭文板瓦瓦当 / 213
Roof-end Tiles

396. 铭文板瓦瓦当 / 213
Roof-end Tiles

397. 铭文板瓦瓦当 / 213
Roof-end Tile

398. 瓷器 / 214
Ceramics

399. 青瓷铁画长鼓 / 214
Drum, Celadon

400. 唐宋瓷器 / 214
Chinese Ceramics

401. 唐宋瓷器 / 214
Chinese Ceramics

402. 罗汉像 / 215
Image of Buddhist Saint

403. 陶器 / 216
Potteries

404. 虎子 / 216
Chamber Pot

405. 石制有盖壶 / 216
Stone Jar with Cover

首尔景福宫
Gyeongbokgung Palace in seoul
国立文化财研究所

406. 景福宫远景 / 221
View of Gyeongbokgung Palace

407. 庆会楼三十六宫地图 / 222
Blueprint of Gyeonghoeru Pavilion
现存于国立中央图书馆

408. 庆会楼全景 / 223
View of Gyeonghoeru Pavilion
存于国立中央博物馆，玻璃原版照片（无1111-1）

409. 龙 / 225
Figure of Dragon
现存于国立古宫博物馆

410. 兴福殿址发掘遗迹平面图 / 226
Drawing of Heungbokjeon Site

411. 烧厨房址发掘遗迹平面图 / 226
Drawing of Sojubang Site

韩国 考古学重大发现（2002~2007）

412.《北阙图形》/ 227
Diagram of Bukgwol, Gyeongbokgung Palace
现存于国立古宫博物馆

413. 景福宫烧厨房址，福会堂址 / 228
Sojubang and Bokhoedang Site, Gyeongbokgung Palace

414. 咸和堂、缉敬堂廊庑址 / 228
Site of Hamhwadang and Jipgyeongdang Halls, Gyeongbokgung Palace

415. 兴福殿 / 229
Heongbokjeon, Gyeongbokgung Palace
《朝鲜古籍图谱》

416. 兴福殿址 / 229
Heongbokjeon Site, Gyeongbokgung Palace

417. 瓷器 / 230
Ceramics

418. 石制盖 / 230
Stone Cover

419. 青花白瓷勺 / 230
Spoons, White Porcelain

420. 粉青砂碟 / 231
Dishes, Buncheong Ware

421."仁寿府"铭 / 231

422."密阳长兴库"铭 / 231

423."内赡"铭 / 231

424. 兴福殿址出土瓷器 / 232
Ceramics

425. 大唐师父杂像 / 233
Decorative Roof Tile

426. 烧厨房址出土瓦当、青瓦 / 233
Roof Tiles

427. 青瓦 / 234
Roof Tiles

428. 瓦当 / 234
Roof-end Tiles

429. 黄瓦、青瓦 / 235
Roof Tiles

| 襄阳洛山寺
Naksansa Temple in Yangyang
国立文化财研究所

430. 洛山寺发掘现场全景 / 237
View of Naksansa Temple Site

431. 圆通宝殿 / 237
Wontong Bojeon in Naksansa Temple Site

432."洛山寺"铭 / 238
Rubbed Copy of the Roof Tile

433."洛山寺"铭板瓦 / 239
Roof Tile

434. 洛山寺远景 / 239
View of Naksansa Temple

435. 郑歆《洛山寺图》/ 240
Painting of Naksansa Temple
现存于国立中央博物馆(德寿2370-36)

436. 金夏钟《洛山寺图》/ 241
Painting of Naksansa Temple
现存于国立中央博物馆(德寿2827)

437."皇帝万岁"铭板瓦瓦当拓片 / 242
Rubbed Copy of Roof-end Tile

438. 莲花纹筒瓦瓦当、"皇帝万岁"铭板瓦瓦当 / 242
Roof-end Tiles

439. 龙纹板瓦瓦当拓片 / 243
Rubbed Copy of Roof-end Tile

440. 凤凰纹筒瓦瓦当、龙纹板瓦瓦当 / 243
Roof-end Tiles

441."梵"字纹筒瓦瓦当、迦陵频伽纹板瓦瓦当 / 243
Roof-end Tiles

442. 迦陵频伽纹板瓦瓦当 / 243
Roof-end Tiles

443. 莲花纹瓦当 / 244
Roof-end Tiles

444. 兽目纹瓦当 / 244
Roof-end Tiles